Medical Negligence and Childbirth

This book is dedicated to mothers and their babies.

Medical Negligence and Childbirth

Doireann O'Mahony BL

Consultant Editor

Roger V Clements, FRCS (Ed) FRCOG FAE, Harley Street, London

Medical Expert Contributors

Dr Peter Dear, MD FRCP FRCPCH,
Consultant in Neonatal Medicine.

Leroy C Edozien, LLB PhD MRCPI FRCOG
Consultant Obstetrician & Gynaecologist Manchester Academic
Health Science Centre, St Mary's Hospital, Manchester.

Professor M R B Keighley, MB BS MS FRCS,
Professor of Surgery & Colorectal Expert.

Dr Ben Lloyd, MD FRCPH, Consultant Paediatrician,
Royal Free Hospital, London. Email: b.w.lloyd@btinternet.com

Dr Simon J Newell, MD FRCPCH FRCP
Consultant and Senior Clinical Lecturer in Neonatal Medicine,
Leeds Teaching Hospitals. Vice President of The Royal College of Paediatrics and
Child Health.

Dr Janet Rennie, MD FRCP FRCPCH Consultant in Neonatal
Medicine EGA Wing, UCLH, London.

Bloomsbury Professional

Published by
Bloomsbury Professional
Maxwelton House
41–43 Boltro Road
Haywards Heath
West Sussex
RH16 1BJ

Bloomsbury Professional
The Fitzwilliam Business Centre
26 Upper Pembroke Street
Dublin 2

ISBN 978 1 78043 8030

© Bloomsbury Professional Limited 2015
Bloomsbury Professional, an imprint of Bloomsbury Publishing Plc

This work is intended to be a general guide and cannot be a substitute for professional advice. Neither the authors nor the publisher accept any responsibility for loss occasioned to any person acting or refraining from acting as a result of material contained in this publication.

While every care has been taken to ensure the accuracy of this work, no responsibility for loss or damage occasioned to any person acting or refraining from action as a result of any statement in it can be accepted by the authors, editors or publishers.

British Library Cataloguing-in-Publication Data
A catalogue record for this book is available from the British Library

Typeset by Marie Armah-Kwantreng, Dublin, Ireland
Printed in Great Britain by
CPI Group (UK) Ltd, Croydon, CR0 4YYL

When a woman is in travail she has sorrow, because her hour has come; but when she is delivered of the child, she no longer remembers the anguish, for joy that a child is born into the world.

John 16:21 RSV

FOREWORD

It is a privilege to be asked to write the foreword for this important work by Ms Doireann O'Mahony BL, a rising star of the Munster Circuit.

When I commenced practice on the Munster Circuit in the mid-1970s, the publication of an Irish law book was, indeed, a rare event. Prof John Maurice Kelly had published the second edition of his *Fundamental Rights in the Irish Constitution,* and the first edition of Wylie on *Irish Land Law,* was about to be launched but we were some six years before the first edition of McMahon and Binchy. The only criminal law textbook had been published some 20 years before. The two works by Judge Kenneth Deale on *Landlord and Tenant* were out of print.

As a result, every practitioner purchased every Irish law book. At that time, most of our pleadings in the Circuit Court were taken from Mr Babbington's second edition of Osborne's *County Court Practice* which was published in 1910, the first edition being published in 1890!

All this has, of course, changed and practitioners, academics and persons interested in legal matters are faced with a vast array of titles competing for attention.

Ms O'Mahony in *Medical Negligence and Childbirth* has, I believe, filled an important gap in legal publishing and it is truly innovative in its combination of legal and medical learning.

Ms O'Mahony provides a brisk accessible summary of the legal principles in relation to medical negligence, along with contributions written by her Consultant Editor, Roger V Clements and a number of other medical experts eg: *Self Determination in Childbirth* by Leroy C Edozien, *What is Cerebral Palsy* by Dr Janet Rennie, *Neonatal Resuscitation* by Dr Simon Newell, *Timing Fetal Brain Damage Caused by Acute Near Total Asphyxia* by Dr Ben Lloyd, *Timing Fetal Brain Damage in Chronic Partial Asphyxia* by Dr Peter Dear and *Pudendal Neuropathy* by Prof Michael Keighley.

It is this combination of the medical and the legal that renders Ms O'Mahony's work unique.

In this regard, while it is true that, for example in Dr John White's great work on *Damages,* basic diagrams and medical terminology were given, the reader of Ms O'Mahony's work will be able to assess the medical, as well as the legal implications, of a given problem to a degree never previously available in one volume.

Accordingly, this work will be of great interest, not alone to barristers, solicitors, students and academics, but also to myself and my colleagues as judges who have, for the first time, in an accessible format, complex medical conditions described in an intelligible manner.

I can recommend this work without any hesitation.

Mr Justice Kevin Cross
High Court
November 2015

PREFACE

There are many great texts, both medical and legal, but what seems to be missing is a simple explanation of the issues giving rise to litigation around childbirth, written for those who do not practice medicine, and in particular for the lawyers who bear the responsibility of handling these important cases. I hope that this book will satisfy the need for information and knowledge, and contribute perhaps, even in some small way, towards helping those who have been injured or bereaved.

I am honoured that Mr Justice Kevin Cross agreed to write the foreword for this book and I wish to thank him for his time and kind words of encouragement along the way.

Heartfelt thanks to each of my contributors: Dr Peter Dear, Leroy Edozien, Prof Michael Keighley, Dr Ben Lloyd, Dr Simon Newell, Dr Janet Rennie and especially my consultant editor, Roger Clements, without whose devotedness these pages would never have seen the light of day.

I gratefully acknowledge the assistance of Roger Murray, David O'Malley, Shauna Keyes, Sheila O'Connor, Cathriona Molloy, James Cross BL, Asim Sheikh BL, John Healy SC, Eddie Walsh SC and Mr Justice Liam McKechnie. Thanks to both of those with whom I devilled, Judge John Cheatle and Michael McGrath BL – the first to hear about my idea for this book. Thanks to my talented friend Leonora Daly for providing her illustrations. Thanks to all at Bloomsbury Professional, in particular Sarah Sheehy, editor. Love and thanks as ever, of course, to my family – John, Louise and Cian. And remembering my friend Michael O'Flaherty.

Doireann O'Mahony BL
Law Library
Four Courts
Dublin 7.

November 2015

ILLUSTRATIONS

Illustrations reproduced courtesy of Sonicaid, Elsevier and Leonora Daly:

- Figures 6.1, 6.2, 6.3, 6.4, 6.5, 6.6, 6.7, 6.9 and 6.10 – Steer, *Fetal Heart Rate Patterns and their Clinical Interpretation* (2nd edn, Sonicaid, c 1984)

- Figure 6.8 – Gibb and Arulkumaran, *Fetal Monitoring in Practice* (3rd edn, Elsevier, 2008)

- Figure 6.11 – Sweet et al, *Mayes` Midwifery* (12th edn, Elsevier, 1997)

- Figure 6.12 – Vacca, *Handbook of Vacuum Extraction in Obstetric Practice* (Elsevier, 1992)

- All other illustrations provided by Leonora Daly

CONTENTS

Foreword vii

Preface ix

Illustrations x

Contents xi

Table of Cases xix

Table of Statutes xxv

Table of Statutory Instruments xxvii

Conventions xxvii

Constitution of Ireland xxvii

PART I
PROCEDURE

Chapter 1: **Litigation and Risk Management** 3
    Introduction 3
    Definition 3
    The history 3
    Elements of risk management 4
    Clinical risk management in obstetrics 6

Chapter 2: **Civil Procedure** 9
    Introduction 9
    Possible causes of action 9
    Negligence: the standard of care 11
    Causation 13
    Medical records 16
    Identity of parties 18
    Letter of claim 19
    Limitation 19
    Delay 24
    Pleadings 29
    Particulars 32
    Discovery 32
    The disclosure rules 34
    Survival of causes of action on death 37
    Trial 38
    A word on costs 38

Chapter 3: Expert Evidence 41

Who is an expert?...41

The expert's duty..42

The overriding duty..42

How to choose an expert 43

How to instruct an expert 44

PART II
CONSENT

Chapter 4: Self-Determination in Childbirth: The Law of Consent 51

Leroy C Edozien

Introduction 51

Medical paternalism 52

Consent to treatment 53

Valid consent..54

The professional standard...55

Departure from the professional standard 57

The causation hurdle 60

The timing of consent...63

Does consent have to be in writing?...64

Refusal of treatment 65

Children under the age of 16 years...67

PART III
CEREBRAL PALSY

Chapter 5: What is Cerebral Palsy? 71

Dr Janet Rennie

Classification of cerebral palsy 72

Typical underlying brain disorders in CP 73

Birth asphyxia and cerebral palsy 79

Other cases of cerebral palsy 80

Causes of cerebral palsy...80

Medico-legal aspects of cerebral palsy 80

Chapter 6: What Causes Cerebral Palsy? 83

Intrauterine fetal surveillance..83

The cardiotocograph trace...83

Decelerations of the fetal heart 86

Baseline artefact..92

Classification of intrapartum trace..94

Fetal scalp blood sampling 95
The significance of meconium in the liquor 96
The abuse of oxytocin 97
Why does the contraction frequency matter? 99
Fetal distress and oxytocin augmentation 100
Cord problems 101
Obstruction to the umbilical cord 101
Abnormalities of the cord 102
Prolapse and presentation of the cord 102
Placental malfunction 104
Chronic placental failure 105
Acute placental failure 106
Rupture of the uterus 106
Obstructed labour 107
Oxytocin abuse 107
Direct injury 108
The scarred uterus 108
The incidence of scar rupture 108
The decision to allow VBAC and consent for it 109
The place of induction/augmentation of labour 110
Operative vaginal delivery 110
Classification of forceps delivery according to station
and rotation 112
The obstetric forceps 112
The ventouse 113
The mal-rotated head 114
Trial of operative delivery 117
Breech delivery 117
Twin delivery 119

Chapter 7: Neonatal Resuscitation 121
Dr Simon Newell
Doing simple things well saves lives and offers lifelong health 121
The underlying physiology 122
Assessment of the newborn 124
Resuscitation 125
A – Airway 127
B – Breathing 130
C – Circulation 130
D – Drugs 130
Post-resuscitation care 131

Special considerations.. 131

Common errors in resuscitation 132

Chapter 8: The Law 133

Breach of duty 133

Antenatal... 133

Labour.. 134

Postnatal.. 134

Causation..134

Resuscitation failure...139

CTGs 142

Placental failure..144

Operative vaginal delivery 149

Quantum 153

Chapter 9: Timing Fetal Brain Damage Caused by Acute Near Total Asphyxia 155

Dr Ben Lloyd

Introduction 155

(a) What is meant by a bradycardia?...156

(b) When does damage occur after the onset of an acute near total hypoxic-ischaemic insult?...157

(c) Review of the working forward method for determining timing of brain damage (the 10–25 minute principle).....................................158

(d) Review of the working backward method for determining timing of brain damage...159

Some considerations limiting the accuracy of the working backwards method 160

How to time the onset of brain damage using the working backward method.. 161

(e) Is it reasonable to consider units of time less than five minutes when reviewing the timing of a baby's brain damage by an acute, near total, hypoxic-ischaemic insult?...163

(f) The implications of the introduction of therapeutic cooling............. 164

(g) Summary..165

Review of evidence that brain damage can ensue well after a bradycardia lasting longer than 10 minutes..................................166

Evidence from work by Kayani and colleagues – 2003 166

Evidence from Naeye and Shaffer – 2005 168

Chapter 10: Timing Fetal Brain Damage Caused by Chronic Partial
Asphyxia 173
Dr Peter Dear
Introduction 173
Timing the damage from chronic partial asphyxia 176

PART IV
OTHER INJURIES

Chapter 11: Failed Pregnancy 183
Introduction 183
Miscarriage 183
Diagnosis 185
Ectopic pregnancy 186
The law 187
Conclusion 194

Chapter 12: Obstetric Brachial Plexus Injury 195
Definitions 195
      Shoulder dystocia 195
      OBPI 195
The anatomy 196
Good practice 198
The defence 201
The mechanism of labour 201
Posterior shoulder injury 202
Maternal propulsion 203
The lesser of two evils 205
The law 206
Conclusion 215

Chapter 13: Obstetric Anal Sphincter Injury 217
Introduction 217
Allegation of failure to prevent third- and fourth-degree tears 220
Allegation of failure to detect injury 221
Allegation of inadequate repair 222
      The surgeon 222
      The circumstances 222
      Suture material 223
      Post-operative care 223
Pudendal neuropathy (*Prof Michael Keighley*) 223
      Clinical testing 223

Neuropathy with or without an anatomical defect
    in the sphincters 223
    Tests of function 224
    Transient or permanent 224
    Clinical effects 224
    Causes 224
Prognosis 225
Recto-vaginal fistula 226
The importance of swab counts and the 'retained swab' cases...............226
The law..227
Conclusion...236

Chapter 14: Failed Sterilisation 237
    Introduction..237
    Tubal ligation 239
    Laparoscopic sterilisation – Filshie clips 239
    Causes of failure...240
    Recanalisation 241
    The law...241
        Introduction 241
        Investigation of the cause of failure....................................... 242
        Pre-operative counselling... 242
        Compensation 243
    Conclusion...250

PART V
QUANTUM OF DAMAGES

Chapter 15: Quantum 253
    Introduction...253
    Compensatory damages 253
    Mechanism of compensation..254
    General damages 258
    Cap on general damages..259
    Special damages: past 262
    Special damages: future 264
    Life expectancy 265
    Real rate of return..267
    Taxation...269
    Cost of care 270
    Physiotherapy..270
    Accommodation 270

Loss of earnings 273
Other headings of future expenses 276
A word on aggravated and exemplary damages 276
Fatal injuries 278
Preparing for trial 279
Payment out of funds 279
Appealing quantum 280
Epilogue 281
Appendix: Support Services 283
I. Bereavement services 283
II. Maternal mental health support services 283
III. Birth injury support services 284
IV. Advocacy services 284
Index 285

TABLE OF CASES

A

A v Bottrill [2003] 1 AC 449 ....15.69
Alcock v Chief Constable of South Yorkshire Police [1992] 1 AC 310 ....2.10
Antoniades v East Sussex Hospitals [2007] EWHC 517 (QB) 7.09
Arden v Malcolm [2007] EWHC 404 (QB) 15.43
Armstrong v Moffatt and Ors [2013] 1 IR 417, [2013] IEHC 148 ....2.77

B

B v The Royal Victoria Infirmary & Associated Hospitals NHS Trust [2002]
    EWCA Civ 348 ....15.43
Barnett v Chelsea and Kensington Hospital [1969] 1 QB 428 ....2.18
Barry v National Maternity Hospital and Anor [2011] 3 IR 80 ....15.55
Bennett v Cullen [2014] IEHC 574 ....15.03
Birch v University College London Hospital NHS Foundation Trust [2008] EWHC
    2237 (QB) 4.23
Bolam v Friern Hospital Management Committee [1957] 1 WLR 582 ....4.16
Bolitho v City and Hackney Health Authority [1998] AC 232, [1997] 4 All ER 771 ....4.23
Bolton v Blackrock Clinic (23 January 1997) SC 4.20
Boyne v Dublin Bus and Anor [2003] 4 IR 47 ....15.24, 15.49–15.50
Brennan v Fitzpatrick [2001] IESC 105 ....2.59
Buckley v O'Herlihy and National Maternity Hospital [2010] IEHC 51 ....14.44
Burke v McKenna [2011] IEHC 449 ....2.102
Byrne v Ryan [2009] 4 IR 54, [2009] IEHC 207 ....14.22
Byrne v Ryan [2009] IEHC 206..14.22

C

Canterbury v Spence [1972] 464 F 2d 772 ....4.24
Carroll v Mater Misericordiae Hospital [2011] 2 IR 411, [2011] IEHC 231 ....2.42
Cassidy v The Provincialate [2015] IECA 74 ....2.66
Chester v Afshar [2004] UKHL 41 ....4.23, 4.29
Children's University Hospital Temple Street v CD and EF [2011] 1 IR 665,
    [2011] 2 ILRM 262 ....4.43
Clarke v O'Gorman [2014] IESC 72 ....2.43
Conley v Strain [1988] 1 IR 628 ....15.30
Connolly v Casey and Murphy [2000] 1 IR 345, [2000] 2 ILRM 226 ....2.68
Conway v INTO [1991] 2 IR 305, [1991] ILRM 497 ....15.67
Cooke v Cronin and Neary [1999] IESC 54 ....2.68
Corrigan v HSE [2011] IEHC 305 ....2.12
Courtney v Our Lady's Hospital Ltd [2011] 2 IR 786, [2011] 2 ILRM 328,
    [2011] IEHC 226 ....2.10, 15.75
Creevy v Barry-Kinsella and Ors [2008] IEHC 100 ....2.64
Croft v Heart of England NHS Foundation Trust [2012] EWHC 1470 (QB) 12.70
Cunningham v Neary and Ors [2004] 2 IR 625, [2004] IESC 43 ....2.72

D

Daly v Mulhern [2008] 2 IR 1 ....15.68
Daniels v Heskin [1954] IR 73 ....4.17, 8.18

Delaney v Southmead Health Authority [1992] EWCA Civ J0609–5 ....2.21
Devlin v National Maternity Hospital [2008] 2 IR 222 ....2.10
Dignam v HSE and Duffy [2015] IEHC 295 ....2.44
Doherty v Bowaters Irish Wallboard Mills Ltd [1968] IR 277 .... 15.31, 15.57, 15.59–15.62
Donnellan v Westport Textiles [2011] IEHC 11 ....2.53
Donoghue v Stevenson [1932] AC 562 ....12.82
Doyle v Dunne [2014] IESC 69 ....2.97
Dunne v Coombe Women and Infants University Hospital [2013] IEHC 58 ....8.22
Dunne v Eastern Regional Health Authority and Ors [2008] IEHC 315 ....2.48
Dunne v National Maternity Hospital and Jackson [1989] IR 91 ....2.12, 4.16, 8.12, 15.52

E

Ellis v Royal Surrey County Hospital [2003] EWHC 3510 (QB) 12.66
Emeh v Kensington, Chelsea and Westminster Area Health Authority [1985] QB 1012 ....14.17
English v South Eastern Health Board and Howard [2011] IEHC 362 ....11.36
Everard v HSE [2015] IEHC 592 ....12.65

F

Fagan v Griffin [2012] IEHC 377 ....15.23
Fairchild v Glenhaven Funeral Services Ltd [2002] UKHL 22, [2003] 1 AC 32 ....2.19, 8.50
Farrell v Ryan [2015] IEHC 275 ....2.48, 2.58
Fitzpatrick v National Maternity Hospital [2008] IEHC 62 ....8.38
Fitzpatrick and Anor v FK and Anor [2008] IEHC 104, [2009] 2 IR 7 ....4.12
Fitzpatrick v White [2008] 3 IR 551, [2008] 2 ILRM 99 ....4.22, 4.31
Fletcher v Commissioners of Public Works [2003] 1 IR 465 ....14.31
Flynn v Bon Secours Health Systems Ltd [2014] IEHC 87 ....2.65
Folkes v Chadd [1782] 3 Doug 157, 99 ER 589 ....3.03

G

Geoghegan v Harris [2000] 3 IR 536 ....4.22, 4.27
Gillick v West Norfolk Area Health Authority [1986] AC 112 ....4.42
Glynn v The Governors and Guardians of the Hospital for the Relief of Poor
    Lying-In Women, Dublin [2000] IEHC 41 ....2.57
Gough v Neary and Anor (15 November 2002) HC 15.26
Gough v Neary and Anor [2003] 3 IR 92, [2003] IESC 39 ....2.47, 2.51, 15.26
Griffin v Patton and Tyndale (21 March 2003) HC 11.20
Griffin v Patton and Tyndale [2004] IESC 46 ....11.29
Gunning v National Maternity Hospital [2009] 2 IR 117, [2008] IEHC 352 ....2.42

H

H West & Son Ltd v Shephard [1964] AC 326 ....15.03
Hamilton v HSE [2014] IEHC 393 ....2.15
Harrington v Cork City Council and Anor [2015] IEHC 41 ....2.94
Hayes v Minister for Finance [2007] 3 IR 190 ....2.18
Hegarty v Mercy University Hospital Cork [2011] IEHC 435 ....2.09
Hepworth v Kerr [1995] Med LR 139 ....8.64
Hewitt v HSE [2014] 2 ILRM 466, [2014] IEHC 300 ....2.97
Holsgrove v South West London Strategic Health Authority [2004] EWHC 501 (QB) 12.73
Hughes v Lord Advocate [1963] AC 837 ....8.64
Hurley Ahern & Ahern v Moore & Southern Health Board [2013] 1 IR 205 ....14.33

I

Ikarian Reefer [1993] 2 Lloyd's Rep 68 ....3.04

J

Jackson v Bro Taf Health Authority [2002] EWHC 2344 (QB) 12.69

K

Kearney v McQuillan and North Eastern Health Board [2012] ILRM 377,
    [2012] IESC 43 ....15.25
Kearney v McQuillan and North Eastern Health Board [2012] IEHC 127 ....15.25
Kearney v McQuillan and North Eastern Health Board [2010] 3 IR 576 ....2.58
Kelly v Board of Governors of St Laurence's Hospital [1988] IR 402,
    [1989] ILRM 877 ....2.15, 2.42
Kelly v Hennessy [1995] 3 IR 253 ....2.10
Kelly v Lenihan [2004] IEHC 427 ....13.52
Keogh v Dowling & Connolly [2005] IEHC 359 ....12.57
Keogh v Wyeth Laboratories Inc (31 July 2003) HC 2.60
Keogh v Wyeth Laboratories Inc [2006] 1 IR 345, [2005] IESC 46 ....2.60
Kiernan v HSE [2015] IEHC 141 ....2.15
Kincaid v Aer Lingus Teoranta [2003] 2 IR 314, [2003] IESC 31 ....2.89, 2.96
Kingsberry v Greater Manchester Strategic Health Authority [2005] EWHC 2253 (QB),
    [2006] 87 BMLR 73, [2011] LS Law Med 334 ....8.77

L

Laffan v Quirke and Anor [2012] IEHC 250 ....15.64
Lalor v National Maternity Hospital [2015] IEHC 423 ....15.22
Laycock v Gaughan and Ors [2011] IEHC 52 ....11.46
Lindsay v Mid-Western Health Board [1993] 2 IR 147 ....2.21
Livingstone v Rawyards Coal Co (1880) 5 App Cas 25 ....15.03
Loraine v Wirral University Teaching Hospital NHS Foundation Trust [2008]
    EWHC 1565 (QB) 8.61

M

M v HSE [2011] IEHC 339 ....13.60
Maguire v Randles and Ors (21 June 1991) HC 11.30
Mangan v Dockery [2014] IEHC 477 ....2.63
MB (Adult, medical treatment), re [1997] 38 BMLR 175 CA 4.03
McBrearty v The North Western Health Board and Ors [2007] IEHC 431 ....2.56
McBrearty v The North Western Health Board and Ors [2010] IESC 27 ....2.56
McCarthy v South Infirmary [2004] IEHC 429 ....2.62
McFarlane v Tayside Health Board [2000] 2 AC 59 ....14.17
McGee v O'Reilly [1996] 2 IR 229 ....2.76
McGhee v National Coal Board [1973] 1 WLR 1 ....2.19, 8.50, 13.59
McGrory v ESB [2003] 3 IR 407 ....2.30
McIntyre v Lewis [1991] 1 IR 121, [1990] IESC 5 ....15.69
McKinley v Minister for Defence [1997] 2 IR 176 ....2.09
McLennan v Newcastle Health Authority [1992] 3 Med LR 215 ....14.14
Montgomery v Lanarkshire Health Board [2015] UKSC 11 ....4.23, 12.76
Murphy v DePuy International Ltd [2015] IEHC 153 ....2.42
Myles v McQuillan and North Eastern Health Board [2007] IEHC 333 ....15.20, 15.69

N

Naessens v Jermyn and O'Higgins [2010] IEHC 102 ....2.48
Nelson v McQuillan and Ors [2013] IEHC 152 ....15.04
Nolan v Murphy [2005] 4 IR 461, [2005] IESC 17 ....15.19
North Western Health Board v HW and CW [2001] IESC 90 ....4.45

O

O'Brien v Derwin and Anor [2009] IEHC 2 ....15.30
O'Brien v Wheeler (23 May 1997) Supreme Court of New South Wales 4.26
O'Domhnaill v Merrick [1984] IR 151, [1985] ILRM 40 ....2.54
O'Donovan v Cork County Council [1967] IR 173 ....8.18
O'Grady v Southern Health Board and Tralee General Hospital [2007] 2 ILRM 51,
    [2007] IEHC 38 ....2.72–2.73
O'Mahony v Tyndale and Anor [2002] 4 IR 101 ....2.29
O'Mahony v Tyndale and Anor [2000] IEHC 43 ....8.33–8.34
O'Neill v National Maternity Hospital [2015] IEHC 160 ....15.10
O'Riordan v Dempsey and Anor [2014] IEHC 523 ....15.24
O'Riordan v Maher [2012] IEHC 274 ....2.61
O'Sullivan v Kiernan & Bon Secours Health Systems Ltd [2004] IEHC 78 ....12.49

P

Parkinson v St James and Seacroft University Hospital NHS Trust [2001] EWCA Civ 530,
    [2001] 3 All ER 97, [2002] QB 266 ....14.19, 14.37
Parry v North West Surrey Health Authority [1994] 5 Med LR 259 ....8.69
Payne v Shovlin and Others [2007] 1 IR 114, [2006] IESC 5 ....2.90
Pearce v United Bristol Healthcare NHS Trust [1998] EWCA Civ J0520–16,
    [1999] PIQR P53 ....4.23
Philp v Ryan [2004] 4 IR 241 ....15.68
Priestley v Harrogate Health Care NHS [2002] EWCA Civ 183 ....13.71
Primor Plc v Stokes Kennedy Crowley [1996] 2 IR 459 ....2.59
Purdy v Lenihan and Ors [2003] IESC 7 ....8.52
Purver v Winchester and Eastleigh Healthcare NHS Trust [2007] EWHC 34 (QB) 8.81

Q

Quinn v Mid-Western Health Board and North Eastern Health Board
    (14 October 2003) HC 8.43
Quinn v Mid-Western Health Board [2005] 4 IR 1, [2005] IESC 19,
    [2005] 2 ILRM 180 ....2.18, 2.19, 8.49

R

R v Collins and others, ex parte S [1998] 3 All ER 673 ....4.37
Rashid v Essex Rivers Healthcare NHS Trust [2004] EWHC 1338 (QB) 12.67
Reddy v Bates [1983] IR 141, [1984] ILRM 197 ....15.63, 15.80
Rees v Darlington Memorial Hospital NHS Trust [2002] EWCA Civ 88 ....14.19
Reeves v Carthy and O'Kelly [1984] IR 348 ....8.18
Reibl v Hughes [1980] 114 DLR (3d) 1 ....4.24
Reidy v National Maternity Hospital [1997] IEHC 143 ....2.68
Ring v Mulcahy and Anor [2015] IECA 148 ....2.79
Roberts v Johnstone [1989] QB 878 ....15.55, 15.59
Robshaw v United Lincolnshire Hospitals NHS Trust [2015] EWHC 923 (QB) 15.46
Roche v Peilow [1985] IR 232 ....8.18
Rogers v Whitaker [1992] HCA 58, (1992) 175 CLR 479 ....4.24

Russell v HSE [2014] IEHC 590 .... 15.07, 15.24, 15.50
Russell v HSE (5 November 2015) Court of Appeal 15.51

S

Sardar v NHS Commissioning Board [2014] EWHC 38 (QB) 12.71
Schloendorff v Society of New York Hospital [1914] 211 NY 125 .... 4.01
Sherry v Primark [2010] 1 IR 407, [2010] IEHC 66, [2010] 2 ILRM 198 .... 2.43
Sidaway v Bethlem Royal Hospital Governors, [1985] AC 871 .... 4.16, 12.76
Simpson v Diamond and Anor (No 2) [2001] NSWSC 1048 .... 8.86
Sinnott v Quinnsworth Ltd [1984] ILRM 523 .... 15.23
Smith v Barking HA [1995] 5 Med LR 285 .... 4.27
Spargo v North Essex Health Authority [1997] 8 Med LR 125, [1997] PIQR 235,
    [1997] EWCA Civ J0313–13 .... 2.47
St George's Healthcare NHS Trust v S 4.37
Sugg v O'Keeffe and Anor [2005] IESC 92 .... 2.68
Sutcliffe v Countess of Chester Hospital NHS Trust [2002] Lloyd's Rep Med 449 .... 12.68
Swaine v The Commissioners for Public Works in Ireland [2003] 1 IR 521,
    [2003] IESC 30 .... 15.67

T

T (Adult, Refusal of Treatment), re [1993] Fam 95 .... 4.02
Toal v Duignan and Ors [1991] ILRM 135 .... 2.54, 8.53
Totham (protected party) v King's College Hospital NHS Foundation Trust [2015]
    EWHC 97 (QB) 15.22

W

Walsh v Family Planning Services Ltd [1992] 1 IR 496 .... 2.06, 4.20
Warnock v National Maternity Hospital [2010] IEHC 25 .... 13.37
Whitehouse v Jordan [1980] 1 All ER 650 .... 2.21
Whitehouse v Jordan [1981] 1 All ER 267 .... 3.04
Willett v North Bedfordshire Health Authority [1993] PIQR, Q 166 .... 15.59
Winston v O'Leary [2006] IEHC 440 .... 4.28
Wisniewski v Central Manchester Health Authority [1998] PIQR 324 .... 8.64
Wright v HSE and Anor [2013] IEHC 363 .... 2.81, 2.103

Y

Yardley v Brophy [2008] IEHC 14 .... 15.34
Yun v MIBI and Anor [2009] IEHC 318 .... 15.23, 15.30

TABLE OF STATUTES

A

Age of Majority Act 1985
  s 3 .... 2.34

C

Civil Liability Act 1961
  s 7(1) 2.97
    (2) 2.97
    8 .... 2.98
    47(1) 15.74
    48 .... 15.74
    58 .... 2.08
    Pt II 2.97
    Pt IV 15.74

Civil Liability and Courts Act 1991
  s 7 .... 2.05

Civil Liability and Courts Act 2004
  s 7 .... 2.40
    8 .... 2.36
    10 .... 2.67
    22 .... 15.21

Courts Act 1981
  s 22(1) 15.33

Courts Act 1988
  s 1 .... 15.02

Courts and Court Officers Act 1995
  45(1)(a)(iii), (iv), and (v) 2.86

Courts of Justice Act 1936
  s 78 .... 2.39

Criminal Justice (Female Genital
  Mutilation) Act 2012 .... 4.09

D

Data Protection Act 1988
  s 4 .... 2.24

Data Protection (Amendment) Act 2003
  s 5 .... 2.24

Debtors (Ireland) Act 1840
  s 26 .... 15.33

E

European Convention of Human Rights
  Act 2003 .... 4.39

F

Female Genital Mutilation Act 2003 ..... 4.09

Finance Act 1990
  s 5 .... 15.52

Freedom of Information Act 2014 .... 2.24

P

Personal Injuries Assessment Board
  Act 2003 .... 15.21
  s 3(d) 2.41–2.44
    50 .... 2.44

Prohibition of Female Genital Mutilation
  (Scotland) Act 2005 .... 4.09

S

Statute of Limitations (Amendment)
  Act 1991
  s 2 .... 2.45
    (1) 2.46
    (2) 2.46
    (3) 2.46
    3 .... 2.05
    (1) 2.40
    6(1)(b) 2.45

Statute of Limitations 1957
  s 49 .... 2.52
    71 .... 2.50

TABLE OF STATUTORY INSTRUMENTS

Civil Liability Act 1961 (Section 49) Order
 2014 (SI 6/2014) 15.76

Freedom of Information Act, 1997 (Section
 28(6)) Regulations 2009
 (SI 387/2009) 2.24

Rules of the Superior Courts
 Ord 1A r 6 .... 2.71
 10(4) 2.75
 8 r 1 .... 2.64, 2.73
 15 r 20 .... 2.35
 19 r 7 .... 2.76
 (1) 2.77

Ord 27 r 9(1) 2.75
 36 r 9 .... 2.102
 39 r 45–51 .... 2.82
 r 46(1) 2.84
 (4) 2.87
 47 .... 2.88
 63 r 12(1) 15.78

Rules of the Superior Courts (No 6)
 (Disclosure of Reports and Statements)
 1998 (SI 391/1998) 2.82, 2.90, 3.19

Rules of the Superior Courts (Personal
 Injuries) 2005 (SI 248/2005) 2.75

CONVENTIONS

European Convention on Human Rights
 Art 6 .... 2.53

CONSTITUTION OF IRELAND

Art 34.1 .... 2.53

Art 42.5 ....4.43, 4.44

PART I
PROCEDURE

Chapter 1

LITIGATION AND RISK MANAGEMENT

INTRODUCTION

[1.01] Clinical risk management was developed initially as a means of controlling medical negligence litigation.[1] Wherever risk management has developed, it has usually been driven by anxiety about litigation. Nevertheless it has the potential to reduce injury to patients and to redress deficiencies in medical audit, particularly audit of outcome. The Health Service Executive says that it 'recognises the importance of risk management as an essential process for the delivery of quality and safe services', describing the concept as 'a key element of good governance [which] underpins the ability to provide safe and effective care to our patients; it refers to strategies that reduce the possibility of a loss or harm'.[2]

DEFINITION

[1.02] A number of definitions have been suggested for clinical risk management either in terms of its form or its function. A useful working definition is: 'A means of reducing the risks of adverse events occurring in clinical care by systematically assessing, reviewing and then seeking ways to prevent their recurrence'.

THE HISTORY

[1.03] The purpose of clinical risk management is to provide the organisation with a memory. Without remembering its shortcomings, the organisation is unlikely to improve. In Ireland, health care services were the responsibility of a number of different organisations until the establishment of the Health Service Executive in 2005. Clinical risk management was sporadic and largely

---

1.   Vincent and Walsh, 'Clinical Risk Management and the Analysis of Clinical Incidents' in *Risk Management and Litigation in Obstetrics and Gynaecology* (RSM Press, 2001).

2.   http://www.hse.ie/portal/eng/about/Who/qualityandpatientsafety/incidentrisk/ Riskmanagement/riskmanagement.html.

ineffective. A number of high profile reports of adverse events at the beginning of the century also provided impetus for the establishment of clinical risk management.

[1.04] Indemnity for health care professionals was provided by a number of different agencies, and litigation was often unnecessarily complicated because, in almost every case, there were several different defendants each represented by a different legal team. Two of the providers of obstetric indemnity withdrew from the market at the beginning of the century and the State Claims Agency, established in 2001, set up a clinical indemnity scheme in July 2002 under which the management of all clinical claims against public hospitals and public community healthcare facilities became its responsibility. The clinical indemnity scheme (CIS) not only provides clinical indemnity for all government healthcare providers but also introduced clinical risk advisers and clinical claims managers in every major facility supplying anonymised data for a central claims management system,[3] NIMS.[4]

ELEMENTS OF RISK MANAGEMENT

[1.05] Clinical risk management at provider level consists of three elements:

- identifying risk;
- analysing risk;
- controlling risk.

[1.06] Such a system has at its foundation the reduction of cost to the organisation but its primary purpose in health facilities is to improve the quality of care and the outcome for the individual patient, whose welfare is at the centre of the process. This individual is no longer identified as a potential litigant.

---

3. Oglesby, 'An Overview of the Clinical Indemnity Scheme of Clinical Risk Management in Ireland', (2010) 16 Clinical Risk 127–129.

4. The National Incident Management System (NIMS) is described by the State Claims Agency as 'the confidential highly secure web based system. It is an end to end risk management tool that allows delegated State authorities (DSAs) to manage incidents throughout the incident lifecycle. This includes: reporting of incidents (including serious reportable events), management of investigations, recording of investigation conclusions, recording of recommendations, tracking recommendations to closure, analysis of incident, investigation and recommendations data and other functionality'.

[1.07] Identifying risk: Every adverse outcome or untoward incident is recorded and reported to a local co-ordinator. In obstetrics, that role is usually assumed by a senior midwife whose role it is to obtain full information from all of the participants and observers at the earliest possible moment before memory fades. Incident reporting is a strictly factual exercise and the aim is to create a culture in which every member of the clinical team takes responsibility for reporting (initially at the local level) an adverse event or a 'near miss'. Only the facts are reported and no opinion is required as to the cause of the incident and certainly no finger is pointed at an individual. In that sense clinical risk management is not a blame exercise.

[1.08] Analysing risk: At the next stage it becomes necessary to identify why the incident has occurred. Adverse outcome, even death, may occur with the best possible care and without any clinical error. The purpose however is to discover those occasions when the adverse outcome might have been prevented. The second phase, the analysis of the error, should therefore be subjected to careful scrutiny. One of the more common forms of such investigation is 'root cause analysis', the purpose of which is to identify the factors that resulted in the nature, magnitude, location and timing of the adverse outcome. Invariably such thorough investigation will identify error where it exists. It is in the nature of clinical misfortunes that in any clinical accident there are usually multiple causes. Each needs to be identified and the question 'why' must follow. This led to the '5 Whys', a concept developed in the motor car industry, illustrating the principle that the initial answer to the question may need further exploration into the system of care that has allowed such an outcome. Asking one 'why' is often not enough. The answer to the 5 Whys is the way into systems design and systems error.

[1.09] Controlling risk: If poor systems or poor compliance are the cause, the action required is usually straightforward. For example, if the registrar/consultant rota on the labour ward allows only for brief six-hour periods of duty, and with lax handovers, the rota needs to be changed and handover periods carefully managed.

[1.10] But what if an individual is shown to have erred? Some have advocated a 'no blame culture' but that is to deny reality and negate the very purpose of clinical risk management. If an individual has clearly failed that individual must be identified. That is not to say that they should be pilloried or disciplined but at the very least they will need re-education, training, support and encouragement not to repeat the exercise. Without the identification of fault there can be no improvement in the standard of care. Unless the midwife, who failed to understand the significance of the CTG, is re-trained so that she does not make the same mistake again, the whole exercise of risk management is a waste of time. There can be no improvement without the identification and correction of fault. Without a proper system of risk management, 'groundhog day' will never end.[5]

CLINICAL RISK MANAGEMENT IN OBSTETRICS

[1.11] What risk management has taught us is that common themes run through clinical error and in almost every obstetric disaster there can be identified:

- failure of communication;

- delay;

- a cascade of events.

[1.12] Most consent complaints are failures in communication. Most asphyxial injuries are the result of delay, either delay in diagnosis or delay in implementation. Errors made in the antenatal clinic are not addressed and when the mother is admitted in labour, no senior clinician takes the responsibility for revising the management plan; junior staff are left to implement the car crash. Unless some clinician has the intelligence and courage to change the direction of travel, an intervention that may mean challenging a prior decision of a senior colleague, the train of events continues to its disastrous outcome. It is all too common that the junior clinicians at the end of a series of mistakes attract the blame because they happen to be there when the final damaging event occurs. An efficient risk management analysis should correct that and draw attention to the early part of the cascade which set the train of events in motion along the wrong track.

[1.13] A number of clinical scenarios will be discussed in this book, all of which demonstrate this cascade effect. They represent familiar clinical circumstances in which injury to mother or baby is common leading to complaints and sometimes litigation:

- perinatal asphyxia;

- abuse of oxytocin;

- vaginal birth after Caesarean section;

- shoulder dystocia;

---

5.   O'Mahony, 'We must end "groundhog day" culture in maternity services' (2015) *Evening Echo*, 15 June.

- anal sphincter injury;
- major obstetric haemorrhage;
- consent issues.

Chapter 2

CIVIL PROCEDURE

INTRODUCTION

[2.01] A case in medical negligence is a tort action for damages for personal injuries and all of the requirements of such an action must be complied with. This chapter will discuss the general legal principles applying to an action in medical negligence as well as limitation periods and those procedural rules that often arise in medical negligence actions.

[2.02] Few triumphs can rival the joy and goodwill that is produced following the birth of a healthy baby. The converse could be equally overwhelming. Harm to mother and/or baby is uniquely dispiriting.[1] It has been observed that the most dangerous journey made by any individual is through the four inches of the birth canal.[2]

[2.03] The patient who has suffered the consequences of negligence, as opposed to bad luck, ought to be compensated. The doctor who was not guilty of negligence, but was unlucky, ought to be vindicated.[3]

[2.04] In order for an injured plaintiff's claim to succeed, a relationship giving rise to a duty of care between the plaintiff and the defendant must be established; this rarely poses a difficulty. It must then be established that there was a breach of the duty of care owed. Further it must be established that injury, loss and damage resulted which was caused by the breach of duty. It is proving this last element, or causation, that can be the more hotly contested aspect of the claim. Realistic expectations of prospects of success and potential liability in respect of costs must be given to a new client from the outset. She needs to understand the legal requirements of proving a claim, the procedures that have to be followed and her responsibility to provide instructions.

POSSIBLE CAUSES OF ACTION

[2.05] Medical negligence cases are, as the name suggests, grounded in common law negligence. Sometimes plaintiffs also plead breach of contract. In

---

1. Mahendra, 'When love's labour is lost' (1996) NLJ 146 (6729) 125–127.
2. Jeffcoate, 'Prolonged Labour' (1961) Lancet ii, 67.
3. Samuels, 'Contraception, Pregnancy, Childbirth – When Things go Wrong' (1986) Med Sci Law 26(1) 39–47.

any event, irrespective of whether one is dealing with a cause of action in common law negligence or in breach of contract the limitation period in a personal injuries action is two years from the date of accrual of the cause of action or from the 'date of knowledge' if such arises later than the date of accrual of the cause of action.[4]

[2.06] Trespass to the person is sometimes pleaded.[5] The tort is actionable per se, that is, without proof of injury or damage. Administration of treatment, and particularly surgery, in the absence of consent, constitutes assault, battery or trespass to the person, which terms, in practice, are used overlappingly.

[2.07] Along with negligence and breach of duty, a plaintiff will sometimes plead breach of statutory duty in cases against public health authorities.

[2.08] The relevant law also applies to an unborn child for her protection in like manner as if she were born, provided she is subsequently born alive.[6] The law on the 'born-alive' rule may not be settled.[7]

[2.09] There are causes of action which might arise in favour of persons other than the plaintiff in the principal action. One type of 'related' cause of action is the action for loss of consortium.[8]

[2.10] A nervous shock claim may be made if the plaintiff can establish on the basis of medical evidence that she has suffered a recognisable psychiatric illness[9] which was shock-induced,[10] caused by the defendant's negligence and sustained by reason of actual or apprehended physical injury to her or another

---

4.   Statute of Limitations (Amendment) Act 1991, s 3 as amended by Civil Liability and Courts Act 1991, s 7.
5.   *Walsh v Family Planning Services Ltd* [1992] 1 IR 496.
6.   Civil Liability Act 1961, s 58.
7.   McMahon and Binchy, *Law of Torts* (4th edn, Bloomsbury Professional, 2013).
8.   *McKinley v Minister for Defence* [1997] 2 IR 176. An action exists for partial as well as total loss of consortium.
9.   This concept must be contrasted with the normal emotions of mental distress, disappointment, fear, grief or sadness. In *Hegarty v Mercy University Hospital Cork* [2011] IEHC 435 the height of the plaintiff's evidence was that he experienced very high levels of stress and anxiety in or about the time he was diagnosed as being MRSA positive. There was no evidence of any recognisable psychiatric injury. Evidence of any actionable injury was lacking and without actionable damage, stress and anxiety alone are insufficient to support a claim. A range of conditions has been accepted by our courts as constituting recognised psychiatric injury, including clinical depression and post-traumatic stress disorder.
10.   In *Devlin v National Maternity Hospital* [2008] 2 IR 222 (contd .../)

and that the defendant owed her a duty of care not to cause her injury in the form of nervous shock.[11] A claim in nervous shock may, for example, be made by parents whose baby has been injured at a traumatic birth, due to negligence on the part of the defendant.[12] Nervous shock is as much a head of damage as physical injury. It must be borne in mind that whilst there may be breathing room in terms of the limitation period for the baby's claim, the limitation period for a nervous shock claim on behalf of the parents is the same as for a physical injury, and the two-year limitation period will ordinarily commence running on the baby's date of birth.

NEGLIGENCE: THE STANDARD OF CARE

[2.11] To bring a successful medical negligence action against a health care professional a plaintiff must prove that harm has been caused by a failure to provide the appropriate standard of care. The court hearing a case must apply certain criteria in order to reach its decision on whether there has been such a failure. Simply put, the professional must give the standard of care expected of a competent member of the relevant professional group.

[2.12] The test that must be satisfied in law in order to establish medical negligence is a difficult one – there is a 'weighty burden of proof demanded of a plaintiff in proceedings of this nature'.[13] The definitive test was set out in *Dunne v National Maternity Hospital and Anor*,[14] which was, coincidentally, a birth injury case.

[2.13] The test is the same for alleged negligent advice, failure to warn, negligent technique in carrying out surgery, development or treatment of

---

10. (contd) Denham J quoted the following passage from the judgment of Lord Ackner in *Alcock v Chief Constable of South Yorkshire Police* [1992] 1 AC 310:'"Shock", in the context of this cause of action, involves the sudden appreciation by sight or sound of a horrifying event, which violently agitates the mind. It has yet to include psychiatric illness caused by the accumulation over a period of time of more gradual assaults on the nervous system'.
11. Hamilton CJ in *Kelly v Hennessy* [1995] 3 IR 253 set out the five principles which are required to be satisfied in order for a plaintiff to recover in nervous shock.
12. In *Courtney v Our Lady's Hospital Ltd* [2011] IEHC 226 a mother was awarded €150,000 in respect of nervous shock resulting from witnessing the death of her child, and €10,500 in respect of legal representation at the child's inquest.
13. Per Irvine J in *Corrigan v HSE* [2011] IEHC 305.
14. *Dunne v National Maternity Hospital and Jackson* [1989] IR 91.

subsequent complications or any other complaint. It applies to diagnosis and treatment alike.

[2.14] Finlay CJ in the Supreme Court set out what have become known as the '*Dunne* principles' which are the legal principles to be applied by courts in determining whether there has been medical negligence and which have been consistently applied ever since. The principles may be summarised as follows:

1. to rebut an allegation of negligence in diagnosis or treatment, it must be proved that the defendant medical practitioner did not depart from what any other medical practitioner of equal specialist or general status and skill would have done if acting with ordinary care;

2. if the medical practitioner has deviated from a general and approved practice, that will not establish negligence unless it is also proved that the course he did take was one which no medical practitioner of similar specialisation and skill would have followed had he been taking the ordinary care required from a person of his qualifications;

3. if a medical practitioner defends his conduct by establishing that he followed a practice which was general and approved of by his colleagues of similar specialisation and skill, he cannot escape liability if the plaintiff establishes that such practice has inherent defects which ought to be obvious to any person giving the matter due consideration.

[2.15] Historically, this deferential test has not been applied to assess negligence on the part of nurses, with courts in such cases favouring the application of the ordinary principles of the standard of care.[15] However in *Kiernan v HSE*[16] Cross J when applying the deferential test to determine the liability of a public health nurse, commented that:

> To apply a different and lesser obligations to a nurse than a doctor is to adopt what, in this day, seems to me to be to be an outdated view dating from a time nursing was a vocational rather than a professional qualification, and to revert to an age in which nurse had little, if any, professional autonomy and deferred entirely to the directions of doctors.[17]

---

15. *Kelly v Board of Governors of St. Laurence's Hospital* [1988] IR 402, [1989] ILRM 877.
16. *Kiernan v HSE* [2015] IEHC 141.
17. Midwives are also recognised as independent practitioners with obstetricians relying on their skills. Midwives are able to make diagnoses, exercise clinical judgment and prescribe treatment. In *Hamilton v HSE* [2014] IEHC 393 Ryan J applied the deferential test to determine the liability of a midwife.

CAUSATION

[2.16] In medical negligence claims, a plaintiff who establishes breach of duty has 'done no more than surmount the first hurdle'.[18] She must thereafter prove causation of injury and this can be the most difficult aspect of the claim. Allegations of obstetric negligence very often raise complex causation issues, for example where a baby is born with a condition that may have been caused by negligence but may also have occurred without any negligence, such as cerebral palsy.[19] The causation issue can be even more contentious where the alleged negligence consisted of an omission rather than an act.

[2.17] Although negligence and causation are theoretically entirely separate from each other, they often come together as a matter of proof. The plaintiff asserts a theory as to why, for example, the child has cerebral palsy which ascribes blame to a doctor or midwife; the defendant then puts forward an opposing theory with a different causal explanation for the plaintiff's condition. In determining the causal question, the court will, as a consequence, also be determining the issue of negligence.[20]

[2.18] The classic test for determining factual causation is the 'but-for' test.[21] The but-for test is satisfied if the plaintiff can prove on the balance of probabilities that but for the defendant's negligence, she would not have suffered injury. If the plaintiff would have sustained the injury in any event then, regardless of the fact that the defendant may have been negligent, liability will not be imposed since the defendant's negligent act or omission did not actually cause the injury.

[2.19] Kearns J in *Quinn v Mid-Western Health Board and Anor*[22] hinted at an openness to alternative causation tests, particularly in cases with a definite

---

18. Seymour, *Childbirth and the Law* (Oxford University Press, 2000) 50.
19. Binchy, 'Causal issues in obstetric and neonatal care', conference paper dated 9 October 2014.
20. Boylan, 'Leading Irish Cerebral Palsy Cases', conference paper dated 13 May 2008
21. *Barnett v Chelsea and Kensington Hospital* [1969] 1 QB 428. In English law there are recognised exceptions to the but-for test, but such exceptions have not yet been established in Irish law. However, the door remains open: see the *dicta* of Kearns J in *Quinn v Mid-Western Health Board and Anor* [2005] 4 IR 1 and in *Hayes v Minister for Finance* [2007] 3 IR 190 where he said '[i]t is worth considering whether policy considerations should encourage this Court to relax the requirements of establishing causation'.
22. *Quinn v Mid-Western Health Board* [2005] 4 IR 1, [2005] IESC 19.

causative link but where the extent of causation is less definite. Nonetheless he commented that 'any approach which had the effect of reversing the onus of proof, or transferring the onus of proof to the defendant, would be one of such importance, even in the few exceptional cases where it might be appropriate, that it would require a full court – or perhaps even legislation – before a change of such magnitude to existing law could take place'. Special circumstances did not exist in *Quinn* to bring it within the one of the exceptions recognised in UK law in cases such as *McGhee v National Coal Board*[23] and *Fairchild v Glenhaven Funeral Services Ltd.*[24]

[2.20] If the plaintiff has established factual causation, the court then addresses the issue of legal causation to establish the extent of injury, loss, and damage in respect of which the plaintiff is entitled to be awarded compensation. Under the heading of legal causation a court may consider factors such as the rules on remoteness, *novus actus interveniens*, and mitigation of loss when considering if there is a reason as to why the extent to which the plaintiff should recover damages should be limited.

[2.21] The present state of science is only slightly further advanced than when Lord Denning stated in 1980 that '... when a baby is stillborn or dies soon after birth or is born damaged or deformed, that fact is no evidence of negligence on the part of the doctor or nurses attending the birth. It does not speak for itself. The doctrine of res ipsa loquitur does not apply'.[25] The maxim of *res ipsa loquitur* ('the matter speaks for itself') might be usefully invoked in some cases. The Supreme Court in *Lindsay v Mid-Western Health Board*[26] described it 'not a rule of substantive law, but simply an aid in the evaluation of evidence which provided a method of inferring a fact or facts in issue from circumstances proved in evidence'. If the doctrine truly applies to the case, then the onus of proof shifts from the plaintiff on to the defendant. But when does it truly apply? There must be reasonable evidence of negligence but if the impugned diagnosis or treatment was under the control of the defendant and the outcome is such as does not ordinarily occur in the normal course, a rebuttable presumption arises that there was want of care. The maxim should never be thrown into pleadings just for the sake of it. *Delaney v Southmead Health Authority*[27] is but one

---

23. *McGhee v National Coal Board* [1973] 1 WLR 1.
24. *Fairchild v Glenhaven Funeral Services Ltd* [2003] 1 AC 32.
25. *Whitehouse v Jordan* [1980] 1 All ER 650.
26. *Lindsay v Mid-Western Health Board* [1993] 2 IR 147.
27. *Delaney v Southmead Health Authority* [1992] EWCA Civ J0609–5.

example of the judicial disapproval of the ready invocation of the plea of *res ipsa loquitur*; the English Court of Appeal was not at all convinced of the applicability of it in medical negligence actions.[28]

[2.22] Complex factual situations can arise in obstetric negligence cases and a number of experts may be required to address both breach of duty and causation. One of the tasks of the lawyers should be to give clear instructions to the experts so that they can address the issues that the court will need to determine. In each case, questions will need to be tailored to the facts but should try to elicit the following:

1. What happened to the plaintiff to leave her with the injury of which she now complains?

2. Did a medical professional who treated/failed to treat her fail to act competently (within the *Dunne* test)?

3. Would competent treatment on the balance of probabilities have avoided some injury?

4. What would have been the plaintiff's condition and prognosis with competent treatment?

[2.23] The plaintiff is not required to prove her case as a matter of certainty, but rather 'on the balance of probabilities'. If the plaintiff is able to establish that it is more likely than not that the defendant's negligence caused the injury of which she complains, then she will succeed.

---

28. In *Lindsay v Mid-Western Health Board* [1993] 2 IR 147 the Supreme Court, in allowing the defendant's appeal, found that the unique and unusual nature of what had happened to the plaintiff, together with the respective positions of the parties, placed a burden on the defendant to displace the inference that the facts spoke for themselves. In showing that there was no negligence, the defendant successfully discharged this burden, and the onus of proof reverted to the plaintiff. While no act of negligence could be identified, it would be in defiance of reason and justice to say that an explanation by the defendant was not called for however, in circumstances where a patient had undergone a routine medical procedure under general anaesthetic, but had not returned to consciousness. Nonetheless, the most the defendant was required to do was to show that it exercised all reasonable care and that it was not negligent. It was not required to take the further step of proving what had actually caused the injury. O'Flaherty J believed it necessary to ensure the rule embodied in the maxim did not place so onerous a burden upon defendants that unjust results were produced and wished to prevent any 'unjustifiable extension of the law'.

MEDICAL RECORDS

[2.24] It is essential at the outset of any potential case that the new client's medical records are obtained. This step should be taken as swiftly as possible bearing in mind that delays are frequently encountered. Often, it may be necessary to obtain records from a number of different hospitals, institutions and/or doctors. Requests for copy sets of medical records made to public hospitals should be made under the Freedom of Information legislation. When seeking the records of an infant or a person of full age who due to disability is unable to exercise her/his rights under the FOI legislation reference should be made to the Freedom of Information Act, 1997 (Section 28(6)) Regulations 2009[29] (which continue to be in force following the coming into force of the Freedom of Information Act 2014). When requesting a copy set of the medical records of a mother following a childbirth the request should state that it is made pursuant to s 4 of the Data Protection Act 1988 as amended by s 5 of the Data Protection (Amendment) Act 2003. A copy set of the records should be sent to the party making the request no longer than 40 days after a properly constituted request has been made under this section.

[2.25] The client's medical records, once obtained, should be organised and paginated by solicitors who should aim to familiarise themselves with the records by sorting and reading through them, after which they will be submitted to the expert who will make his report based on them and any other relevant information. As complete a set of records as possible should be obtained for the purposes of submitting to an expert (see **Chapter 3**). Records of treatment from other hospitals earlier or later than the impugned treatment may well illuminate aspects of the claim. GP records are very often relevant.[30] The expert may identify sequential or chronological gaps within the records sent to him, indicating missing pieces of the picture. If there are any such gaps then this aspect should be investigated and remedied. If the records are relevant they should be relentlessly sought, by way of discovery if necessary. A cooperative approach towards early discovery of relevant records can assist in avoiding unnecessary cost in litigation. Parties should exercise their minds in relation to what is actually required by way of medical records and later in discovery.

[2.26] Records do not strictly speaking prove themselves. It is usually accepted that the records are not going to be challenged unless a party has put the

---

29.   Freedom of Information Act, 1997 (Section 28(6)) Regulations 2009 (SI 387/ 2009).

30.   Lewis and Buchan, *Clinical Negligence A Practical Guide* (7th edn, Bloomsbury Professional, 2012), 449.

opposition on notice that the timing or content or altering of a particular note is not accepted.

[2.27] It is now well established that hospitals and doctors own the medical records that they create, subject to the patient's right of access to them.[31]

[2.28] Medicine has its own language and many medical words are derived from Latin and Greek. Additionally, notes are often written in a hurried fashion as a result of which they can be almost illegible, containing a lot of shorthand and abbreviations. In order properly to read and understand medical notes and records a good, up-to-date medical dictionary is helpful. There are also useful handbooks[32] to assist in the understanding of records and the terminology in them.

[2.29] Medical records must be retained by the authors for a certain number of years.[33] In *O'Mahony v Tyndale and Anor* the Supreme Court considered the maxim *omania praesumuntur spoliatorem* whereby inferences may be drawn against a party who has destroyed relevant evidence[34] but found it did not apply. The maxim is intended to ensure that no party to litigation is subjected to a disadvantage in the presentation of their case because an opponent had acted wrongly by destroying or suppressing evidence. Its application will depend entirely on the circumstances of the particular case in which it is invoked.

[2.30] It goes without saying that a patient's records are confidential and normally records are not to be disclosed to anyone other than their doctor. Medical negligence litigation is, of course, a principal exception to this as the plaintiff is taken to have waived the right to confidentiality. All of the defendants are entitled to see all of the relevant records.[35]

[2.31] Privileged documents must be discovered but can be withheld from inspection. If challenged, privilege has to be proven. Medical reports on liability, causation, condition and prognosis are privileged and a party cannot be required

---

31. Healy, *Medical Malpractice* (Round Hall, 2009) 2–48.
32. Maddock, *Cracking the Code* (M&K Publishing, 2015).
33. There is often confusion amongst healthcare organisations in relation to how long records should be retained. There are HSE guidelines in relation to records retention. The best advice, especially in relation to maternity cases, is that they should be kept indefinitely.
34. *O'Mahony v Tyndale and Anor* [2002] 4 IR 101, [2001] IESC 62.
35. *McGrory v ESB* [2003] 3 IR 407.

to produce them. The disclosure rules (see para **[2.82]**) for medical reports on the plaintiff's condition and prognosis mean that if she does intend to produce such evidence in court she must disclose it first.

IDENTITY OF PARTIES

[2.32] It is essential to correctly identify all of the defendants and to sue appropriately. The distinction between public and private patient is vitally important.

[2.33] It goes without saying that care is required in ensuring that the appropriate defendants are named on a summons. Claims against public hospitals are managed by the State Claims Agency (SCA). As and when appropriate, confirmation should be sought from the SCA in relation to indemnity – the normal position is that clinical staff at a public hospital will be indemnified by the hospital/the HSE but this is subject to confirmation in each case, and if such indemnity arrangement is in place the practice of the SCA has been to request that a single defendant is named to represent the hospital/HSE in legal proceedings (the SCA should agree to the title of the defendant: for Dublin hospitals nominee defendants (such as the chief executive of the hospital) have commonly been used, for some hospitals there is a corporate entity which is named as defendant, for some hospitals the HSE is named as defendant, and another alternative is that the name of the hospital is used as title for the defendant).

[2.34] If the plaintiff is under 18 years when proceedings commence she is known as a minor plaintiff and, because 'under a disability', must sue through a next friend.[36] A person of unsound mind is also described as a person under a disability and cannot bring proceedings other than by a next friend. If the plaintiff is made a ward of court she must sue through a committee, that is, the person appointed by the President of the High Court to look after her affairs.

[2.35] Before proceedings are issued on behalf of a minor plaintiff, a form of consent of the next friend must be prepared.[37]

---

36. Age of Majority Act 1985, s 3.
37. This form must be signed by the next friend, witnessed by the solicitor and filed in the Central Office when issuing proceedings (RSC, Ord 15, r 20). Remember that the plaintiff's name must appear in the title of proceedings exactly as it is on the birth certificate, including any middle names.

LETTER OF CLAIM

[2.36] Section 8 of the Civil Liability and Courts Act 2004 requires a plaintiff in a personal injuries action (which includes a medical negligence action) to serve notice in writing on the proposed defendant stating the nature of the wrong alleged to have been committed. This step is to be taken within two months of the date on which the plaintiff's cause of action accrued or the date on which the plaintiff first obtained the requisite knowledge or as soon as practicable thereafter. There is no specified format for the letter of claim, but where a plaintiff fails to serve one without reasonable cause, she may be penalised by a court.

[2.37] Section 8 is impractical in the context of medical negligence. The requirement to dispatch a letter of claim in most cases will be impossible to comply with. It is standard for patients not to seek advice from solicitors until well after two months from the date the incident arose or injury occurred as they may be still coming to terms with what has happened. Moreover, it could take several months for solicitors to obtain the medical records, brief an expert and establish grounds for a claim – so the nature of the wrong alleged to have been committed cannot reasonably be outlined in the stipulated format.

[2.38] It is good practice properly to investigate a case prior to dispatching a letter of claim as once this step has been taken it may be difficult to expand the scope of the claim. It is important within a letter of claim to say why s 8 has not been capable of being complied with. In the circumstances, a court should look reasonably at any delay on the part of a plaintiff in dispatching.

[2.39] In a case involving multiple potential wrongdoers then the letter of claim should be served along with a traditional O'Byrne letter. This differs from the standard letter of claim by stating that the injury in question happened as a result of the negligence of the recipient and/or the negligence of other potential defendants but that the plaintiff is not in a position to say which of them is responsible.[38]

LIMITATION

[2.40] Section 7 of the Civil Liability and Courts Act 2004[39] reduced from three years to two, the time limit for bringing medical negligence proceedings. The

---

38. Courts of Justice Act 1936, s 78 provides for situations where an unsuccessful defendant in proceedings can be liable for the costs of the successful defendants as well as for the plaintiff's costs.
39. This amended Statute of Limitations (Amendment) Act 1991, s 3(1).

two-year limitation period runs from the date on which the cause of action accrued or the plaintiff's date of knowledge, if later. The two-year limitation period which applies to personal injuries generally is too restrictive, not taking account of the particular complexities associated with medical negligence claims and the extent of their reliance on expert evidence. There is significant pressure on potential plaintiffs and their legal advisors to initiate proceedings within the two-year statutory limitation period. It is crucial that practitioners investigate a potential claim in a timely fashion so as to be in a position to issue proceedings within the two-year limitation period.

[2.41] Pursuant to s 3(d) of the Personal Injuries Assessment Board Act 2003, medical negligence claims are specifically excluded from the scope of the Injuries Board. They have only a two-year limitation period with no possibility of a temporary 'stopping of the clock' while an Injuries Board assessment takes place. These cases have a considerably shorter limitation period than routine personal injuries cases as in the latter, the running of the clock may be put on hold for several months while the claim is with the Injuries Board. This is so despite the fact that these types of cases are likely to be much more complex and difficult to investigate than ordinary personal injury claims.

[2.42] In some borderline cases, however, it may be dangerous to proceed without PIAB authorisation. A patient falling in a hospital was classified as nursing negligence and not medical negligence in *Kelly v Board of Governors of St Laurence's Hospital*.[40] The plaintiff in *Carroll v Mater Misericordiae Hospital*[41] relied on *Kelly* to argue that he needed a PIAB authorisation and so time stopped running when the case was in PIAB, but the court disagreed and held that the particular fall in *Carroll* was medical negligence and not nursing negligence, and so there was no need to go to PIAB and the claim was statute barred. The only clear statement of principle for the application of s 3(d) is that set out by O'Neill J in *Gunning v National Maternity Hospital*[42] that one must look at the factual circumstances of what happened to the patient rather than classifying something as 'medical negligence' or 'nursing negligence' or 'product liability'. Accordingly one must analyse each factual situation individually. If in doubt, remember that it is always safer to pay for an application to PIAB for authorisation, thereby removing the potential hurdle of the defendant bringing a motion to dismiss for limitation. In *Murphy v DePuy International Ltd*[43] Faherty J ruled that the plaintiff required an authorisation

---

40.   *Kelly v Board of Governors of St Laurence's Hospital* [1988] IR 402.
41.   *Carroll v Mater Misericordiae Hospital* [2011] 2 IR 411, [2011] IEHC 231.
42.   *Gunning v National Maternity Hospital* [2009] 2 IR 117, [2008] IEHC 352.
43.   *Murphy v DePuy International Ltd* [2015] IEHC 153.

from PIAB prior to commencement of the proceedings for negligence arising out of the insertion of a hip replacement system manufactured by the defendant into the plaintiff which was subsequently recalled.

[2.43] The statutory limitation rules may be expressly asserted by a defendant in its defence. If a plea of statute bar is successfully raised it means that proceedings will be dismissed. In *Clarke v O'Gorman*[44] the Supreme Court overruled *Sherry v Primark*[45] and held that the absence of a PIAB authorisation was a matter of defence, not jurisdiction.

[2.44] *Dignam v HSE and Duffy*[46] was a Circuit Court appeal following rejection of the appellant's claim that the claim was statute barred. The respondent had contended that the cause of action was for personal injuries suffered due to distress at witnessing his late wife sitting on a chair in the accident and emergency department for three days and that he was obliged to submit an application to PIAB. The appellant had contended that an application to PIAB was not required as it was exempted under s 3(d). McDermott J upheld the appeal. The respondent would not be entitled to the benefit of s 50 of the Act (which deals with the reckoning of time for the purposes of the Act) as the application to PIAB was made one day after the expiration of the limitation period. The respondent's action was statute barred and his claim was dismissed.

[2.45] The date that the cause of action accrued is not always straightforward in medical negligence. In some cases plaintiffs will seek to rely on the 'date of knowledge' saver contained in s 2 of the Statute of Limitations (Amendment) Act 1991[47] and argue that they lacked the requisite knowledge for time to begin running from the date of the alleged negligence. A plaintiff relying on s 2 bears the burden of establishing that she falls within its ambit. It is difficult to rely on s 2 with confidence because prediction of when a court would fix a plaintiff with the requisite knowledge is so difficult. Wherever possible, a claim should be issued within the primary limitation period.[48]

[2.46] A person's date of knowledge is the date on which that person first had knowledge of the following facts as set out in s 2(1):

> (a)   that the person alleged to have been injured had been injured;

---

44.   *Clarke v O'Gorman* [2014] IESC 72.

45.   *Sherry v Primark* [2010] 1 IR 407, [2010] IEHC 66, [2010] 2 ILRM 198.

46.   *Dignam v HSE and Duffy* [2015] IEHC 295.

47.   A similar provision for fatal injury claims is contained in Statute of Limitations (Amendment) Act 1991, s 6(1)(b).

48.   Wainwright, 'Medical negligence: limitation periods', insight on westlaw-uk.

(b)   that the injury was significant;

(c)   that the injury was attributable in whole or in part to the act or omission which is alleged to constitute negligence, nuisance or breach of duty;

(d)   the identity of the defendant; and

(e)   if it is alleged that the act or omission was that of a person other than the defendant, the identity of that person and the additional facts supporting the bringing of an action against the defendant.

Knowledge that any acts or omissions did or did not, as a matter of law, involve negligence, nuisance or breach of duty is irrelevant. Section 2(2) provides that knowledge includes knowledge that a person might reasonably be expected to acquire: (a) from facts observable or ascertainable by that person; or (b) from facts ascertainable by that person with the help of medical or other appropriate expert advice which it is reasonable for that person to seek. Section 2(3) goes on to say that, notwithstanding the foregoing: (a) a person shall not be fixed with knowledge of a fact ascertainable only with the help of expert advice so long as that person has taken all reasonable steps to obtain (and, where appropriate, to act on) that advice; and (b) a person injured shall not be fixed with knowledge of a fact relevant to the injury which that person has failed to acquire as a result of that injury.

[2.47] The correct interpretation of s 2 was given by the Supreme Court in *Gough v Neary*[49] where the defendant performed an unnecessary hysterectomy on the plaintiff, made false representations to the effect that the operation had been necessary, and used his professional position in an overbearing and melodramatic manner to prevent her, until the limitation period had run, from making further enquiries. The 'date of knowledge' principles enunciated by Brooke LJ in the English Court of Appeal in *Spargo v North Essex Health Authority*[50] were cited:

(1) The knowledge required ... is a broad knowledge of the essence of the causally relevant act or omission to which the injury is attributable;

(2) 'attributable' in this context means capable of being attributed to, in the sense of being a real possibility;

(3) a plaintiff has the requisite knowledge when she knows enough to make it reasonable for her to begin to investigate whether or not she has a case against the defendant. Another way of putting this is to say that she

49.   *Gough v Neary* [2003] 3 IR 92, [2003] IESC 39.

50.   *Spargo v North Essex Health Authority* [1997] EWCA Civ J0313–13, [1997] 8 Med LR 125, [1997] PIQR 235.

will have such knowledge if she so firmly believes that her condition is capable of being attributed to an act or omission which she can identify (in broad terms) that she goes to a solicitor to seek advice about making a claim for compensation;

(4) on the other hand, she will not have the requisite knowledge if she think she knows the acts or omissions she should investigate but in fact is barking up the wrong tree: or if her knowledge of what the defendant did or did not do is so vague or general that she cannot fairly be expected to know what she should investigate; or if her state of mind is such that she thinks her condition is capable of being attributed to the act or omission alleged to constitute negligence, but she is not sure about this, and would need to check with an expert before she could be properly said to know that it was.

[2.48] In *Naessens v Jermyn and O'Higgins*[51] Irvine J stated that the issue was 'to ascertain the point at which it could be said that the plaintiff had sufficient knowledge to justify embarking on the preliminary to issue a writ'. That point was found to be when the plaintiff had the relevant hospital notes and records in her possession in *Farrell v Ryan*,[52] where a plea of statute bar by the defendant was rejected. The plaintiff may have been aware at an earlier stage that the impugned symphysiotomy procedure was carried out on her but 'was not armed with any information that could have justified her issuing proceedings against the defendants or going to a solicitor to instruct that solicitor to issue proceedings'. Mention should be made of a judgment of Peart J relating to the procurement of expert evidence on liability in a medical negligence case and when time for the purpose of the Statute of Limitations should be deemed to commence running: *Dunne v Eastern Regional Health Authority and Ors*.[53] The content of Peart J's judgment in that case – good and all as it may be from a plaintiff's point of view – should not affect the applicability of the interpretation of the relevant statutory provision as was applied by Hardiman J in *Gough v Neary*.

[2.49] It is often very difficult to determine precisely when the statute has begun to run, and it would be very unwise to assume that the date of knowledge can always be postponed until such time as a supportive medical-liability report comes to hand. It is always safer to issue proceedings within two years of the earliest point in time at which the alleged negligence could be said to have arisen. When it comes to limitation a plaintiff cannot 'wait and see'. If she

---

51. *Naessens v Jermyn and O'Higgins* [2010] IEHC 102.
52. *Farrell v Ryan* [2015] IEHC 275.
53. *Dunne v Eastern Regional Health Authority and Ors* [2008] IEHC 315.

knows of any injury, even if minor, the limitation period may have started running.

[2.50] Another mechanism for establishing that the plaintiff may not have had the requisite knowledge is by pleading equitable fraud as against the defendant. Section 71 of the Statute of Limitations 1957 provides that the period of limitation does not begin to run until the plaintiff has discovered fraud.

[2.51] In the exceptional *Gough v Neary*,[54] what had transpired between the doctor and the patient in that case was such that, had equitable fraud been pleaded, the necessary ingredients to meet that plea were present. Hardiman J said:

> All this took place between doctor and patient. Having regard to the relationship I consider that the content and language of the doctor's communications and the express discouragement of further inquires were, prima facie, unconscionable on his part and capable of amounting to … a deliberate concealment of the true facts of what occurred, and an attempt both overbearing and underhand to forestall further enquiry on her part.

[2.52] In minor cases, s 49 of the Statute of Limitations 1957, as amended, provides that the plaintiff who, on the date her cause of action accrued, was suffering from a relevant disability (including legal minority) has until two years after the disability ceases or she dies to issue proceedings in negligence. Thus, where a baby suffers injury at birth as a result of alleged negligence, she has until the eve of her 20th birthday to institute an action because time does not begin to run until she reaches 18 years of age. If that baby's mother also suffered injury at her baby's birth due to alleged negligence, she has two years from the date the cause of action accrued or the date of knowledge, within which to bring a case in negligence.

DELAY

[2.53] Striking out for delay is a matter of grave concern to the plaintiff and understandably so as it may cost her a good claim. In *Donnellan v Westport Textiles*[55] Hogan J observed that the speedy and efficient dispatch of civil litigation is of necessity an inherent feature of the court's jurisdiction under Art 34.1 of our Constitution and found support for that proposition in art 6 of the European Convention on Human Rights, stating 'one might add that this duty also extends to protecting the public interest in ensuring the timely and effective administration of justice'.

---

54. *Gough v Neary* [2003] 3 IR 92, [2003] IESC 39.
55. *Donnellan v Westport Textiles* [2011] IEHC 11.

[2.54] Particular caution should be heeded to older cases which can be risky, such as a cerebral palsy case where the client or their parents come to a solicitor not long before their child's 20th birthday. In those circumstances the case is clearly within the statutory time limit, but the events complained of go back a very significant length of time. It is a scenario where every action by the solicitor will be judicially scrutinised.[56] In this regard a court has the power to strike out for delay which predates the commencement of proceedings and which is of no fault of the solicitor.[57] 'While justice delayed may not always be justice denied, it usually means justice diminished'.[58]

[2.55] The *O'Domhnaill* jurisdiction tends to be employed where, at the time the application to dismiss is brought, such a significant length of time has elapsed between the events giving rise to the claim and the likely trial date that the defendant can maintain that, regardless of the absence of blame of the part of the plaintiff for that delay, it would be unjust to ask to the defendant to defend the claim.[59] The test for determining whether there was pre-commencement delay such as to justify dismissal of a claim may be summarised as: Is there by reason of the lapse in time a real and serious risk of an unfair trial or unjust result; and is there by reason of the lapse of time a clear and patent unfairness in asking the defendant to defend the action?

[2.56] In *McBrearty v The North Western Health Board and Ors*[60] the Supreme Court refused to strike out a 26-year-old plaintiff's claim against the Health Board that he suffered injury at birth as a result of which he suffered severe cerebral palsy. McMenamin J in the High Court[61] found that there had been inordinate and inexcusable delay in bringing the proceedings but had allowed them to proceed on the balance of justice. On appeal the Supreme Court found no inordinate and inexcusable delay and so the action would be allowed to proceed unless it would be fundamentally unfair to any particular defendant because of his special circumstances to have to defend the action. The two defendant doctors, a long time after the events in question, were faced with huge

---

56. Murray, 'Introduction to Medico Legal Claims Handling from a Plaintiff's Perspective' (Law Society Certificate in Healthcare Law and Practice, 2013)
57. *O'Domhnaill v Merrick* [1984] IR 151, [1985] ILRM 40; *Toal v Duignan* [1991] ILRM 135.
58. Per Henchy J in *O'Domhnaill v Merrick* [1984] IR 151, [1985] ILRM 40.
59. Many of the decisions which have considered the *O'Domhnaill* jurisdiction have been delivered in what may be described as historic sexual abuse cases where proceedings were commenced very many years after the acts of abuse were alleged to have been perpetrated.
60. *McBrearty v The North Western Health Board and Ors* [2010] IESC 27.
61. *McBrearty v The North Western Health Board and Ors* [2007] IEHC 431.

expense and having to pay their own lawyers and so it was fundamentally unfair that they would have to face trial and it was not necessary to consider the balance of justice, but the Health Board was in an entirely different position and would be indemnified by its own insurance company. The mishap occurred in a small hospital and the available medical records were more than adequate.

[2.57] In *Glynn v The Governors and Guardians of the Hospital for the Relief of Poor Lying-In Women, Dublin*[62] O'Sullivan J similarly held that the plaintiff's case should continue and dismissed the defendant's application to strike out. The plaintiff was born in 1981 and suffered cerebral palsy but proceedings were not issued until 2000. Certain documents relating to the birth had never been discovered and neonatal notes had only been discovered in 1998. The defendant claimed the delay had prejudiced its defence and claimed that certain witnesses were no longer available or could not recall the events in question. While much of the delay was in fact inordinate and inexcusable, the plaintiff was in her minority during all the relevant period of inordinate and inexcusable delay. The court was not satisfied that allowing her case to proceed would be unjust.

[2.58] In *Farrell v Ryan*[63] there was a delay of 51 years but, on the reformulation of the plaintiff's claim[64] she succeeded in defeating the defendant's plea of delay. Cross J described the inherent jurisdiction of the court to dismiss for delay as being 'clearly a draconian measure' and said that 'the right to a speedy trial … must, I believe, be subordinate to the right to a trial in the first place'.

[2.59] Of even more concern than the jurisprudence in relation to pre-commencement delay, is that in relation to post-commencement delay.[65] There is a line of authorities stemming from *Primor Plc v Stokes Kennedy Crowley*[66] which involves examination of whether any delay is inordinate or inexcusable (the burden of proving which is on the defendant) and whether, assuming it is both, the balance of justice favours dismissal. The *Primor* jurisdiction is usually exercised in proceedings where there has been post-commencement delay or a

---

62. *Glynn v The Governors and Guardians of the Hospital for the Relief of Poor Lying-In Women, Dublin* [2000] IEHC 41.
63. *Farrell v Ryan* [2015] IEHC 275.
64. The reformulation of the plaintiff's case to proceed on the single basis that 'there was no justification whatsoever in any circumstances for the performance of the symphysiotomy on the plaintiff at the time it was performed' followed the reformulation by the plaintiff appellant in *Kearney v McQuillan and North Eastern Health Board* [2010] 3 IR 576 which precluded any complaint about the manner in which the operation was carried out as opposed to the decision to carry it out at all.
65. *Brennan v Fitzpatrick* [2001] IESC 105.
66. *Primor Plc v Stokes Kennedy Crowley* [1996] 2 IR 459.

combination of pre- and post-commencement delay. Old cases are risky cases, even if they are brought within the statutory time period. Once taken on, every single letter and every single time gap on the solicitor's file will be scrutinised most carefully; the solicitor will be heavily criticised and runs the risk of the action being struck out if there is culpable delay in terms of prosecution of the case.

[2.60] In *Keogh v Wyeth Laboratories Inc*[67] the plaintiff had issued proceedings in 1989. The defendants had issued a motion seeking to have the plaintiff's action dismissed for want of prosecution or alternatively for inordinate and inexcusable delay. In reply the plaintiff submitted that the case was a complex one which required much detailed investigation and, unlike the defendants, she had very limited resources. She also alleged that the defendants by their inactivity and attitude had acquiesced in any delay that had taken place. McKechnie J refused the defendant's application to strike out. Despite the fact that on the face of it the relevant time period looked appalling, the balance of justice did not favour the dismissal of the action. McKechnie J stated that if he did so he 'would have a real sense of doing an injustice to the plaintiff'.

[2.61] The defendants in *O'Riordan v Maher and Ors*[68] were refused their application to set aside renewal of the plaintiff's summons or in the alternative, to dismiss for want of prosecution. The defendants' ability to defend had not been impaired and Birmingham J found that 'if one has regard to the very serious difficulties in which the plaintiff found himself that the interests of justice are served by allowing the parties to litigate this dispute. Both sides have a case to make and both sides are in a position to do so'.

[2.62] Abbott J in *McCarthy v South Infirmary*[69] refused an application to dismiss for inordinate and inexcusable delay and for want of prosecution on the basis that death of one of the defendants should not be a reason to dismiss the case as death alone had never been a reason for not allowing a case to go on.

[2.63] In *Mangan v Dockery*[70] Costello J dismissed an application to set aside renewal of a summons. The plaintiff suffered severe and permanent injury as a consequence of severe respiratory distress in the postnatal period and claimed that this was caused by negligence on the part of the defendant consultant obstetrician. The personal injury summons was issued in 2008 but no attempt was made to serve this summons on the defendant. However, the lapse in time

---

67. *Keogh v Wyeth Laboratories Inc* (31 July 2003) HC, McKechnie J. This was overturned on appeal to the Supreme Court: [2006] 1 IR 345; [2005] IESC 46.
68. *O'Riordan v Maher* [2012] IEHC 274.
69. *McCarthy v South Infirmary* [2004] IEHC 429.
70. *Mangan v Dockery* [2014] IEHC 477.

between then and the date of issue, and renewal in 2013 was attributable to the efforts taken by the solicitor in complying with the careful and necessary directions of counsel as to the issues that needed to be fully addressed before the summons could be properly served upon the defendant. Costello J found that it would neither be possible nor proper for the plaintiff's case to proceed without the appropriate expert paediatric neurological evidence being available to justify the bringing of proceedings against the defendant. It was only possible to gain paediatric neurological evidence at a later stage. The court held that there existed a good or potentially good reason to renew the summons.

[2.64] The duty of a solicitor who delays in serving proceedings was examined in *Creevy v Barry-Kinsella and Ors.*[71] The plaintiff claimed negligence in her care following the delivery by Caesarean section of her twins in 2001. Following the birth she suffered a significant haemorrhage. In order to resolve the haemorrhage, a decision was taken to perform a hysterectomy on the plaintiff. She alleged that her treatment post-haemorrhage was negligent, particularly the decision to perform a hysterectomy. Proceedings issued in 2004 and were served in 2006. The first and fourth defendants and the sixth defendant sought an order seeking to set aside the order of the High Court renewing the summons. Dunne J stated:

> 'The question therefore arises, does the need to carry out such an investigation provide the necessary "other good reason" as set out in Order 8(1)? In my view, the answer to that question in the context of this case, and having regard to all the circumstances of this case, is undoubtedly yes.'

It was clear that there was other good reason for the failure of the plaintiff to serve within the time permitted. The delay, although inordinate, was not inexcusable. Dunne J accepted the principle that 'the need to investigate the basis of the claim is not a licence to delay' but on the facts, was satisfied that the plaintiff and her advisors had not overstepped the boundaries of what was permissible. It was found that the prejudice to the plaintiff in not renewing the summons far outweighed the prejudice to the defendants, and so their application was dismissed.

[2.65] In *Flynn v Bon Secours Health Systems Ltd*[72] Hogan J overturned permanent stays which had been placed on medical negligence actions by the Circuit Court as a result of the plaintiff's inability to produce an expert medical report. Of significance was the fact that the claims were not made against medical professionals but against their hospitals, a report in the

---

71. *Creevy v Barry-Kinsella and Ors* [2008] IEHC 100.
72. *Flynn v Bon Secours Health Systems Ltd* [2014] IEHC 87.

possession of one of the defendants indicated that the basis of the plaintiff's complaint was, at least to some degree, well founded and the balancing of rights rendered permanent dismissals premature.

[2.66] When dealing with an application to dismiss on grounds of delay, a court should factor into its considerations Ireland's obligations under art 6 of the Convention.[73] In assessing the balance of justice in the context of delay, courts have traditionally favoured plaintiffs. The rule to remember, however, is that prejudicial delay will defeat a claim even if it is brought within the limitation period.

PLEADINGS

[2.67] Medical negligence actions, like all personal injuries actions, must be commenced by way of a personal injuries summons containing full particulars of negligence and damage alleged to have been suffered by the plaintiff.[74] Precision is key – give a concise statement of the facts on which the plaintiff will rely in support of her allegations of negligence. Plead what you mean and mean what you plead.

[2.68] In some cases it may be impossible for the claim to be particularised to the necessary extent within the two-year limitation period, because delays have been encountered in taking up medical records and/or obtaining expert opinion. The courts have in the past condemned practitioners for commencing medical negligence cases without firstly obtaining an expert report supportive of a claim.[75] In one passage from a High Court judgment that has subsequently been quoted with approval in both the High and Supreme Courts, Barr J stated that:

> It is irresponsible and an abuse of the process of the court to launch a professional negligence action against institutions such as hospitals and professional personnel without first ascertaining that there are reasonable grounds for so doing. Initiation and prosecution of an action in negligence on behalf of the plaintiff against the hospital necessarily required appropriate expert advice to support it.[76]

In the professional negligence context the Supreme Court has said: 'Proceedings must have an appropriate basis. Counsel have a duty of care'.[77] On one appeal to the Supreme Court the naming of a medical practitioner as a respondent without

---

73. Per Irvine J in *Cassidy v The Provincialate* [2015] IECA 74.
74. Civil Liability and Courts Act 2004, s 10.
75. *Sugg v O'Keeffe and Anor* [2005] IESC 92.
76. *Reidy v National Maternity Hospital* [1997] IEHC 143.
77. *Connolly v Casey and Murphy* [2000] 1 IR 345, [2000] 2 ILRM 226.

proper cause was described as 'deplorable' and 'in no way excused'.[78] In the latter decision Keane J referred to the 'serious responsibility which rests on both branches of the legal profession in the institution and conduct of proceedings for negligence against professional persons'.

[2.69] On the other hand, it has been held that time can begin to run against a plaintiff even in the absence of being in possession of a supportive report.

[2.70] A practical solution to the problem posed is that practitioners, as a precautionary measure, issue but do not serve proceedings until such time as the claim has been properly investigated and supportive expert opinion obtained. Under no circumstances should a personal injury summons which is simply issued for the purpose of beating the clock be served without a supportive independent expert report. The only circumstances in which it is permissible to issue medical proceedings in the absence of appropriate supportive expert reporting is where the claim is about to become statute barred. A summons issued in such circumstances is usually referred to as a 'precautionary', 'protective' or 'safety' summons, and a summons issued in such circumstances is issued purely to prevent the cause of action from becoming statute barred. Other procedural steps such as serving a letter of claim, serving the summons, and swearing/filing/serving an affidavit of verification are not taken until such time as appropriate expert evidence supporting the plaintiff's claim is procured.

[2.71] In such a scenario, there should be included a statement to the effect that the plaintiff reserves the right to add further and better particulars and that the summons was issued to avoid the claim becoming statute barred.[79]

[2.72] A period of 12 months is allowed for service of a summons following issue, and if necessary a plaintiff can apply *ex parte* for renewal of a summons which operates to allow six months for service from date of renewal. The device of the precautionary summons was described as 'perfectly possible and legitimate' by McGuinness J in the Supreme Court,[80] and the legitimacy of the device was also recognised by O'Neill J in a later High Court judgment.[81]

[2.73] A summons may be renewed for a period of six months once the court is convinced that reasonable efforts have been made to serve or that there was

---

78. *Cooke v Cronin and Neary* [1999] IESC 54.
79. RSC, Ord 1A, r 6.
80. *Cunningham v Neary and Ors* [2004] 2 IR 625, [2004] IESC 43.
81. *O'Grady v Southern Health Board and Tralee General Hospital* [2007] 2 ILRM 51, [2007] IEHC 38.

good reason for the failure to serve.[82] In medical negligence cases it should, per *O'Grady v Southern Health Board and Tralee General Hospital*[83] be sufficient to show that proceedings were not served as expert opinion confirming negligence was awaited – subject to a duty to act diligently in obtaining the reports. In any case where a summons has been renewed on an *ex parte* application, any defendant shall be at liberty before entering an appearance to serve a notice of motion to set aside such order. Rule 2 imposes a burden of proof on a defendant to point to evidence which would have prompted a court hearing the *ex parte* application for renewal to refuse same.

[2.74] If when the matter has been properly investigated it is decided that a sustainable case in medical negligence arises and if at that point in time a decision is made to proceed with the case then detailed particulars of claim can be drafted.

[2.75] If given the liberty to do so a defendant might allow a very significant amount of time to pass by before entering its personal injuries defence. Plaintiff lawyers should make appropriate diary entries to remind them to take the appropriate steps at the appropriate times to prevent such delay. An important fact to remember is that in a High Court case (the specifics of the rules in the Circuit Court, which are different, will not be covered here) the eight-week time period a defendant has within which to enter its defence only commences running when the plaintiff has served an affidavit of verification covering the contents of the indorsement of claim on the personal injuries summons.[84] Because of this it is wise, if possible, to serve an affidavit of verification at the same time as service of the personal injuries summons. When the eight-week time period allowed to the defendant to enter its defence has elapsed the plaintiff must dispatch a 21-day warning letter before proceeding with a motion for judgment in default of defence – such warning letter should consent to late delivery of the defence within 21 days of the date of the letter and state that if within such 21-day period of time the defendant does not deliver its defence the plaintiff shall, without further notice, proceed with a motion for judgment in default of defence, and the warning letter will be opened to the court to support an application for the costs of such motion.[85]

---

82. RSC, Ord 8, r 1.
83. *O'Grady v Southern Health Board and Tralee General Hospital* [2007] 2 ILRM 51, [2007] IEHC 38.
84. RSC, Ord 1A, r 10(4) as inserted by Rules of the Superior Courts (Personal Injuries) 2005 (SI 248/2005).
85. RSC, Ord 27, r 9(1).

PARTICULARS

[2.76] Requests for particulars[86] should arise out of the pleadings – they should not amount to a detailed cross-examination on every issue or stray into matters of evidence. *McGee v O'Reilly*[87] concerned a plaintiff's request for particulars in a medical negligence case. The Supreme Court, in dismissing the appeal, held that the purpose of pleadings and particulars were to define the issues between the parties, to confine the evidence of the trial to the matters relevant to those issues and to ensure that neither party was taken at a disadvantage by the introduction of matters not fairly to be ascertained from the pleadings.

[2.77] Hogan J in *Armstrong v Moffatt and Ors*[88] refused the vast majority of particulars raised by the defendant for reason of lack of necessity or prematurity, referring to the 'misplaced enthusiasm' for the practice of raising particulars which had 'been allowed to proliferate in many areas of legal practice far beyond the boundaries stipulated by Order 19 rule 7(1)' with 'many pleaders [who] have simply gone astray in their enthusiasm to interrogate every possible detail of their opponent's claim'. This decision is frequently cited by plaintiffs in response to inappropriately onerous requests for further and better particulars which are still raised by defendants in medical negligence litigation. This very sensible decision is frequently cited in response to inappropriately onerous requests for further and better particulars.

DISCOVERY

[2.78] Experience has shown that (for whatever reason) it is not very unusual that a person investigating a query in a medical negligence matter will be furnished with an enormous bundle of hospital records and there will be one or more crucial pages missing from the records. Usually a lawyer or an expert witness notices this and the records absent from the bundle received will be procured after some time has been spent chasing the matter up with the holder of the original records. Requests for all relevant records to be covered in discovery are routinely made in medical negligence cases, and it is accepted that a plaintiff is entitled to discovery of her medical records covering an appropriate period of time.

---

86.   RSC, Ord 19, r 7.
87.   *McGee v O'Reilly* [1996] 2 IR 229.
88.   *Armstrong v Moffatt and Ors* [2013] 1 IR 417, [2013] IEHC 148.

[2.79] In *Ring v Mulcahy and Anor*,[89] Kelly J in the Court of Appeal dismissed a plaintiff's appeal of a decision made in the High Court to dismiss a discovery application in a medical negligence action. The plaintiff had originally succeeded in obtaining an order for discovery of documents as against the second defendant hospital. She then brought a subsequent motion seeking discovery as against the first defendant, an orthopaedic surgeon, which the High Court refused on the basis that it was merely an application to duplicate and replicate relief which had already been obtained as against the second defendant.

[2.80] It would be entirely wrong for a discovery order of the type which was sought as against the first defendant be made, in circumstances where there was already going to be discovery of three of those categories as a result the order made as against the second defendant. The appeal was dismissed but the original High Court order for discovery as against the second defendant was varied to reflect the inclusion of the first defendant. Irvine J, concurring with Kelly J's decision, added the following observation on the course of action adopted by the plaintiff:

> Not only does that have significant costs implications in the context of proceedings of this nature, it also has the effect of slowing down proceedings of this type, but most importantly it puts a very substantial and significant drain on the resources of the Health Service ... To ask the [first defendant] to conduct the same exercise in my view, places an unwarranted pressure and unnecessary pressure on a defendant in such circumstances.

[2.81] The greater use of the discovery procedure has led to the introduction and reliance upon increased numbers of medical records in the course of proceedings. In *Wright v HSE*[90] the preparation of the discovery documentation by the plaintiff was said to have been 'a perfect example' of how medical records should be prepared and presented.[91]

---

89. *Ring v Mulcahy and Anor* [2015] IECA 148.
90. *Wright v HSE* [2013] IEHC 363.
91. The court and all witnesses had the benefit of paginated books of typed notes of the relevant clinical records laid out in the same format as the originals and interleaved so that the typed note could be read from the left hand page of the folder with the witness having the benefit of a copy of the hand written note on the opposite page.

THE DISCLOSURE RULES

[2.82] The current disclosure rules[92] introduced significant reform for all High Court personal injuries proceedings whereby there must be disclosure by all parties to a case of the reports and statements of expert witnesses they intend to call to give evidence at trial. Parties are not permitted to call any expert to give evidence whose report has not been disclosed in accordance with the rules.

[2.83] It is very important to ensure that any UK experts are aware of the difference in terms of discoverability and disclosability of reports that apply in this jurisdiction versus those which apply in the UK. Remember that any of the material supplied to any expert is also disclosable.

[2.84] Order 39, r 46(1) RSC states that the plaintiff must furnish the other parties with a schedule listing all reports from expert witnesses intended to be called within one month of the service of the notice of trial or within such further time as may be agreed by the parties permitted by the court. Disclosure must be made by the defendant within seven days of receipt of the plaintiff's schedule. Within a further period of seven days exchange of copies of reports listed in both sides' respective schedules must take place.

[2.85] It is important to ensure that exchange of experts' reports is only carried out by way of contemporaneous physical handover of experts' reports, and before such exchange takes place the plaintiff's team should ensure that the release of reports by the defendant will be adequate – ie a plaintiff's team should not hand over to a defendant all of the plaintiff's reports if the defendant will be holding back one or more important reports which it will be relying on at the trial.

[2.86] Within one month of service of notice of trial or within such further period as may be agreed by the parties or permitted by the court, the parties shall exchange the information/statements referred to in s 45(1)(a)(iii), (iv), and (v) of the Courts and Court Officers Act 1995 – this includes details of witnesses as to fact to be called to give evidence at the trial, details of the claim for items of special damages together with supporting documentation, and details in respect of social welfare payments received by the plaintiff (nowadays it is the defendants who procure a statement of recoverable benefits).

[2.87] The disclosure obligation is ongoing. Any party who, after disclosure and exchange has taken place, obtains any report within the meaning of the section

---

92. Rules of the Superior Courts (No 6) (Disclosure of Reports and Statements) (SI 391/1998) inserted new rr 45–51 into Rules of the Superior Courts 1986, Ord 39.

or the name and address of any further witness, must deliver a copy of any such report or statement or details of the name and address of any such witness to the other side.[93]

[2.88] A motion for directions may be brought by any party to a case for failure on the part of their opponent to comply with their requirements.[94] Importantly if at any stage it appears to the court that there has been non-compliance with any provision of the rules, the court may make such order as it deems fit including an order prohibiting the adducing of evidence in relation to which such non-compliance relates or may adjourn the action to permit compliance.

[2.89] In *Kincaid v Aer Lingus Teoranta*[95] Geoghegan J held that 'the purpose of the rules is not to disclose the strengths and weaknesses of each other's case but, rather, to prevent surprise evidence being thrown up at trial with which the other party, at that stage, is unable to deal'.

[2.90] In *Payne v Shovlin and Others*,[96] the Supreme Court dealt with the issue of what exactly constituted a report pursuant to SI 391/1998. The plaintiff contended that a preliminary/draft report which did not contain an expert's final views was not disclosable on the basis that SI 391/1998 should be confined to a report or reports which contain the intended evidence in chief of the expert witness and this was the obvious inference to be drawn from the repeal of the more onerous obligations contained in the previous 1997 rules. Giving judgment in the Supreme Court, Kearns J directed that both the preliminary report and the final report be disclosed to the defendant, stating that:

> while it is correct to say that SI 391/1998 introduced an exception to the general privilege attaching to the communications made in contemplation or in furtherance of litigation it should be remembered that litigation privilege is in itself an exception to the general principle that all relevant information should be before the Court, and the consequent need to construe this latter exemption strictly has been recognised frequently by the Courts ...

[2.91] Kearns J then went on to state that:

> the failure to produce an earlier report providing it contains the substance or part of the substance of the evidence which at the time of its compilation was intended to give may lead to a situation where the course

---

93.   Order 39, r 46 (4).
94.   Order 39, r 47.
95.   *Kincaid v Aer Lingus Teoranta* [2003] 2 IR 314, [2003] IESC 31.
96.   *Payne v Shovlin and Others* [2007] 1 IR 114, [2006] IESC 5.

of cross examination it may emerge that the author expressed a different view, for example in relation to causation in a medical negligence action at an earlier time and adverted to same in the first report. How can the interests of expedition and efficiency be served when such information only emerges in cross examination? It may well require that the trial be adjourned while further lines of enquiry are pursued [or] the claim be dropped altogether. All of these costly and undesirable consequences are avoided by disclosure of all reports which contain any of the substance of the evidence intended to be led.

[2.92] Clearly there is a very broad obligation dealing with all reports which contain any of the substance of the evidence intended to be met. If, therefore, an expert writes a letter to the plaintiff's solicitor pointing out certain weaknesses in the case, then that could be construed as containing at least some of the substance of the evidence and therefore is disclosable.

[2.93] It is wise to ensure that experts are properly instructed from the outset, and to ensure that there is no embarrassment caused by an obligation to disclose, for example, a covering letter which contains an injudicious phrase, or an earlier draft of a report which is unfortunately worded.

[2.94] In *Harrington v Cork City Council and Anor*[97] the plaintiff was ordered to furnish expert reports to the defendant, where the defendant had disclosed no expert witnesses or reports but reserved the right to call any expert evidence or produce expert reports pursuant to the proceedings 'as matters may arise', subject to an undertaking by the defendant that the plaintiff's reports not be furnished to any expert retained by the defendant until such expert had furnished his own report. The defendant thereafter requested the plaintiff to furnish it with copies of the reports referred to in its disclosure schedule. The plaintiff refused to do so absent an undertaking from the defendant that it would not divulge the contents of the plaintiff's expert reports to any experts which the defendant chose to commission in advance of the trial. The defendant refused to limit the conduct of its defence in such a way, therefore the plaintiff refused to deliver copies of the reports to the first defendant and an impasse arose between the parties which fell upon the court to adjudicate on.

[2.95] Kearns P was:

> satisfied by reference to the various authorities cited that the requirements of fairness require a simultaneous exchange of expert reports and that requirement is not abrogated by the non-existence at this point in time of expert reports to the defendants. While specific cases have not been

---

97.   *Harrington v Cork City Council and Anor* [2015] IEHC 41.

opened to the Court, the jurisprudence of the European Court of Human Rights in recent years has repeatedly emphasised the concept of 'equality of arms' in litigation and I think it fair to say that this concept has increasingly permeated judicial thinking in this jurisdiction also. The plaintiff's apprehension that the first defendant will secure a litigious advantage in the current circumstances obtaining in this case is not one without any foundation.

[2.96] In accordance with the Supreme Court decision in *Kincaid v Aer Lingus Teoranta*,[98] the plaintiff's disclosure of his reports was to be conditional upon the defendant's undertaking that those reports would not be given, directly or indirectly, to any expert retained by the defendant until after such expert has furnished his report.

SURVIVAL OF CAUSES OF ACTION ON DEATH

[2.97] Part II of the Civil Liability Act 1961 provides for the survival of a cause of action vested in a person for the benefit of her estate.[99] It preserves a cause of action commenced or entitled to be commenced by a person before her death.[100] However, the extent of recovery is limited and does not include exemplary damages, or damages for any pain or suffering or personal injury or for loss or diminution of expectation of life or happiness.[101] In *Doyle v Dunne*[102] the Supreme Court dismissed an appeal in a medical negligence action where the plaintiff had died before the hearing of her appeal was concluded, as under the legislation, none of the heads of damage in her claim survived her death. An application was made by the defendant in *Hewitt v HSE*[103] to strike out the claims for being statute barred. The court struck out that part of the plaintiff's action brought for the benefit of his wife's estate on the basis that the two-year time limit in the medical negligence claim had elapsed by the time of her death, but refused to strike out the wrongful death claim brought for the benefit of the deceased's dependents as that cause of action did not accrue until the time of her death.

[2.98] On the death of a defendant, any cause of action subsisting against him survives against his estate.[104]

---

98. *Kincaid v Aer Lingus Teoranta* [2003] 2 IR 314, [2003] IESC 31.
99. Civil Liability Act 1961, s 7(1).
100. Per Baker J in *Hewitt v HSE* [2014] 2 ILRM 466, [2014] IEHC 300.
101. Civil Liability Act 1961, s 7(2).
102. *Doyle v Dunne* [2014] IESC 69.
103. *Hewitt v HSE* [2014] 2 ILRM 466, [2014] IEHC 300.
104. Civil Liability Act 1961, s 8.

TRIAL

[2.99] Kearns P issued a practice direction in November 2012 directing that all medical negligence trials were to be set down for trial in Dublin. Even before then the standard practice was for medical negligence trials to be heard in Dublin – they were too long for provincial venues, and most expert witnesses travelling from abroad to give evidence, having heavy clinical and other commitments in England or elsewhere, wished to fly in and fly out of Dublin as soon as possible before and after giving evidence.

[2.100] Medical negligence cases should be specially fixed for trial, instead of being put into the ordinary personal injuries list.

[2.101] It is standard practice that prior to trial the parties agree on a paginated set of the hospital and medical records to facilitate ease of reference to entries in the hospital and medical records during the trial.

[2.102] In some cases it is arguably reasonable, convenient and just to have a modular trial, thus separating out issues of liability and quantum. Ryan J in *Burke v McKenna*[105] exercised his discretion under Ord 36, r 9 RSC to order separate trials on liability and quantum, stating that:

> complex brain injury cases, especially when they give rise to causation issues as well as sequelae questions, very often involve detailed technical evidence by busy experts who may have travelled far to testify. Such witnesses find it difficult to understand how their evidence cannot be scheduled for a precise time. The court can have difficulty accommodating them. It is not very professional to lump all the witnesses whether they are lay or technical together in the hope that somehow the arrangements will work out. It seems to me to make sense to direct separate trials of liability and damages in cases involving complex or lengthy technical, scientific or medical questions. In fact, the difficulty is to explain or justify why any other arrangement should be made.

The modular trial in certain situations may in fact be more costly and defeat the purpose of finality. Each application is fact specific.

A WORD ON COSTS

[2.103] *Wright v HSE and Anor*[106] saw a departure from the ordinary rule that costs follow the event and serves as a warning to plaintiffs of the danger of

---

105. *Burke v McKenna* [2011] IEHC 449.
106. *Wright v HSE and Anor* [2013] IEHC 363.

bringing claims with certain allegations which cannot be substantiated. Irvine J stated that:

> Just because a plaintiff has one good point they should not ... be permitted to litigate a myriad of others and have the court make an order requiring the successful defendant on such issues to pay for that luxury.

[2.104] The court noted that there is now a growing body of case law which suggests that in complex litigation, the court, prior to makings its award of costs, should consider engaging in a more detailed analysis of the precise circumstances which give rise to that order before making its final decision.

[2.105] The following principles were emerging, namely:

(i) The costs of proceedings in any court are ultimately a matter for the discretion of the trial judge.

(ii) In non-complex litigation a successful plaintiff will usually be entitled to an order for the reasonable costs of bringing their case to court to secure their rights. Similarly, a successful defendant will normally be entitled to an order providing for their reasonable costs of defending the action.

(iii) In complex litigation, where there are several events or relatively discrete issues which have not all been resolved in favour of the party who may be considered to have been the successful party in the overall sense, the court should look with greater scrutiny as to how the costs should be treated.

(iv) Where in complex litigation it can be concluded with some degree of certainty that the trial of any discrete issue of law and/or fact which was not resolved in favour of the successful party had the effect of increasing the costs of the proceedings by extending the duration of the hearing then the court should reflect this fact in its order for costs.

(v) Where in complex litigation the party who is in the overall sense considered to have been the successful party has unsuccessfully litigated an issue requiring evidence to be heard from witnesses directed solely towards that issue, the court should disallow the costs of that party's witnesses and should consider making an order that the party who was successful on the issue be paid their costs which should then be set off against any order for costs made against them.

(vi) In complex litigation the court should seek to fashion an order for costs that will do more than award the costs to the winning side so as to discourage parties from raising additional unmeritorious issues.

[2.106] The court was satisfied that regardless of the fact that the plaintiff only succeeded on the last of what was considered to have been four separate legs of her claim, she must nonetheless have been deemed to be the overall winner of proceedings in which the defendants denied any liability and in the course of which she established a right to compensation. However, the proceedings were of a complex variety and warranted the court applying a greater degree of scrutiny to the order for costs which it had to make.

[2.107] The plaintiff argued it was not a balancing exercise as to who won the most points in the match but rather who won the game. The defendants argued that the normal approach could be departed from on the basis that the court was required to spend a great deal of time and expense considering allegations that went unproven. The plaintiff was ultimately awarded 65 per cent of her costs. There is no authority for the proposition that the overall successful plaintiff should be directed to pay the defendant's costs of any issue on which they were unsuccessful, but as *Wright* shows, the imposition of a penalty on the overall winner by directing a percentage reduction in their costs is a possibility.

Chapter 3

EXPERT EVIDENCE

WHO IS AN EXPERT?

[3.01] It is the function of the expert to explain technical matters so as to assist the court in understanding the issues; but uniquely amongst witnesses, experts are permitted to express their opinion about matters before a court, often to give an opinion on the principal issue. The responsibilities of the expert witness are correspondingly great.

[3.02] In the beginning, witnesses called before the courts, both civil and criminal, were permitted only to give eye-witness factual evidence. Opinion evidence was by nature hearsay and if witnesses were allowed to give opinion evidence on ultimate issues there was a serious danger that the jury would be unduly influenced.

[3.03] Nevertheless from the 16th century onwards expert evidence has been permitted when matters before the court were not within the everyday knowledge of judge and jury.[1] If expert evidence was to be called so as to explain certain 'scientific' matters then the calling of the expert should be the responsibility of the court. It was not until the second half of the 18th century that expert evidence, called by a party, was permitted. The case of *Folkes v Chadd*[2] is usually referred to as the first occasion on which the judge (Lord Mansfield CJ), in a case concerning the silting up of a harbour, permitted a chartered engineer to give evidence on behalf of one of the parties.

[3.04] The rules governing expert evidence have evolved over the last 250 years and were encapsulated in modern times by Cresswell J in *The Ikarian Reefer*,[3] a case involving allegations of the deliberate scuttling of a ship. Over 80 days much expert evidence was heard of varying quality, leading the judge to set down the principles which should govern such evidence. He quoted, with apparent approval, the hyperbole of Lord Wilberforce in *Whitehouse v Jordan*:[4] 'Expert evidence presented to the court should be, and should be seen to be, the

---

1. Blom-Cooper and Cooper, 'Historical Background' in Blom-Cooper (ed), *Experts in the Civil Courts* (Oxford University Press, 2006).
2. *Folkes v Chadd* [1782] 3 Doug 157, 99 ER 589.
3. *The Ikarian Reefer* [1993] 2 Lloyd's Rep 68.
4. *Whitehouse v Jordan* [1981] 1 All ER 267.

independent product of the expert uninfluenced as to form or content by the exigencies of litigation'.

[3.05] We know what he meant, but of course the expert's report would not exist at all but for the requirements of litigation. The principles set out by Cresswell J have been incorporated into protocols and rules in various jurisdictions.

THE EXPERT'S DUTY

[3.06] In many jurisdictions the expert, in preparing a report for the court, must make a declaration covering all relevant matters of propriety and rectitude. In some jurisdictions, including in Northern Ireland, the expert's declaration is set out in precise terms and is to be appended to all expert reports presented to the court.

[3.07] As well as the duties set out in such declarations there is a requirement for truth. The courts in England and Wales now require a 'statement of truth' appended to every expert report, the wording of which is obligatory and may not be changed. The statement of truth has the same importance, weight and relevance as the swearing in of a witness to give oral evidence.

THE OVERRIDING DUTY

[3.08] There is no doubt that the expert in adversarial legal proceedings has a duty to the client. When first instructed by a plaintiff the expert's only duty is to the client. If the expert's report is negative, that will be the only duty the expert incurs. When, however, the expert prepares a report which may someday reach the court or when giving oral evidence to the court the expert has another duty, a duty to the court. It is commonly said that this duty overrides any duty the expert may have to his client.

[3.09] The expert owes his client a duty to present his evidence as clearly and persuasively as possible; he has a duty to identify clearly the facts on which his opinion depends, to consider, and be in a position to explain in evidence how his opinion would be affected if the facts were found to be different from those for which his client contends, and to explain clearly the process of reasoning by which he supports his opinion. He has a duty to explain the 'range of opinion' concerning such matters – a duty to include opinions of which he is aware but with which he does not agree. Such a balanced view is required by his duty to the court and in no way conflicts with his duty to the client. If he fails to express such a balanced opinion the trial judge is likely to disregard his evidence as partisan.

[3.10] In an adversarial process the overriding duty might be said positively to reside in the duty to the client. It is perhaps less confusing to summarise the expert's duty as a duty to assist the court.[5]

HOW TO CHOOSE AN EXPERT

[3.11] The best way to go about choosing an expert is to seek the advice of specialist counsel who will have built up a database of tried and tested experts – those they have worked with in the past and are satisfied to recommend. Specialist counsel are always best placed to provide the contact details of an appropriate and reliable expert.

[3.12] It would generally, save with the most limited exceptions, be unwise for a plaintiff solicitor to instruct an expert within the jurisdiction in a medical negligence case. The small population of clinicians and the current cultural climate can discourage doctors and other clinical staff from giving evidence on the instruction of plaintiff solicitors. This is particularly true for breach of duty experts, but is probably best observed in relation to all experts in contested areas.

[3.13] There are published directories of expert witnesses. Experts generally pay for entry into these directories but the entry criteria are not rigorous and there is no guarantee of quality. A few organisations advertise to solicitors that they can provide experts on clinical matters but caution is advised. The aphorism that 'if you want something done quickly you should ask someone who is busy' is never more true than in the context of expert witnesses.

[3.14] There is a large plaintiff support organisation in the UK, AvMA (Action Against Medical Accidents), who provide a list of experts for their members. There is also the Irish organisation, MIA (Medical Injuries Alliance), who provide a list of experts for their members. There are also expert bodies, organisations that exist to support and train experts, such as the Expert Witness Institute and the Academy of Experts.

[3.15] Solicitors have, of course, ready access to specialist counsel who should always be the first port of call.

---

5. Blom-Cooper and Clements, 'Duty to the Court' in Blom-Cooper (ed), *Experts in the Civil Courts* (Oxford University Press, 2006).

[3.16] The initial approach should be to the expert best suited to advise on breach of duty. In birth-related cases that will almost always be an obstetrician, midwife or neonatologist – rarely an anaesthetist. Causation will usually require additional experts. In the most complex cerebral palsy cases that will involve (in addition to the obstetrician and/or midwife advising on breach of duty) a neonatologist, paediatric neurologist and a paediatric neuroradiologist, and the investment in expert evidence will run into many thousands of euros. In such cases several quantum reports will be required. Similarly – but slightly less expensive – a brachial plexus injury will require input from an orthopaedic surgeon with special experience in the treatment of such injuries – a very rare breed. Increasingly frequent are actions for the mother in relation to anal sphincter injuries, negligently caused or negligently repaired. Causation, condition and prognosis in such cases are the prerogative of the colorectal surgeon. Maternal injuries will almost always have psychiatric and/or psychosexual consequences and appropriate experts will be required for causation, condition, prognosis and quantum.

[3.17] If the breach of duty expert is trusted and experienced he will often act as a lead expert and give advice to the instructing solicitor on the choice of experts to be brought in for causation.

[3.18] Whilst expert agencies are an inevitable fact of life in the world of personal injury, there is no place for them in medical negligence. Because there is absolutely no place for any intermediary between solicitor and expert in a medical negligence case, agencies are to be avoided. The relationship between solicitor and expert must be personal and close if the team assembled is to be effective.

HOW TO INSTRUCT AN EXPERT

[3.19] Your relationship with your lead expert will be greatly facilitated if you observe the following suggestions:

1. Enquire first. Do not send the expert several kilos of ill-sorted, semi-legible clinical records until you have ascertained that your expert is:

    *   appropriate;

    *   available;

    *   willing; and

    *   unconflicted.

2. Once accepted, ascertain the expert's terms and conditions and if appropriate agree terms so that the relationship begins on a proper professional footing.

3. Agree a timescale for the provision of the initial report.

4. The letter of instruction should contain:

   • an outline of the plaintiff's case;

   • a statement/attendance note from the plaintiff/mother; and

   • a list of all the clinical documents to be provided.

   (Most experienced experts will not welcome a homily on the law but if you think the expert may be inexperienced, by all means include one.)

   Experts from the UK will be used to working in a system where litigation privilege between solicitor and expert applies. As in most jurisdictions, only the expert's final report will, under normal circumstances, be discoverable. Draft reports and other correspondence will be privileged. It is essential when instructing a UK expert for the first time to explain the draconian provisions of SI 391/1998 Rules of the Superior Courts (No 6) (Disclosure of Reports and Statements) 1998, under which all written communication between solicitor and expert is not only discoverable but is routinely disclosed. He should be warned to put nothing in writing unless it is fit to be disclosed.

5. The medical records should be presented in a professional manner:

   • legible;

   • paginated;

   • copied; and

   • indexed.

   Legible – it is not necessary to hold a medical degree to tell whether a document is legible or not. Do not accept documents from defendants that you cannot read. If you cannot read them the chances are the expert cannot read them either. You will simply be wasting his time by sending them. Do not accept documents from defendants with edges missed by careless photocopying. Suggest to the defendants that they instruct their staff to copy such documents with 95 per cent magnification! They are unlikely to think of it themselves. If there is no writing on a piece of paper, it is unlikely that it will be of interest to your expert. Do not send large numbers of blank sheets. Clinical records should be produced in the format in which they were created, A4 as A4, A3 as A3, etc. Several standard documents are frequently created in A3 format; these include antenatal records, partograms and intensive care unit charts. Cutting them into two sheets of A4 leads to loss of information in the middle. Most importantly, cardiotocograms (CTGs) are produced as continuous rolls of paper; they cannot properly be interpreted if chopped up into A4 slices. There are shops capable of copying long documents and solicitors should not accept CTGs in any other form.

Paginated – ideally the notes should be collated by someone who understands them, such as a nurse or a medical student. If that cannot be afforded, it does not particularly matter, but the notes should be paginated, even if it is in the same haphazard order in which the defendants have supplied them. Without pagination your expert cannot direct you to the pages in the records from which he quotes or to which he will refer.

Copied – once paginated you should make as many copies of the notes as you think you will need for your initial investigation – more can be made later. Do not send your only copy of the records to the first expert and then ask for them to be returned. Everyone involved in litigation (solicitor, counsel, experts and the plaintiff – remember they are her notes and she is entitled to see them, own them and, in as far as she is inclined, to understand them in the light of the experts' reports) will need their own copy.

Indexed – clinical records derive from different sources (eg different hospitals or different departments such as obstetrics/paediatrics) and should be collated and paginated in different bundles. A list should then be made of the different categories.

6.   Acknowledge receipt of the report and pay the bill within the timescale agreed. Experts are usually willing and able to deal with points of clarification promptly and without additional charge.

7.   Do not serve the particulars of negligence without checking that your expert is able to support all the allegations.

8.   As soon as the defence is served send a copy to your expert but do not invite written comments; a supplementary report may be appropriate if there are matters in the defence that raise new issues – but not until after a telephone conference.

9.   Keep your expert informed of progress of the case, and as other reports are received, copy them to all of your other experts.

10. Before applying to specially fix the case for trial check the availability of all your experts. Before applying to the Deputy Master for the case to be specially fixed for trial, check the availability of all your experts.

PART II
CONSENT

Chapter 4

SELF-DETERMINATION IN CHILDBIRTH: THE LAW OF CONSENT

Leroy C Edozien

INTRODUCTION

[4.01] The pregnant woman, like any other recipient of medical treatment, has the right to determine what treatment to accept or to decline. This was famously expressed by Cardozo J in the landmark US case of *Schloendorff v Society of New York Hospital*: '... every human being of adult years and sound mind has a right to determine what shall be done with his own body; and a surgeon who performs an operation without his patient's consent, commits an assault'.[1]

[4.02] It was reaffirmed by Lord Donaldson MR in the English case, *Re T*: 'An adult patient who ... suffers from no mental incapacity has an absolute right to choose whether to consent to medical treatment, to refuse it or to choose one rather than another of the treatments being offered ... This right of choice is not limited to decisions which others might regard as sensible. It exists notwithstanding that the reasons for making the choice are rational, irrational, unknown or even non-existent'.[2]

[4.03] In the same vein, Butler-Sloss J said in *Re MB* that: 'A mentally competent patient has an absolute right to refuse to consent to medical treatment for any reason, rational or irrational, or for no reason at all, even where that decision may lead to his or her own death'.[3]

[4.04] This right is commonly referred to in legal and other texts as 'autonomy' but this word can mean different things to different persons and in different contexts, so this author prefers to use the term 'self-determination'. Self-determination includes not only the right to bodily integrity but also the right to make choices (eg regarding lifestyle, family life, social relations and, in the context of health care, whether or not to accept any particular treatment). In exercising the right to self-determination in pregnancy care, the woman relies on

---

1. *Schloendorff v Society of New York Hospital* [1914] 211 NY 125.
2. *Re T (Adult: Refusal of Treatment)* [1993] Fam 95.
3. *Re MB (Adult, medical treatment)* [1997] 38 BMLR 175 CA.

the information provided by the doctor or midwife, and the right cannot be said to have been upheld if the woman is not in a position to make an informed choice. Unfortunately, interventions are frequently (in some cases, routinely) delivered in the absence of informed choice. The traditional explanation for this disregard of the patient's informed choice was paternalism.

MEDICAL PATERNALISM

[4.05] Medical paternalism is acting in the perceived best interests of the patient irrespective of whether this line of action contradicts the patient's own wishes. By definition, it entails infraction of self-determination. Further, it is a manifestation of the values and attitudes of the doctor or midwife, and reflects their concept of professionalism. As a consequence of developments in modern society, such as the ascendancy of rights thinking, improved levels of public awareness and decreasing social gradients, paternalism is ebbing and health professionals have an obligation to understand and respect their patients' wishes – even in situations where the doctor or midwife does not agree with the expressed wish of a competent woman. To illustrate this, in the past a doctor could perform a Caesarean section against the wishes of a woman in situations where the doctor recognised that not doing the operation could result in serious harm (for example, rupture of the uterus) or death to the woman or her baby. In today's practice, the doctor undertaking a Caesarean section without the consent of the woman will be breaking the law. It does not follow, however, that a patient can demand any particular treatment or that the doctor is obliged to accede to this demand.

[4.06] The protection of patient self-determination entails:

(a) recognition of, and respect for, the patient's right to decide what treatment to have or not to have;

(b) provision of an enabling climate for the patient to make self-determined choices (ensuring effective communication and building trust); and

(c) having regard for the context (social, cultural, emotional, etc) in which the patient has to make her decision.

Self-determination should be viewed not in isolation but in the context of the doctor–patient relationship. The extent to which patients are able to make decisions about their treatment is largely dependent on the style of communication adopted by their doctor.

CONSENT TO TREATMENT

[4.07] The mechanism by which the law aims to protect the patient's right to self-determination is consent. The term 'informed consent' is frequently used in clinical practice and in the legal and medical literature, but it could be confusing. There is no such thing as an uninformed consent; consent must always be informed if it is to be legally and ethically acceptable. On the other hand, the term 'informed consent' has been used in a technical sense to refer to the legal doctrine that requires full disclosure of material risks to the patient, with the standard of disclosure being determined not by the medical profession but by the court, taking account of the patient's expectations. Except when used in this technical sense, the term should be avoided.

[4.08] A doctor or midwife undertaking treatment without consent commits a trespass against the person (assault or battery), regardless of whether their motive was beneficent. Battery is an intentional, unauthorised touching of another person, irrespective of whether any injury results and whether or not the defendant acted in good faith. This includes the situation where a doctor obtains consent from the patient to perform one type of treatment and subsequently performs a substantially different treatment for which consent was not obtained. Across various jurisdictions, the courts have generally avoided applying battery in cases of failure to obtain a valid consent (that is, where there was a failure to disclose information), but have not hesitated to apply it in some cases where the doctor has performed an operation different from the one that the patient actually consented to. Generally, however, most actions relating to non-disclosure of information are brought under negligence law rather than battery.

[4.09] If a doctor performs an illegal operation, he or she cannot use the patient's consent to the operation as an acceptable defence. In obstetrics and gynaecology, this is particularly pertinent to female genital mutilation (FGM), which is illegal in the Republic of Ireland under the Criminal Justice (Female Genital Mutilation) Act 2012 and in the UK under corresponding legislation.[4] Reversal of a defibulation after childbirth is an offence under this legislation, so a doctor who attempts this at the request or 'consent' of the woman or her husband faces criminal prosecution.

---

4.   In England, Wales and Northern Ireland, the Female Genital Mutilation Act 2003, and in Scotland, the Prohibition of Female Genital Mutilation (Scotland) Act 2005.

VALID CONSENT

[4.10] For consent to be valid the following must apply:

    (a) the patient must have the capacity to make the decision;

    (b) there must be no undue influence;

    (c) the patient must have been given (or offered) sufficient information about the proposed treatment.

[4.11] No-one can give consent on behalf of an adult who has capacity. In maternity care the husband cannot give a legally valid consent on behalf of his pregnant wife who does not lack capacity. Where the woman lacks capacity (eg due to unconsciousness or mental ill-health), the clinician should, in consultation with colleagues and the woman's family, provide treatment that is deemed to be in the best interests of the woman.

[4.12] An adult is presumed to have capacity, and a full assessment of capacity is required only in those cases where the clinician has reason to rebut this presumption. In such cases, the clinician must determine whether the patient has capacity to make a decision in respect of the particular treatment that is being offered. To determine capacity, the clinician finds out if the patient is capable of retaining the pertinent information, weighing the options against her values, beliefs and attitudes, and arriving at a decision. In *Fitzpatrick and Anor v FK and Anor*,[5] Laffoy J stated that in assessing capacity a distinction should be made between misunderstanding or misperception of the treatment information in the decision-making process on the one hand, and a decision made for irrational reasons, on the other hand. The former may be evidence of lack of capacity but the latter is irrelevant to the assessment.

[4.13] The Irish Medical Council gives the following guidance on the care of patients who lack capacity[6]: If a patient is unable to understand, retain, use or weigh up the information they have been given to make the relevant decision, or if they are unable to communicate their decision, they may be regarded as lacking the capacity to give consent to the proposed investigation or treatment. A judgment that a patient lacks the capacity to make a particular decision does not imply that they are unable to make other decisions or will be unable to make this or other decisions in the future. Where an adult patient is deemed to lack capacity to make a healthcare decision, you should take reasonable steps to find

---

5.   *Fitzpatrick and Anor v FK and Anor* [2008] IEHC 104, [2009] 2 IR 7.

6.   Medical Council, *Guide to Professional Conduct and Ethics for Registered Medical Practitioners* (7th edn, 2009), para 34.5.

out whether any other person has legal authority to make decisions on the patient's behalf. If so, you should seek that person's consent to the proposed treatment. If no other person has legal authority to make decisions on the patient's behalf, you will have to decide what action to take. In doing so, you should consider:

- which treatment option would provide the best clinical benefit for the patient;

- the patient's past and present wishes if they are known;

- whether the patient's capacity is likely to increase;

- the views of other people close to the patient who may be familiar with the patient's preferences, beliefs and values; and

- the views of other health professionals involved in the patient's care.

[4.14] Consent is invalid if it is obtained by physical force or coercion or, as more commonly obtained in clinical practice, by more subtle forms of undue influence. The well-publicised cases of unnecessary hysterectomies performed in Ireland illustrate the reality and the degree of harm to both bodily integrity and self-esteem when 'consent' is obtained under undue influence and misinformation.

[4.15] For consent to be valid, the patient must be given sufficient information, but what constitutes sufficient information? Two standards have been employed in various jurisdictions: the professional standard and the 'prudent (or reasonable) patient' standard. To determine under the professional standard what constitutes sufficient information, the court relied on medical opinion. Where, on the other hand, the prudent patient standard is applied, the court considers what a reasonable person would want to know in order to make an informed choice.

THE PROFESSIONAL STANDARD

[4.16] The standard for establishing medical negligence was articulated by *Dunne*[7] in Irish law and *Bolam*[8] in English law. In the UK, a doctor is not guilty of negligence if he has acted in accordance with a practice accepted as proper by a responsible body of medical men skilled in that particular art. This standard is known as the '*Bolam* test'. It initially applied to diagnosis and treatment but was

---

7.   *Dunne v National Maternity Hospital and Jackson* [1989] IR 91.
8.   *Bolam v Friern Hospital Management Committee* [1957] 1 WLR 582.

extended to cases of non-disclosure of information. In *Sidaway,*[9] a landmark case in the UK, the House of Lords (in a majority judgment) declined to apply the doctrine of informed consent and opted to apply the *Bolam* test, which favoured the defendant clinician.

[4.17] Although *Bolam* attracted by far greater publicity, an Irish case, *Daniels v Heskin*[10] had established the same principle before *Bolam*. The plaintiff in this case underwent repair of a perineal tear immediately following childbirth. The end of the needle broke and was retained in the perineal tissue. The defendant anticipated that the small piece of metal would either cause no problem or worm its way out of the skin, but failed to inform the plaintiff or her husband about the broken needle. The court determined that withholding this information was acceptable practice and found in favour of the defendant. Kingsmill-Moore J stated that:

> Any attempt to substitute a rule of law or even a rule of thumb or practice for the individual judgment of a qualified doctor, doing what he considers best for the particular patient would be disastrous ... I cannot admit any abstract duty to tell patients what is the matter with them ... all depends on the circumstances – the character of the patient, her health, her social position ... In the present case the patient was passing through a post-partum period in which the possibility of nervous or mental disturbance is notorious ... husband and wife were of a class and standard of education which it would incline them to exaggerate the seriousness of the occurrence and to suffer needless harm.

[4.18] In 1989, the Supreme Court in *Dunne* established principles that were similar to the *Bolam* test. The plaintiff was a twin who had suffered severe hypoxic brain injury at birth. The other twin did not survive. In labour, only the first twin was monitored; as was common practice at the time, the heartbeat of the second twin was not auscultated.

[4.19] Finlay CJ outlined the following principles, which have subsequently become foundational in Irish negligence law:

> 1. To rebut an allegation of negligence in diagnosis or treatment, it must be proved that the defendant medical practitioner did not depart from what any other medical practitioner of equal specialist or general status and skill would have done if acting with ordinary care.
>
> 2. If the medical practitioner has deviated from a general and approved practice, that will not establish negligence unless it is also proved that the course he did take was one which no medical practitioner of similar

---

9.   *Sidaway v Bethlem Royal Hospital Governors* [1985] AC 871.
10.   *Daniels v Heskin* [1954] IR 73.

specialisation and skill would have followed had he been taking the ordinary care required from a person of his qualifications.

3. If a medical practitioner defends his conduct by establishing that he followed a practice which was general and approved of by his colleagues of similar specialisation and skill, he cannot escape liability if the plaintiff establishes that such practice has inherent defects which ought to be obvious to any person giving the matter due consideration.

[4.20] Medical lawyers have long argued that issues of diagnosis (which are essentially technical) should be separated from issues of information disclosure and consent (where not only medical but also non-medical concerns of the patient could be decisive), and opportunities arose for the courts to determine whether the *Dunne* principles applied not only to diagnosis but also to consent. In *Walsh v Family Planning Services*[11] (failure to warn of the risk of orchialgia and impotence following an elective vasectomy) and in *Bolton v Blackrock Clinic*[12] (undisclosed risk of laryngeal nerve injury at surgery), Finlay CJ declared that the *Dunne* principles applied. In other words, the professional standard was upheld. Thus, in relation to (non-)disclosure of information, the Chief Justice felt that the test should be whether the medical profession generally, or a recognised school of opinion within it, would regard a warning as necessary; in the event that a general and approved practice contained inherent defects which should be obvious to any person giving the matter due consideration, then the fact that a medical practitioner followed general medical practice would not be sufficient defence. It should be noted that there was a difference of opinion among the judges in the *Walsh* case, even though they arrived at the same decision in favour of the defendant (on the basis that the plaintiff had been appropriately warned). While the Chief Justice felt that the *Dunne* principles applied, O'Flaherty J felt that the starting point was not the *Dunne* principles (ie the professional standard applied to disclosure of information) but the patient's right to be informed of any material risk, given her own particular context.

DEPARTURE FROM THE PROFESSIONAL STANDARD

[4.21] The courts do, however move with the times. With the ascendance of consumer advocacy and rights thinking, a gradual but steady shift away from the professional standard occurred in both Ireland and the UK.

---

11.   *Walsh v Family Planning Services Ltd* [1992] 1 IR 496.
12.   *Bolton v Blackrock Clinic* (23 January 1997) SC.

[4.22] In *Geoghegan v Harris*[13] the plaintiff sued the defendant for failing to disclose to him in advance of a dental operation the risk that chronic neuropathic pain might eventuate as a consequence of the procedure. The risk of nerve injury and resultant severe, chronic pain was statistically remote – less than 1 in 100. The medical experts all testified that it was acceptable practice not to warn of the remote risk of neuropathic pain. Nonetheless, Kearns J held that the defendant had an obligation to warn the plaintiff of this material risk. In other words, the professional standard was rejected in favour of the prudent patient standard. Rather than adopt the professional standard (and use the 'inherent defect' argument to find in favour of the plaintiff), Kearns J applied the prudent patient standard. Kearns J stated unequivocally that '[c]urrent Irish law requires that the patient be informed of any material risk, whether he inquires or not, regardless of its infrequency'. In 2007, the Supreme Court reiterated in *Fitzpatrick v White*[14] that the prudent patient test was the applicable standard in Ireland.

[4.23] A similar transition from the professional standard to the prudent patient standard took place in the UK. The case of *Bolitho* was not about consent, but it established that if the professional opinion is not capable of withstanding logical analysis, the judge is entitled to hold that the body of opinion is not reasonable or responsible.[15] In *Pearce* the Court of Appeal stated that 'a doctor's decision not to disclose risks will now have to be subjected to logical analysis, and if he has withheld without a good reason information that should have been disclosed then he will be liable even though his decision may have been consonant with ordinary professional practice'.[16] Two further cases showed that the courts no longer deferred routinely to medical opinion. In the first of these, *Chester*, the House of Lords side-stepped the requirement to prove causation (ie had the plaintiff been warned of the risk that had not been disclosed, she would not have had the treatment at any time), in order to protect the patient's right to self-determination.[17] In the other, *Birch*, the High Court stated that the duty to disclose significant risks (that would affect the decision of a patient) included disclosure not only of information about the particular treatment being offered, but also of information about alternative treatments.[18] In the *Montgomery* case

---

13.   *Geoghegan v Harris* [2000] 3 IR 536.

14.   *Fitzpatrick v White* [2008] 3 IR 551, [2008] 2 ILRM 99.

15.   *Bolitho v City and Hackney Health Authority* [1998] AC 232, [1997] 4 All ER 771.

16.   *Pearce v United Bristol Healthcare NHS Trust* [1998] EWCA Civ J0520-16, [1999] PIQR P53.

17.   *Chester v Afshar* [2004] UKHL 41.

18.   *Birch v University College London Hospital NHS Foundation* Trust [2008] EWHC 2237 (QB).

decided in 2015 the UK Supreme Court finally reached the position that the Irish Supreme Court had taken 15 years earlier.[19] The case concerned a woman with diabetes whose son was born with serious and permanent disabilities after a shoulder dystocia during vaginal delivery. Montgomery's obstetrician had not warned her of the risk of shoulder dystocia during vaginal delivery or discussed alternatives such as Caesarean section. The court held that the doctor should have done both: doctors have a duty to ensure that each patient is aware of any material risks of any recommended treatment and of any reasonable alternative treatments. The test of materiality is whether a reasonable person in that particular patient's position would be likely to attach importance to the risk, or whether the doctor is – or should reasonably be – aware that that particular patient would be likely to attach importance to it.

[4.24] Thus both the Republic of Ireland and the United Kingdom have effectively adopted the 'doctrine of informed consent' which was articulated in the US case of *Canterbury v Spence*[20] where it was held that it was for the court to determine the extent of, and any breach of, the doctor's duty to inform. The claimant was a 19-year-old man with severe pain between his shoulder blades who was referred to a neurosurgeon. The doctor told him that he would have to undergo an operation (laminectomy) to correct a suspected ruptured disc. The patient did not object to the operation or ask any questions, but in answer to his mother's question the doctor said the operation was not any more serious than any other operation. The day after the operation, the claimant fell from his hospital bed; he was paralysed in the lower half of his body and became permanently disabled. The claimant sued the doctor and hospital on the ground that the doctor was negligent in failing to disclose a risk of serious disability inherent in the procedure. In a landmark decision, Robinson J upheld the claim that the 1 per cent risk of paralysis should have been disclosed. Significantly, the court decided that the standard for determining whether adequate information had been given was not that of professional opinion but of the reasonable patient. The professional standard was also abandoned in favour of the prudent patient standard in the Canadian case of *Reibl v Hughes*[21] and the Australian case of *Rogers v Whitaker*.[22]

---

19. *Montgomery v Lanarkshire Health Board* [2015] UKSC 11.

20. *Canterbury v Spence* [1972] 464 F 2d 772.

21. *Reibl v Hughes* [1980] 114 DLR (3d) 1.

22. *Rogers v Whitaker* [1992] HCA 58,(1992) 175 CLR 479.

THE CAUSATION HURDLE

[4.25] The adoption of the prudent patient standard does not necessarily mean that the plaintiff in consent cases has an easy ride. There are two related obstacles that remain. In medical negligence cases, the plaintiff has to prove not only that there was a breach of the duty of care but also that an injury was suffered as a result of the breach and that but for the breach the injury would not have occurred. In other words, the plaintiff has to prove causation. In consent cases, the plaintiff has to prove that but for the failure of the defendant to warn of the risk that materialised, the injury would not have happened, and that had the plaintiff been warned of the risk, she would not have accepted the treatment.

[4.26] In determining causation, the courts will consider either what this particular patient, the plaintiff, would have done if she had been warned ('the subjective application of the prudent patient standard') or what the reasonable person in the plaintiff's shoes would have done ('the objective application'). It is argued by some judges and commentators that the subjective application gives the plaintiff an unfair advantage over the defendant by virtue of hindsight bias. This concern led the court in *Canterbury v Spence* and in *Reibl v Hughes* to apply the objective test in determining causation (that is, requiring the plaintiff to show that disclosure of the particular risk would have caused a reasonable person in the plaintiff's position to decline the treatment offered). On the other hand, it is also argued that the objective application substitutes the wishes of the plaintiff with those of a hypothetical person and so fails to protect the patient's right to self-determination. As pointed out in the Australian case *O'Brien v Wheeler*:[23] 'An adult patient who is in a position to make a choice has the right to elect a surgical procedure which the hypothetical "reasonable" person in his or her shoes would avoid, and refuse a procedure which the hypothetical "reasonable" person in his or her shoes would embrace'.

[4.27] The pros and cons of these arguments were addressed at length by Kearns J in *Geoghegan v Harris*.[24] The learned judge settled for an approach which combines the objective and the subjective, a 'dual and combined approach'. After reviewing the comments of judges and academic commentators on the subject, he said:

> It seems to this Court that both approaches are valuable in different ways and that both should be considered. In the first instance it seems to me that the Court should consider the problem from an objective point of view. What would a reasonable person, properly informed, have done in

23. *O'Brien v Wheeler* (23 May 1997) Supreme Court of New South Wales.
24. *Geoghegan v Harris* [2000] 3 IR 536.

the Plaintiff's position? This is the yardstick against which the particular plaintiff's assertion must be tested.

The phrase 'in the Plaintiff's position' can be taken as meaning the Plaintiff's age, pre-existing health, family and financial circumstances, the nature of the surgery – in short, anything that can be objectively assessed, though personal to the Plaintiff.

Purely subjective factors would include not only the matters referred by Hutchison J in *Smith v Barking*, (which may overlap to some degree)[25] but also the dialogue between the particular patient and the medical practitioner, information to be gleaned from contemporaneous notes or correspondence, admissions to third parties (particularly contemporaneous admissions), and, perhaps most importantly, evidence of the actual conduct of the patient prior to surgery, given that actions generally speak louder than words.

There may be many instances where there is a shortfall of subjective material or information in which case the Court will have to decide a causation issue on its own best estimate from the evidence of what a reasonable person would have done in the particular circumstances. That is another good reason for starting with the objective test.

However, it seems to me that any objective test must sometimes yield to a subjective test when, but only when, credible evidence, and not necessarily that of the Plaintiff, in the particular case so demands. While obviously the Court must accord due deference to the testimony both of the patient and the medical practitioner, the cases already cited highlight the difficulties each may have in providing an account on which the Court can safely or absolutely rely. Wherever possible, the Court should look elsewhere for credible confirmation. If a reliable picture in fact then emerges, the Court can act on it to reach a conclusion one way or the other. If this dual and combined approach smacks of pragmatism so be it. It is in my view well justified if it achieves a better result in terms of deciding what probably would have occurred. At the end of the day it seems to me that the different approaches are more about methodology than any legal principle. It is an exercise in 'fact construction'. In any such hypothetical though necessary exercise, there are dangers in

---

25. These matters are: 'religious or some other firmly held convictions: particular social or domestic considerations justifying a decision not in accordance with what, objectively seems the right one: assertions in the immediate aftermath of the operation made in a context other than that of a possible claim for damages: in other words, some particular factor that would suggest that the plaintiff had grounds for not doing what a reasonable person in her situation might be expected to have done'. *Smith v Barking HA* [1995] 5 Med LR 285, 288.

dogmatically adopting one approach to the exclusion of the other, and certain aides to analysis would be forsaken by doing so.

[4.28] This 'dual and combined approach' was subsequently applied in *Winston v O'Leary*[26] where MacMenamin J, having rejected the subjective approach as being unfair to the defendant, decided that there was nothing to suggest that the plaintiff would have avoided the operation if he had been informed of the remote risk of post-operative pain. The plaintiff suffered chronic pain after a vasectomy performed by the defendant. He alleged that he had not been fully informed of all of the risks associated with the operation and had, therefore, not given a valid consent. The defendant failed to scale the causation hurdle.

[4.29] In the celebrated English case of *Chester v Afshar*,[27] the Supreme Court was so keen to promote the patient's right to self-determination that it side-stepped the causation hurdle. A journalist underwent a spinal operation in the hands of a neurosurgeon. The risk of cauda equina syndrome complicating this operation was about 1–2 per cent but this risk materialised, and it was established at first instance that the defendant did not warn the claimant of the risk. It was accepted that the defendant was not negligent in his conduct of the operation, but the question of causation was contentious and was the subject of an appeal to the apex court. The claimant stated that if she had been informed of the risk of cauda equina syndrome, she would have still had the operation but she would have taken time to consider her options and would not have had the operation on that particular day, 21 November 1994. The traditional rule of causation required the claimant to show that had she been warned of the risk that materialised, she would not have undergone the operation. The Supreme Court was concerned that she had not been warned of the risk of cauda equina syndrome, but the claimant's truthfulness left it in a quandary: it was keen to protect her right to be informed of risks that may determine her decision whether to proceed, but causation was a stumbling block. While two of the judges stuck to the traditional causation rule, the majority felt that the right to self-determination was so fundamental that it had to be upheld at the expense of a legal tradition. The majority judges were unequivocal in asserting the primacy of self-determination and by a majority of 3–2 the House of Lords decided in favour of the claimant. In doing so, the court broke the traditional principles of causation and placed greater emphasis on policy and corrective justice.

---

26. *Winston v O'Leary* [2006] IEHC 440.
27. *Chester v Afshar* [2004] UKHL 41.

THE TIMING OF CONSENT

[4.30] It is good practice to allow an appropriate interval between the time that consent is obtained from a patient and the time that treatment is delivered. Legally and ethically, there is no fixed period. What is important is that the patient is allowed time to reflect and, if necessary, change her mind or ask for further information. In non-elective treatment this may not be possible. In all cases, however, emphasis should be on providing the patient with tailored, pertinent information (so that she understands what is proposed, why it is proposed and what her options are) rather than bombarding her with a truckload of generic information and shoving a consent form in front of her before she has digested the information.

[4.31] The issue of timing of consent in non-elective surgery was addressed in *Fitzpatrick v White.*[28] The plaintiff was a professional musician who had a cosmetic operation to correct a squint in his left eye. Unfortunately he suffered a rare complication of the operation – slippage of the medial rectus muscle behind the left eye – and had double vision and headaches. He alleged that he had not been warned of this risk and that, had he been warned, he would not have undergone the operation. The High Court found that he had been warned and held that the plaintiff would have had the operation even if he had not been warned of the risk of muscle slippage. The plaintiff then filed an appeal with the Supreme Court arguing that the warning was given too late – 30 minutes before the operation. The Supreme Court accepted that it was not good practice to obtain consent at such a late stage, especially for a non-emergency procedure. It found, however, that a valid consent had been obtained – because the plaintiff was capable of making a rational decision at the time consent was obtained. In other words, the court found that the defendant did not breach the duty of care by obtaining consent so late in the process of care. This does not sit well with the court's expressed view that it was not good practice to obtain consent at such a late stage. The cause of patient self-determination would have been better served if the court held that obtaining consent so late in the process was a breach of the duty of care; the court could then have achieved the result it wanted by holding that since the plaintiff was still capable of making a rational decision at the time, the claim failed on causation.

[4.32] It should be noted that the plaintiff was in his bed on the ward and had not had his pre-anaesthetic medication. The court determined that at this point he was still in a position to make a rational decision whether or not to proceed with the treatment. His case is different from that of a woman in the throes of labour

---

28. *Fitzpatrick v White* [2008] 3 IR 551, [2008] 2 ILRM 99.

who is made to sign a consent form while on a trolley en route to the operating theatre or after arrival in the theatre. It is likely that a court will deem this woman, who is in severe pain and may even have had a narcotic analgesic, not to be in a position to make a well-considered choice. The way to protect the woman's right to self-determination in such cases is to ensure that she is provided with pertinent information throughout the care pathway from antenatal care through intrapartum care and beyond, so that she is aware of unfolding events and what potential developments and options are on the horizon. That is to say, consent should be viewed not just as an event (the signing of a form) but as a process. The Irish Medical Council advises: 'It is not recommended to seek consent when a patient may be stressed, sedated or in pain and therefore less likely to make a calm and reasoned decision. Where possible, you should explain risks well in advance of an intervention'.[29]

DOES CONSENT HAVE TO BE IN WRITING?

[4.33] A *bona fide* consent is given when the patient makes an informed choice after a dialogue with the doctor, in a collaborative relationship. It appears, however, that clinicians often obtain a contrived consent rather than a *bona fide* one. In contrived consent, the patient is presented with a menu of choices, or a menu of one, and invited to say yes. The menu may be accompanied by a large quantity of information, most of it not specific to the patient, or little or no information. The emphasis is not on the patient's understanding of information but on his or her signal that the doctor may proceed with treatment. In most consultations the signal is verbal, but for surgery it is usually a signature on a consent form. It is this signature that is understood by hospital staff as 'consent'. Most clinicians are unaware that consent can be valid without a signed consent form. It is the patient's informed choice that constitutes consent, not the form. It is also not widely appreciated that consent can be invalid even though a consent form has been signed – if the patient has not made a self-determining, informed choice.

[4.34] The Irish Medical Council advises that doctors 'should explain the process in such a way as to ensure that patients do not feel that their consent is simply a formality or a signature on a page'.[30] The Council also states: 'If a patient is simply presented with a form to sign, it loses all significance as it

---

29. Medical Council, *Guide to Professional Conduct and Ethics for Registered Medical Practitioners* (7th edn, 2009), para 37.2.
30. Medical Council, *Guide to Professional Conduct and Ethics for Registered Medical Practitioners* (7th edn, 2009), para 35.1.

becomes an undemanding formality that must be complied with for legal purposes. This does not serve the ethical objectives of consent'.[31]

[4.35] This appears to give the consent form stronger legal standing than the form actually commands. It is fair to say that if the patient is simply presented with a form to sign, neither the legal nor the ethical objectives of consent are served.

[4.36] There are only a few instances where statutes require consent to be in writing. These include some mental health treatment and (in the UK) some fertility treatments. In other cases, a valid consent should be obtained but this does not necessarily entail the signing of a consent form. The UK General Medical Council recommends[32] that written consent should be obtained if:

(a) the investigation or treatment is complex or involves significant risks;

(b) there may be significant consequences for the patient's employment, or social or personal life;

(c) providing clinical care is not the primary purpose of the investigation or treatment;

(d) the treatment is part of a research programme or is an innovative treatment designed specifically for their benefit.

REFUSAL OF TREATMENT

[4.37] It is well-established that a competent woman has the right to make an informed choice not to have a treatment recommended by clinicians even if the attending staff consider this choice irrational. This is illustrated by cases where a woman has refused to undergo an emergency Caesarean section despite medical advice that this would put her life and/or that of her baby at risk. In one English case,[33] the woman was detained under the Mental Health Act and a Caesarean section was performed under a court order, but she appealed against this decision. Her appeal was upheld and the use of mental health legislation to enforce obstetric treatment was deplored. The court reaffirmed the position that

---

31. Medical Council, *Good medical practice in seeking consent to treatment* (2008), s 3.

32. General Medical Council, *Consent: patients and doctors making decisions together* (2008).

33. *St George's Healthcare NHS Trust v S; R v Collins and others, ex parte S* [1998] 3 All ER 673.

a competent pregnant woman has the right to refuse medical intervention and it provided detailed procedural guidelines for dealing with future cases.

[4.38] Some difficulty arises where clinical staff believe that capacity is temporarily absent due to confusion, fatigue, pain, drugs or panic induced by fear. The issue here is that while a decision made by a competent adult does not have to be rational, irrationality could indicate incompetence. Doctors and lawyers could hasten to declare that a patient lacks capacity if any of the aforesaid factors is present. Also, doctors' concern for fetal wellbeing may conflict with the woman's right to self-determination.

[4.39] These issues are illustrated by an Irish case where the High Court was asked to decide whether a woman who refused blood transfusion after heavy obstetric haemorrhage lacked capacity and whether she could legally be compelled to have the treatment.[34] The woman was a French-speaking Congolese immigrant who gave birth to a baby boy at the Coombe Hospital in September 2006. She suffered a post-partum haemorrhage and cardiovascular collapse but declined blood transfusion, stating (for the first time) that she was a Jehovah's Witness. The hospital was concerned that she would die without the transfusion and, following the hearing of an *ex parte* application, obtained an emergency High Court order allowing the transfusion to go ahead at the time. The judge held that the constitutional rights of the child to be nurtured and reared by his mother trumped the mother's rights to refuse the transfusion. At a subsequent plenary hearing, the hospital sought a declaration that its application was appropriate and that the transfusion was valid. The patient counterclaimed that that her rights had been breached under the European Convention of Human Rights Act 2003 and that the hospital had committed a trespass on her person. Laffoy J found that the patient lacked capacity, because: (a) she did not sufficiently understand and retain the information given to her by the hospital personnel as to the necessity of the blood transfusion to save her life; (b) she did not believe that information and, in particular, that she did not believe that she was likely to die without a blood transfusion being administered; and (c) in making her decision to refuse a blood transfusion, she had not properly balanced the risk of death inherent in her decision to refuse the transfusion and its consequences, including its consequences for her new-born baby, against the availability of a blood transfusion that would save her life.

---

34. For a detailed critique, see Wilson and Weller, 'Benevolent paternalism or a clash of values: Motherhood and refusal of medical treatment in Ireland' (2011) Journal of Mental Health Law 108–119.

[4.40] There are a number of inconsistencies and contradictions in this case. For example, the hospital did not claim during the *ex parte* motion that the patient lacked capacity. Also, the judge appeared to equate capacity with the ability to make a choice that would be regarded by doctors and most others as rational. This case suggests that a gap exists between the rhetoric and the reality of patients' rights to decline treatment.

CHILDREN UNDER THE AGE OF 16 YEARS

[4.41] Patients aged 16 years and over may give a legally valid consent to treatment. In this context, 'treatment' excludes donation of organs or blood and participation in research. If the patient is a child (under the age of 16 years), the parents will usually be asked to give their consent to the child's treatment. In certain cases, however, the child may wish to have the treatment without the knowledge or consent of her parents. In such cases the Irish Medical Council advises that the doctor 'should encourage the patient to involve their parents in the decision, bearing in mind (the doctor's) paramount responsibility to act in the patient's best interests'.[35]

[4.42] This is consistent with what is known in English law as '*Gillick* competence', after the case in which Mrs Victoria Gillick sought to stop a general practitioner from prescribing the contraceptive pill for her daughter without the mother's consent. In dismissing the mother's appeal, Lord Fraser said: 'It seems to me absurd to suggest that a girl or boy aged 15 could not effectively consent, for example, to have a medical examination of some trivial injury to his body or even to have a broken arm set. Of course the consent of the parents should normally be asked but they may not be immediately available. Provided the patient, whether a boy or a girl, is capable of understanding what is proposed, and of expressing his or her own wishes, I see no good reason for holding that he or she lacks a capacity to express them validly and effectively and to authorise the medical man to make the examination or give the treatment which he advises'.[36]

[4.43] While an adult with capacity may legally refuse medical treatment for religious or other reasons, she does not have the same right to refuse treatment on behalf of her child. In a case where a parent withheld consent on behalf a minor on religious grounds, the court invoked Art 42.5 of the Constitution to

---

35. Medical Council, *Guide to Professional Conduct and Ethics for Registered Medical Practitioners* (7th edn, 2009), para 43.5.
36. *Gillick v West Norfolk Area Health Authority* [1986] AC 112.

authorise a blood transfusion.[37] It states that: 'In exceptional cases, where the parents for physical or moral reasons fail in their duty towards their children, the State as guardian of the common good, by appropriate means shall endeavour to supply the place of the parents, but always with due regard for the natural and imprescriptible rights of the child'.

[4.44] Hogan J said:

> The use of the term 'failure' in this context is perhaps a somewhat unhappy one, since there is no doubt but that CD and EF, acting by the lights of their own deeply held religious views, behaved in a conscientious fashion vis-à-vis Baby AB. The test of whether the parents have failed for the purposes of Article 42.5 is, however, an objective one judged by the secular standards of society in general and of the Constitution in particular, irrespective of their own subjective religious views.

[4.45] This case can be contrasted with that of *North Western Health Board v HW and CW*[38] where the Supreme Court held that parents may refuse medical treatment for their child if the treatment is elective and not a life-saving intervention.

---

37. *Children's University Hospital Temple Street v CD and EF* [2011] 1 IR 665, [2011] 2 ILRM 262.
38. *North Western Health Board v HW and CW* [2001] IESC 90.

PART III
CEREBRAL PALSY

Chapter 5

WHAT IS CEREBRAL PALSY?[1]

Dr Janet Rennie

[5.01] Cerebral palsy (CP) is a common cause of physical disability in children, with an incidence of around two per 1,000 in the Western world. The underlying disorder of the brain is not progressive and is permanent, but because CP presents in early childhood the physical limitations do vary with age because the brain is developing so rapidly at this time. The motor disorder of CP, which causes limitation of physical activity, is often accompanied by problems with intellect, epilepsy, and behavioural difficulties.[2] The motor disability is variable in severity but many individuals with CP struggle to execute action sequences (such as bringing a loaded spoon to the mouth) which are simple for most people. CP does not get better, but services for adults with the disorder are scarce and patchy. Children usually receive input from multi-professional teams including community paediatricians, paediatric neurologists, physiotherapists, orthopaedic surgeons, speech and language therapists and benefit from support in school via a statement of special educational needs. All this ceases when the child reaches 18, and at this stage an adolescent who was previously occupied on a daily basis often becomes isolated at home and in the care of elderly parents ill equipped to cope.

[5.02] The underlying brain problem involves some part of the motor pathway, which begins with neurones in the cortex (the 'motor strip' is located in the pre-central gyrus). The neuronal pathway then travels in the myelinated axons (the 'white matter' below the cortex) through the internal capsule, crosses over in the

---

1.   References: Cans, 'Surveillance of cerebral palsy in Europe: a collaboration of cerebral palsy surveys and registers' (2000) 42 Developmental Medicine & Child Neurology 816–824; Cowan, Rutherford, Groenendaal, Eken, Mercuri, Bydder, Meiners, Dubowitz and de Vries, 'Origin and timing of brain lesions in term infants with neonatal encephalopathy' (2003) The Lancet 361, 736–742; Freeman and Nelson, 'Intrapartum asphyxia and cerebral palsy' (1988) Pediatrics 82, 240–249; Hope and Moorcraft, 'Cerebral palsy in infants born during trial of intrapartum monitoring' (1990) The Lancet 228; Maclennan, 'A template for defining a causal relation between acute intrapartum events and cerebral palsy: international consensus statement' (1999) BMJ 319, 1054–1059; Rosenbaum, Paneth, Leviton, Goldstein and Bax, 'Definition and classification of cerebral palsy' (2007) 49 Developmental Medicine & Child Neurology 8–14.

2.   Rosenbaum *et al*, 'Definition and classification of cerebral palsy' (2007) 49 Developmental Medicine & Child Neurology 8–14.

decussation and carries on down the spinal cord. The pathway receives input from the deep grey matter of the brain, and from the cerebellum. From this brief explanation of the neuroanatomy it can be seen that a lesion at any level which affects any part of this pathway can result in the motor disability of CP.

CLASSIFICATION OF CEREBRAL PALSY

[5.03] CP is generally described in terms of the parts of the body which are affected, and this can give some clue to the underlying brain disorder. When all four limbs are affected the term 'quadriplegia' or 'tetraplegia' (Latin or Greek for four) is used. When an arm and leg on one side are involved the term 'hemiplegia' is used, and when the legs are more affected than the arms the label 'diplegia' is often applied. There are problems with this classification – such as when does diplegia become tetraplegia? More recently the registry of Surveillance of Cerebral Palsy in Europe (SCPE)[3] has proposed that the classification should be into unilateral or bilateral CP.[4] The SCPE proposes an algorithm for classification.

[5.04] The motor impairment not only affects different parts of the body, but also has different manifestations of muscle tone. Tone is the term used to describe the state of muscle, which at rest is not completely flabby in healthy people. When muscle tone is increased the tendon reflexes (knee jerk, etc) are brisk and the term 'spastic' is used; spastic CP can be unilateral or bilateral. SCPE found that at least 60 per cent of CP was bilateral spastic, with about 33 per cent diplegic and 10 per cent quadriplegic. CP (hemiplegia) comprises about 25 per cent of cases. When the affected individual has muscle tone which varies, often associated with unwanted involuntary movements, the CP is termed 'dyskinetic'; people with generally reduced activity have 'dystonic' CP and those with increased activity and troublesome involuntary movements are said to have 'choreo-athetoid' CP. The movements may not emerge until the child is four years old or so. Dystonic CP is relatively rare, about 10 per cent of all cases. Ataxic CP is another rare subtype involving uncoordinated movements but with a particular pattern usually suggesting a disorder of the cerebellum. This is a subtype of CP which is generally genetically inherited.

[5.05] The functional impact of the disability due to CP in an individual child is generally assessed by a clinical scoring system, such as the Gross Motor

---

3.   http://www.scpenetwork.eu/.
4.   Cans, 'Surveillance of cerebral palsy in Europe: a collaboration of cerebral palsy surveys and registers' (2000) 42 Developmental Medicine & Child Neurology 816–824.

Function Classification System (GMFCS).[5] This has five levels of severity and has been shown to be reliable across users and relatively stable over time once the child is more than two years old. The GMFCS is used all over the world and is important because it is often used to quantify claims, and estimate life expectancy. There are other functional classification systems, including the Manual Ability Classification.

Typical underlying brain disorders in CP

[5.06] MRI has revolutionised our thinking about CP, and in a modern era should be a standard investigation for an affected child in the developed world. Both the European Surveillance group and the American paediatric neurology groups recommend MRI in affected children.

[5.07] Some clues to the likely underlying problem can be gained from the clinical presentation.

[5.08] Dystonic, choreo-athetoid CP is the subtype which is most likely to be due to damage to the deep grey matter of the brain. This is a term used to describe the structures of the thalami and the lentiform nuclei, sometimes referred to as basal ganglia thalami (BGT) in the literature. The BGT are uniquely vulnerable to damage from a short period of profound asphyxia, 'acute profound' or 'acute near-total' hypoxic ischaemia. This is the type of CP which is most likely to be due to an asphyxial insult in labour at term. Although as a subtype of CP this is not the most common, probably more than 50 per cent of cases do have an asphyxial aetiology. Choreo-athetoid CP can also be caused by kernicterus (chronic bilirubin encephalopathy due to unconjugated bilirubin entering the brain). In kernicterus the part of the deep grey matter which is affected is the globus pallidus, not the putamina of the lentiform nucleus, but the clinical manifestations are similar.

[5.09] Hemiplegic cerebral palsy is typically caused by a 'stroke'. Stroke is surprisingly common in the neonatal period, and is usually an arterial ischaemic stroke. The most common artery to be affected is the left middle cerebral artery, which arises from the common carotid artery. A block to flow in this major artery supplying the brain causes death of tissue ('infarction') often in a large volume of brain including the deep grey matter on that side, part of the cortex, and the internal capsule. Arterial stroke is not caused by hypoxic ischaemia; it is thought likely that emboli travel into the cerebral circulation from the fetal side of the placental circulation towards the end of pregnancy or in labour. The fetus

---

5.   www.canchild.ca.

has several places in the circulation where such emboli can cross from the venous to the arterial side of the circulation. From this brief description it can be seen that a child with hemiplegic CP is less likely to have a medico-legal case than a child with dystonic CP. Nonetheless if there is suspicion about the perinatal period MR should be considered because some children with hemiplegia have bilateral asymmetrical 'borderzone' damage. Of course, MR might also reveal a congenital malformation of the brain such as schizencephaly.

[5.10] Diplegic CP is a term which has fallen out of favour, but it is the case that this is the most common pattern of disability seen in ex-preterm babies when they are affected by CP. The upper limbs are affected to a varying degree. MR imaging usually reveals periventricular leukomalacia (PVL), the characteristic pattern of damage to the white matter around the lateral ventricles of the brain. Children who have PVL on their MR images can be born at term, and are often assumed to have acquired their brain damage during intrauterine life at a preterm stage of gestation (particularly if they remain well in the neonatal period). Rarely the brain can react this way to a hypoxic ischaemic injury at term, and children with cyanotic congenital heart disease seem to be vulnerable to PVL at term.

[5.11] Quadriplegic cerebral palsy has a very variable clinical presentation and can be caused by a mixture of underlying disorders, including hypoxic ischaemia. Severe BGT damage can result in quadriplegic CP, as can cortical damage to the borderzones due to 'prolonged partial' hypoxic ischaemia.

Figure 5.1 Diagram showing common MR imaging patterns in CP

Figures 5.1.1 and 5.1.2 show basal ganglia thalamic pattern. The areas marked in black indicate the typical parts of the brain which are damaged in 'acute profound' hypoxic ischaemia namely the posterior part of the putamina and the lateral nuclei of the thalami.

Figures 5.1.3 and 5.1.4 show the borderzone pattern. The areas marked in black indicate the parts of the brain which are characteristically damaged by 'prolonged partial' hypoxia ischaemia, which lie in the borderzones of the territory supplied by the three major arteries of the brain on each side (anterior, middle and posterior).

Figures 5.1.5 and 5.1.6 show the pattern seen in periventricular leucomalacia. This is the pattern seen after the preterm brain is injured (rarely the brain at term can react this way). The lateral ventricles are enlarged and the margins are usually irregular. There is often abnormal signal on MR images in the brain around the ventricles (glial reaction), shown here by the dark hatching.

Figures 5.1.7 and 5.1.8 show the pattern seen in cerebral infarction (stroke). The commonest arterial territory to be involved in the newborn is that of the left middle cerebral artery; the volume of tissue which is damaged is variable but often considerable. Other arteries can be affected and sometimes there is more than one part of the brain involved. The dark areas indicate the territory of the left middle cerebral artery.

Figure 5.1.1

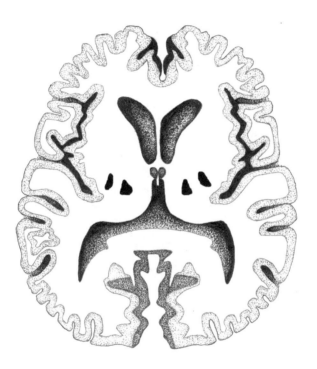

Figure 5.1.2

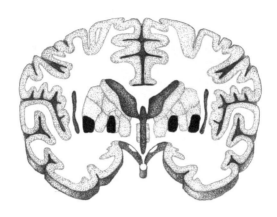

Figure 5.1.3

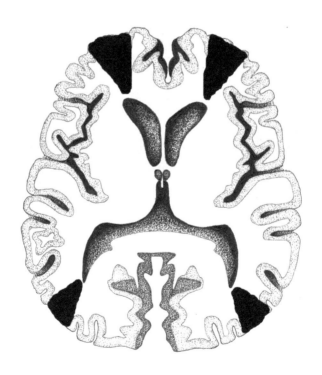

Figure 5.1.4

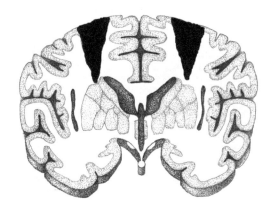

Figure 5.1.5

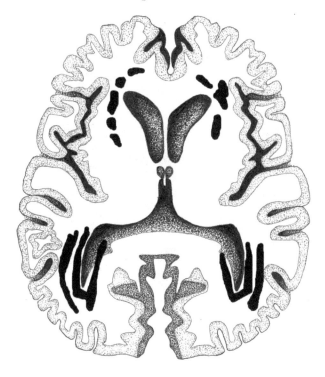

Figure 5.1.6

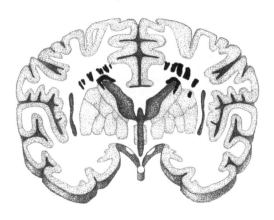

Figure 5.1.7

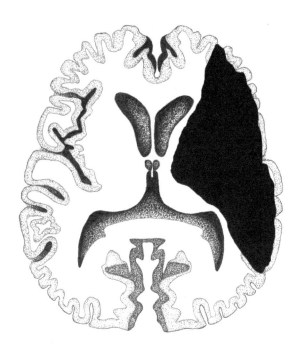

Figure 5.1.8

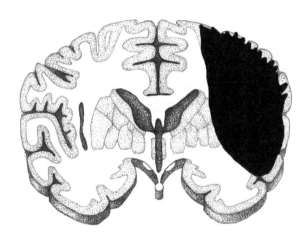

Birth asphyxia and cerebral palsy

[5.12] The link between 'birth asphyxia' and CP was first suggested by Little and Osler in the 19th century, and was for a time thought to be of little importance in most cases. Peter Hope noted in 1990 that:

> It is no longer a matter for conjecture whether asphyxia and cerebral damage are causally related, or merely occur in the same antenatally imperfect individual. Ultrasonography, and many other objective tests of cerebral structure and function allow us to follow the time course of evolving neuronal damage in the postnatal period following severe asphyxia.[6]

Peter Gluckman pointed out that one of the potential barriers to the implementation of cooling as a treatment for perinatal hypoxic ischaemic brain injury could be the failure to convince those delivering intrapartum care that the cause of the damage could lie within that timeframe, hence opening up the management to scrutiny and criticism. In fact, cooling has become a standard of care in the developed world, and is offered to babies born in poor condition who remain 'encephalopathic' – in other words whose neurological status is not normal in the early hours of life. Research has shown that the majority of babies who develop an early neonatal encephalopathy have experienced intrapartum hypoxic ischaemia.[7] Sometimes, it can be shown that different management of

---

6. Hope and Moorcraft, 'Cerebral palsy in infants born during trial of intrapartum monitoring' (1990) The Lancet 228.

79

labour and delivery would (on the balance of probability) have led to a different outcome, and this is the basis for litigation practice in CP. Because the lifetime costs of care for these children are so great, the stakes are very high for this type of litigation.

Other cases of cerebral palsy

[5.13] There are many causes of CP other than birth asphyxia (see below), and some of these are potentially preventable. Kernicterus is the term used to describe the disability due to high levels of bilirubin damaging the brain in the newborn period. Some have suggested that kernicterus should be a 'never event' and many cases are potentially preventable by the appropriate and timely use of phototherapy.

Causes of cerebral palsy

[5.14]

- Intrauterine infection, eg toxoplasma, cytomegalovirus;
- malformation of the brain, eg schizencephaly;
- intracranial haemorrhage;
- infarction (stroke, arterial or venous);
- kernicterus;
- hypoxic ischaemia (intrapartum, twin-twin transfusion, feto-maternal haemorrhage, placental insufficiency);
- meningitis;
- inflammatory response syndrome (cytokines).

Medico-legal aspects of cerebral palsy

[5.15] The starting point for investigating a potential claim of CP possibly due to birth asphyxia is to have a secure diagnosis. Usually this is easy and is available from the clinical records but there can be doubt about the nature of subtle motor disability or whether or not incoordinated movements are ataxic or choreo-athetoid. In general a child needs to be at least two years old before a reliable diagnosis can be made, but in the modern era a neonatal MRI can give a likely prognosis allowing claims to be investigated earlier. There is no substitute for a high quality clinical examination by an experienced paediatric neurologist.

[5.16] Few cases proceed without MR imaging of the brain (see figure 5.1). MR imaging is now widely available but unfortunately the images obtained by some

---

7.   Cowan *et al*, 'Origin and timing of brain lesions in term infants with neonatal encephalopathy' (2003) The Lancet 361, 736–742.

institutions are of very poor quality. The changes in the BGT are often subtle and require the appropriate sequences to be used, and the images need to be reported by a neuroradiologist who is trained in paediatrics. It is not unusual to request to review images which were originally reported as normal only to find that there is evidence of abnormal signal in the posterior putamina and the thalami, characteristic of acute profound hypoxic ischaemia.

[5.17] It is important to examine the maternal history in detail, consider the pregnancy and labour, and to assess whether or not there was any evidence of a neonatal encephalopathy. Seizures are the hallmark of encephalopathy, and can be difficult to diagnose in the newborn.

[5.18] From the information which is outlined above, it can be seen that children with dyskinetic or spastic CP affecting all four limbs who have either the BGT or 'borderzone' pattern on MR imaging and who had a neonatal illness characterised by seizures are those whose disability was most likely to have been acquired as a result of an intrapartum hypoxic ischaemic insult. These 'ground rules' are not absolute but are the basis of criteria which have been suggested by various authorities.[8] That is not to say that the case will be easy, or that the time at which the damage occurred will be obvious, but in general these features do indicate that the cause did not lie earlier in the pregnancy. When the damage occurs in the run-up to delivery the anaerobic metabolism which is inevitably associated with hypoxic ischaemia will cause a metabolic acidosis (a lactic acidosis). Evidence of acidosis is a low pH and high base deficit, which should be sought on cord blood samples which are now generally routine, or from samples of blood taken from the baby in the first hour of life. Babies who have experienced a recent hypoxic ischaemic brain injury are generally born in poor condition, require resuscitation and have low Apgar scores. The Apgar scoring system is universal, being a measure of heart rate, respiratory effort, colour, tone and response to stimulation (see Table at para [7.10]). Each item can score 0, 1 or 2; a baby born in good condition will have a score of more than 8 whereas a baby who requires resuscitation will have a score of 3 or less at one minute.

---

8.   Freeman and Nelson, 'Intrapartum asphyxia and cerebral palsy' (1988) Pediatrics 82, 240–249; Maclennan, 'A template for defining a causal relation between acute intrapartum events and cerebral palsy: international consensus statement' (1999) BMJ 319, 1054–1059.

Chapter 6

WHAT CAUSES CEREBRAL PALSY?

INTRAUTERINE FETAL SURVEILLANCE

[6.01] Babies are damaged during labour most often by oxygen lack but sometimes by haemorrhage. Such babies often give warnings by their conduct, warnings which, if heeded in time, may provide a mechanism for preventing injury. 'Fetal distress' is a loose term used to indicate those responses by the fetus which alarm birth attendants. Fetal distress in labour is recognised by:

- abnormalities of the fetal heart.

- the passage of meconium.

The cardiotocograph trace

[6.02] By far the most effective way of observing changes in the fetal heart is by the cardiotocograph trace (CTG).[1] The CTG machine is an electronic apparatus for monitoring both fetal heart rate and maternal uterine contractions. The contractions are monitored usually by an external tocodynamometer (a disc within a disc, placed on the maternal abdominal wall) but occasionally by an intrauterine transducer.

[6.03] The fetal heart may be recorded by ultrasound, using an external monitoring transducer. Alternatively, once the fetal membranes are ruptured, the fetal heart may be captured, more efficiently and reliably, by the application of a fetal scalp electrode to the baby's head.

---

1. FIGO, 'The Guidelines for the Use of Fetal Monitoring' (1987) 25 International Journal of Gynaecology and Obstetrics 1159–67; Gibb and Arulkumaran, (3rd edn, Churchill Livingston Elsevier, 2008); Beard and Finnegan, *Fetal Heart Patterns and Their Clinical Interpretations* (Sonicaid Ltd, 1974); Klavan, Laver and Boscola, *Clinical Concepts of Foetal Heart Monitoring* (Hewlett-Packard, 1977); Parer, *Handbook of Fetal Heart Rate Monitoring* (W B Saunders Company, 1983); Boylan, (1987) 'Chapter 5 Intra-Partum Fetal Monitoring' in Whittle (ed), *Bailliere's Clinical Obstetrics and Gynaecology* (1987) Vol 1(1) March 1987 'Fetal Monitoring'.

[6.04] These two recordings are combined on a single CTG printout, the main features of which are illustrated in figure 6.1.

Figure 6.1

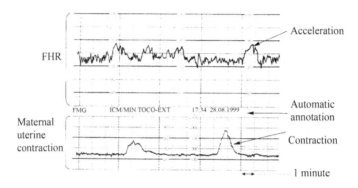

[6.05] The terms used in describing the changes in the cardiotocograph are explained in figure 6.2.

Figure 6.2

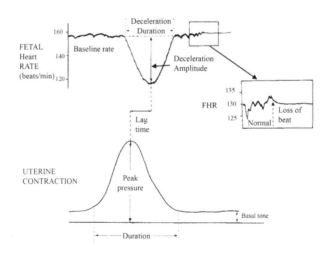

Terms used in the study of continuous records of FHR

[6.06] Traditionally the normal fetal heart rate was regarded as 120–160 beats per minute but in 1987 normal rate was redefined by the International Federation of Obstetrics and Gynaecology (FIGO) as 110–150 beats per minute.

[6.07] The significance of some of the heart rate patterns is illustrated in figure 6.3.[2]

Figure 6.3

Significance of FJR traces relative to pH

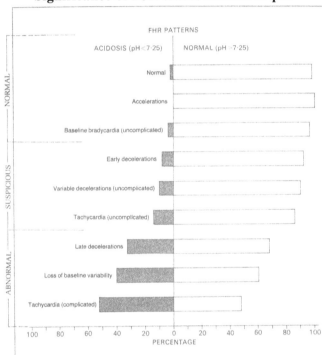

[6.08] Continuous electronic monitoring may result in a higher incidence of intervention (operative vaginal delivery or Caesarean section), sometimes unnecessarily. The final arbiter of fetal welfare is examination of the blood so as to estimate its acidity (pH). The use of fetal scalp blood sampling (see below) helps to reduce the incidence of unnecessary intervention.

[6.09] In the 1980s a Dublin trial of intrapartum fetal heart rate monitoring appeared to demonstrate that there was no advantage, in terms of the prevention of cerebral palsy, in continuous fetal heart monitoring. In other words listening

---

2.   Beard, Filshie, Knight and Roberts, 'The Significance of the Changes in the Continuous Fetal Heart Rate in the First Stage of Labour' (1971) 78 Journal of Obstetrics and Gynaecology of the British Commonwealth 865.

to the baby some of the time was as good as listening to the baby all of the time. No matter how counterintuitive that suggestion, it was nevertheless believed by a significant proportion of obstetricians and midwives. We now know that that trial was hopelessly underpowered. As recent authors have pointed out:

> Even if the number had been doubled in the auscultation group, this would not have been statistically significant … Even the meta analyses are underpowered to address the question of perinatal mortality, let alone long-term outcome. It should always be remembered that absence of evidence is not evidence of absence and one needs to be aware of the possibility of a type II error (i.e., there is a difference which by chance has not been found to be significant).[3]

[6.10] Whilst it is right that mothers should be advised that electronic fetal monitoring is the gold standard, maternal choice is nevertheless paramount and if, after appropriate explanation, the mother prefers to be mobile and rely on intermittent auscultation, she should be allowed to do so with the option to resort to electronic fetal monitoring if auscultation casts doubt on fetal wellbeing.

Decelerations of the fetal heart

[6.11] Decelerations are traditionally classified into three types. An early deceleration is one occurring simultaneously with the uterine contraction which provokes it, without a lag time. The decelerations are typically shallow and by definition must not exceed a depth of more than 40 beats per minute.[3] They are commonly associated with compression of the fetal head. When the fetal head is compressed by a uterine contraction there is a rise of intracranial pressure associated with stimulation of the vagus nerve and an accompanying immediate bradycardia. Head compression decelerations are most frequently seen in the late stage of labour when the descent of the fetal head is occurring through the maternal bony pelvis. Decelerations due to head compression are also seen at the time of vaginal examination and when artificial rupture of the membranes is performed.

[6.12] Late decelerations follow the uterine contraction; they are late with respect to the uterine contraction which provokes them and they have a lag time (figure 6.2). They occur because of the depletion of the reservoir of oxygenated blood in the retroplacental space. If placental function is poor or the uterine

---

3.   Steer and Daniellian (2006) 'Chapter 71 Fetal Distress in Labour' in James, Steer, Weiner and Gonik (eds), *High Risk Pregnancy Management Options* (3rd edn, Saunders Elsevier, 2006).

contraction excessive the retroplacental space may be emptied of oxygenated blood by the uterine contraction and the baby subsequently hypoxic. As the contraction begins the fetus uses up the reservoir of oxygen in the retroplacental space and because that supply is restricted a hypoxic deceleration phase follows. That phase continues through the remainder of the contraction and does not recover fully until some time after the contraction when full oxygenation has been restored. The speed of recovery on the ascending limb may reflect the blood flow and the resilience of the fetus. The decelerations may be subtle, as illustrated in figure 6.4.[4]

Figure 6.4

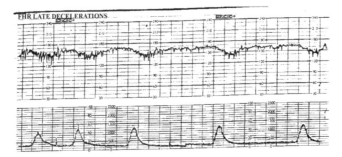

Trace 25   It would be quite easy to miss these recurrent late decelerations. The decelerations are very shallow but each one lasts approximately 2–3 mins. The baseline rate between decelerations is 153 beats per minute, and this falls to a nadir of 135 beats per minute during the trough of the deceleration. Note once again the increase in variability associated with the peak of hypoxia, at the bottom of each deceleration.

[6.13] Variable decelerations are common. They are called variable because they vary in shape and size and sometimes in timing with respect to each other and with respect to the uterine contractions which provoke them. They vary because they are a manifestation of compression of the umbilical cord and it is compressed in a slightly different way each time. On some occasions it may not be compressed at all and there is no deceleration with that particular contraction. Variable decelerations are more often seen when the amniotic fluid volume is reduced. In the United States they are often referred to as 'cord compression decelerations'.

---

4.   Figures 6.4, 6.5, 6.6, 6.7 and 6.8 and the accompanying commentaries are taken from Steer, *Sonicaid Handbook: Fetal Heart Rate Patterns and Their Clinical Interpretations*.

Figure 6.5
Variable decelerations

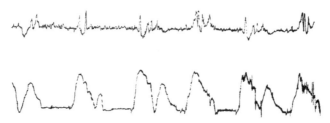

[6.14] Because the umbilical vein has a thinner wall and a lower intra-lumenal pressure than the umbilical arteries, the vein tends to be occluded first when the compression begins. The fetus therefore loses some of its circulating blood volume; when a healthy individual or fetus has its blood volume reduced the natural response, effected by the autonomic nervous system, is a rise in pulse rate to compensate for reduced blood volume. A small acceleration will often appear at the start of a variable deceleration when the fetus is not compromised. After that the umbilical arteries are also occluded and with both vein and artery occluded the baroreceptors of the fetus are stimulated and there is a precipitous fall in the heart rate. The deceleration is at its nadir when both vessels are occluded. During release of the cord compression arterial flow is restored first with a consequent autonomically mediated sharp rise in heart rate; there is often a small acceleration after the deceleration. These accelerations before and after decelerations are called shouldering. They are a manifestation of the fetus coping well with cord compression. The way in which the cord is being compressed will vary depending on exactly how it is positioned with respect to the structure compressing it. Variable decelerations may change if the posture of the mother is changed. Early decelerations and variable decelerations due to cord compression are illustrated in figures 6.6 and 6.7.

Figure 6.6
Variable FHR decelerations

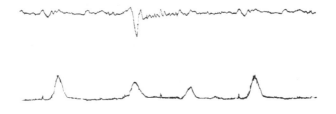

[6.15] This shows typical early decelerations due to mild cord compression. In this example an acceleration precedes each deceleration. This is attributed to the earlier stages of cord compression, in which only the venous flow is obstructed. This results in a decrease in venous return to the fetal heart, and there is a compensatory tachycardia to maintain blood pressure. Once the arterial flow in the cord is occluded, blood pressure rises due to the increase in peripheral resistance. This leads to stretching of the aorta, and activation of the aortic stretch receptors. This in turn leads to activation of the vagal centre in the brain, producing a bradycardia, which restores blood pressure to a more normal level. Once the occlusion of the cord is over, there is a reactive tachycardia once more. Baseline rate and variability are normal and fetal blood sampling is not necessary at this stage.

Figure 6.7
Variable FHR decelerations

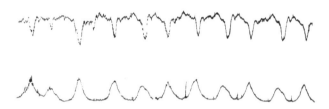

[6.16] In this example the decelerations are essentially the same as in the previous example, except that the amplitude of the deceleration is larger than 40 beats per minute. By definition, therefore, these cannot be called early. This type of deceleration is by tradition called variable. In this example, baseline rate, variability and reactivity remain normal.

[6.17] This indicates one of the reasons why these types of synchronous decelerations receive the term 'variable'. Here we see a normal baseline rate. There is some reduction in the baseline variability.

[6.18] Three contractions are seen during this section of trace. There is no deceleration with contractions 1 or 3, but there is a large synchronous deceleration with contraction 2. The occurrence of decelerations with contractions is therefore variable. The fact that this is probably a cord compression pattern is revealed by the accelerations just before and just after the deceleration (the so-called 'M' shaped pattern). The reduced baseline variability does indicate the possibility of a degree of acidosis, and a fetal blood sampling would be appropriate in this case. The increase in variability seen after the deceleration is a common accompaniment of mild hypoxia.

[6.19] In their simplest form, as illustrated in figures 6.7 and 6.8, variable decelerations are not associated with hypoxia. They simply reflect changes in fetal blood volume and in peripheral resistance. However, as Gibb and Arulkumaran point out:

> Normal well-grown fetuses can tolerate cord compression for a considerable length of time before they become hypoxic. Small growth-retarded fetuses do not have the same resilience. To assess this process it is necessary to analyse the features of the decelerations and also the character of the trace as it evolves.[5]

[6.20] The authors then list six variations on the pattern of variable decelerations with the following comments (Gibb and Arulkumaran 4.21 is reproduced here as figure 6.9).

---

5.   Gibb and Arulkumaran, *Fetal Monitoring in Practice* (3rd edn, Elsevier, 2008), p 38.

Figure 6.8

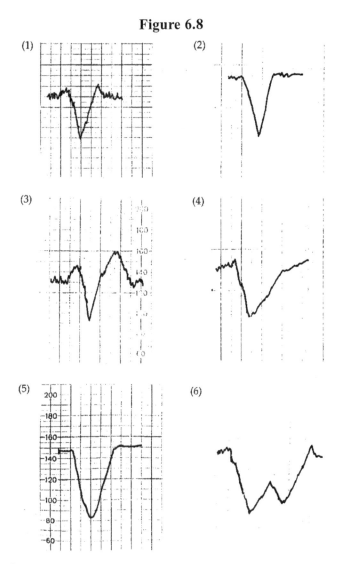

Figure 6.8 shows:

(1) normal shouldering;

(2) exaggeration of shouldering or overshoot (indicates that additional circulations are needed to normalise which is thought to be pre pathological);

(3) loss of shouldering – pathological;

(4) smoothing of the baseline variability within the deceleration which is associated with loss of variability at the baseline and therefore pathological;

(5) late recovery – (variable and late deceleration components merged together) has the same pathological significance as late deceleration;

(6) biphasic deceleration (variable and late decelerations seen as separate components) requiring the same consideration as a late deceleration.

If the duration of the deceleration is more than 60 seconds and the depth greater than 60 beats, progressive hypoxia becomes more likely.[6]

[6.21] The commentary continues: 'The most critical feature, however is the evolution of the trace with time. A change in the baseline rate and change in the baseline variability are the key signs of developing hypoxia and acidosis.'[7]

Baseline artefact

[6.22] The CTG monitor is programmed to 'prefer' a heart rate close to the normal range for the fetus (110–150) and will generally record faithfully heart rates close to or above that range. However if the fetal heart rate is very slow (bradycardia) the monitor sometimes doubles the rate so that a fetal heart rate of 80 may be interpreted by the machine as 160 beats per minute.

6.   Gibb and Arulkumaran, *Fetal Monitoring in Practice* (3rd edn, Elsevier, 2008) p 40.

7.   Gibb and Arulkumaran, *Fetal Monitoring in Practice* (3rd edn, Elsevier, 2008) p 40.

Figure 6.9

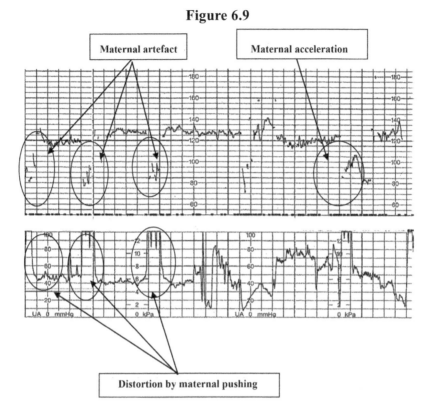

[6.23] At other times, particularly with a severe baseline bradycardia, the monitor may 'prefer' the maternal heart rate, derived from the abdominal aorta. Particularly in the second stage of labour when the external transducer is temporarily moved by the efforts of maternal propulsion, there may be intermittent loss of fetal cardiogram in favour of the mother. Such an occurrence is illustrated in figure 6.10. On this occasion the maternal heart was around 80–90 beats per minute, well below the range expected for the fetus. This sometimes leads to a doubling artefact of the maternal heart, illustrated in figure 6.10.

Figure 6.10

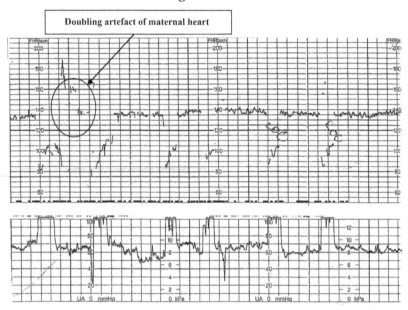

Classification of intrapartum trace

[6.24] The categorisation of CTG traces is not always helpful in the clinical context. Mothers are not managed by CTG alone, but by the whole context of labour; the CTG is but one influence on decision making. Nevertheless for research purposes it is important to be able to use terms of art to distinguish types of CTG traces. Unfortunately there is no universally accepted classification of CTGs and, from time to time, various international and national bodies make up new classifications.

[6.25] Antenatal cardiotocographs are interpreted differently from intra-partum traces. In 1994 the FIGO classification was current and popular and a simplified version of the FIGO classification of intrapartum traces was provided by Gibb and Arulkumaran and is reproduced below.

[6.26]

- **Normal** baseline rate 110–150 bpm; baseline variability 10–25 bpm; two accelerations in 20 minutes and no decelerations;

- **Suspicious** absence of accelerations (first to become apparent – important) and any *one* of the following: abnormal baseline rate < 110 bpm or > 150 bpm; reduced baseline variability < 10 bpm (of greater significance if < 5 bpm) for greater than 40 minutes; variable decelerations without ominous features;

- **Abnormal** absence of accelerations and any of the following: abnormal baseline rate and variability (< 5 bpm for greater than 40 minutes); repetitive late decelerations; variable decelerations with ominous features (duration > 60 s, beat loss > 60 bpm, late recovery, late deceleration component, poor baseline variability between and/or during decelerations);

- Other specific traces categorised as abnormal are sinusoidal pattern, prolonged bradycardia (below 100 bpm) for greater than three minutes and shallow decelerations in the presence of markedly reduced baseline variability (below 5 bpm) in a non-reactive trace.

Fetal scalp blood sampling

[6.27] Although electronic fetal monitoring remains the most reliable method of intra-partum assessment of the fetus, abnormalities of fetal heart rate pattern – even when pronounced – are not invariably associated with poor neonatal outcome. Reliance upon cardiotocographic evidence alone for the diagnosis of fetal distress may result in an unnecessary increase in operative intervention.

[6.28] Fetal blood sampling, used as an adjunct to electronic fetal monitoring, has been shown to facilitate the detection of fetal acidaemia and rationalise the management of labour. However, randomised control trial in high risk patients has not always demonstrated any difference in the Caesarean section rate or neonatal outcome, whether or not the facility of scalp pH measurement was employed.

[6.29] The technique of fetal blood sampling is described in the standard textbooks of the time and has been the subject of numerous review articles.[8]

[6.30] It should be clearly understood however that false positive and false negative results occur in up to 10 per cent of samples and the results need to be interpreted within the clinical context.

[6.31] The pH of the blood sample is currently believed to be the most reliable indicator of fetal oxygenation. The base excess, although derived from the pH, will usually indicate whether the hypoxic insult to the fetus has been a short-lived event or is of a more long standing nature. These are the most basic

---

8. Gibb and Arulkumaran, *Fetal Monitoring in Practice* (3rd edn, Elsevier, 2008).

principles in interpreting fetal blood sampling, with which every obstetric registrar should be familiar.

[6.32] There are occasions when fetal scalp samples should not be performed. Gibb and Arulkumaran explain:

> Fetal scalp sampling is often not appropriate under the following circumstances:
>
> (1)   when the clinical picture demands early delivery … 42 weeks gestation, cervix 3 cm dilated, thick meconium;
>
> (2)   when an ominous trace prompts immediate delivery;
>
> (3)   when the FHR trace is reassuring;
>
> (4)   when the changes are due to oxytocin stimulation;
>
> (5)   when there is associated persistent failure to progress in labour;
>
> (6)   during or soon after an episode of prolonged bradycardia;
>
> (7)   if spontaneous vaginal delivery is imminent or easy instrumental vaginal delivery is possible.[9]

The significance of meconium in the liquor

[6.33] The authors of *Active Management of Labour*[10] describe their approach to meconium, an approach that would be approved by responsible obstetricians of the time:

> Meconium is regarded as a clinical sign of great potential significance. At the outset, women in labour are divided into two groups: those with clear liquor and those with meconium. The division into low-risk and high-risk cases is made on this evidence, which is of fetal origin.
>
> Not all meconium, however, is accorded the same significance. There is a world of difference between light meconium staining of a large volume of liquor and meconium that is virtually undiluted, with umbilical cord, membranes and even endometrium coloured green through its entire depth when subsequently exposed at caesarean section.
>
> Meconium is interpreted as evidence of placental insufficiency of some duration and not as evidence of short-term fetal distress. Moreover, meconium seldom appears for the first time during the course of normal labour.

---

9.   Gibb and Arulkumaran, *Fetal Monitoring in Practice* (3rd edn, Elsevier, 2008), pp 197–199.

10.   O'Driscoll, Meagher and Robson, *Active Management of Labour: The Dublin Experience* (4th edn, Bailliere Tindall, 2003).

Three grades of meconium are recognized, as follows:

Grade I – a good volume of liquor, lightly stained with meconium;

Grade II – a reasonable volume of liquor, with a heavy suspension of meconium;

Grade III – thick meconium, which is undiluted and resembles sieved spinach.

All grades of meconium must be reported to the senior registrar. A wide margin of discretion is permitted in Grade I; after careful review of the clinical circumstances no further action is taken in most cases. In Grade II, treatment is determined by the fetal heart rate pattern. Caesarean section is performed in Grade III unless an easy vaginal delivery is imminent; as not only hypoxia but also meconium inhalation is a real possibility here.[11]

THE ABUSE OF OXYTOCIN

[6.34] Oxytocin is a hormone produced by the pituitary gland. Its principal effect is to increase the activity of smooth (involuntary) muscle in the uterus and in the breast. Oxytocin from the mother's pituitary is an important agent in the 'let down' of milk in the puerperium. It is doubtful whether maternal oxytocin has much to do with the physiology of labour.

[6.35] The causes of the onset of labour remain one of the unsolved mysteries of physiology but it appears to be the result of a combination of factors in both mother and baby, oestrogen levels in the mother increasing the sensitivity of oxytocin receptors in the uterus, together with formation and release of prostaglandins from the lining of the uterus and membranes. It is almost certain that the fetus initiates labour and there is evidence of increased oxytocin levels in the fetal circulation in the period immediately preceding labour.

[6.36] Both prostaglandins and oxytocin are employed therapeutically to induce and to augment labour in appropriate circumstances. Oxytocin can be produced synthetically and is marketed as Syntocinon. It is Syntocinon that drives an active management of labour.[12]

---

11. O'Driscoll, Meagher and Robson, *Active Management of Labour: The Dublin Experience* (4th edn, Bailliere Tindall, 2003), pp 107, 108.
12. O'Driscoll, Meagher and Robson, *Active Management of Labour: The Dublin Experience* (4th edn, Bailliere Tindall, 2003).

[6.37] The uterus contracts regularly but infrequently throughout the second half of pregnancy. These contractions (Braxton Hicks) are painless but the mother may become conscious of them for some weeks before the onset of labour. The difference between Braxton Hicks contractions and labour is one of degree. Labour contractions are much more powerful, longer lasting and are associated with pain in most cases. The contractions (pains) change the shape of the uterus, collecting the muscle fibres into the upper part of the body of the uterus, pushing the baby downwards through the lower segment, towards the pelvis. The contractions also dilate the cervix, opening a canal for the baby to escape into the vagina. The contractions have a profound effect upon the placenta and its blood supply.

[6.38] The placenta is the organ which allows the fetus to obtain nutrients and gas exchange from the mother. Protrusions (villi) from the fetal surface are suspended in a pool of blood (the intervillous space) fed by maternal vessels. Fetal capillaries within the villi are then separated from the pool of maternal blood only by a fine semi-permeable membrane which permits exchange of gases and small molecules. The circulation of blood through the intervillous space is critical, so that the quality of the blood within the space is high. If the circulation through the intervillous space is sluggish then the rate of exchange will be impaired.

[6.39] Towards the end of a normal pregnancy the rate of flow through the intervillous space is entirely dependent upon the maternal heart action, pumping blood from the left ventricle through the aorta, the common iliac arteries, the internal iliac arteries and the uterine arteries, and finally to their branches serving the placental site. It is a common misconception that during labour the fetus is at a disadvantage because of the contraction of the uterus. The reverse is the reality. During normal labour blood flow to the fetus improves as the secondary pump action of the uterus helps to clear maternal blood through the placental site. Each time the uterus contracts the placenta, rather like a sponge held under water, is squeezed empty of blood and, as the uterus relaxes, refills with fresh maternal blood. The effect of this secondary pump action (added to the primary pump activity of the maternal heart) is to improve fetal blood flow and improve fetal oxygen exchange. The normal labour pH of the baby (a proxy for oxygenation) improves in comparison with the mother because of this improved oxygen exchange.

[6.40] However, that mechanism only works to the advantage of the fetus when there is a sufficient recovery (diastole) period between contractions to allow refilling to take place. If the placenta is inefficient, even normal intervals between contractions may not be enough to replenish the blood flow. A healthy placenta will continue to function well at a contraction rate of about four in ten minutes, perhaps five in ten minutes, but above that the period of diastole may be shorter than the period of systole, and blood flow will be reduced. This is the mechanism of fetal distress, caused by excessive rates of uterine contraction or by contractions of excessive power and duration.

Why does the contraction frequency matter?

[6.41] Contractions of a frequency more than four in ten minutes are likely to lead to fetal hypoxia because of the inadequate intervals between the contractions, so as to allow for placental refilling:

> Every uterine contraction above 4-6 kPa causes a cessation of maternal intervillous placental blood flow. This produces a period of relative hypoxia for the fetus, such that the fetal PO_2 falls by about 0.5-0.75 kPa during each contraction, reaching its lowest level at the end of the contraction, following which the flow is restored and the PO_2 recovers. Because it takes sometime for the oxygen – depleted maternal blood to be replaced, recovery takes about 60-90 s. The total period of reduced oxygenation is therefore 120-150 s emphasizing the importance of an adequate intercontraction interval to ensure fetal oxygenation. Poorly controlled oxytocin infusions, which produce excessively frequent contractions, can therefore result in iatrogenic fetal hypoxia and acidosis.[13]

[6.42] When oxytocin infusion is given to induce or augment labour, the infusion can be used to achieve a contraction pattern of the desired frequency. What then is the optimum frequency to be aimed for?

> If oxytocin titration to achieve a preset frequency gives a good obstetric outcome what should this frequency be? In a prospective study, two-thirds of women who showed failure to progress despite no evidence of cephalopelvic disproportion had two or fewer contractions in 10 min, whereas one-third had a contraction frequency of three in 10 min over a period of 4 h. Oxytocin titration to achieve a contraction frequency of four in 10 min with each contraction duration lasting >40 s was associated with normal progress of labour ($\geq$1 cm/h) and vaginal delivery of babies in good condition in 96% (24/25) of these women. If there is no progress in labour with suboptimal frequency of contraction, oxytocin dose should

---

13. Steer and Danielian, 'Chapter 64 Fetal Distress in Labour' in James, Steer, Weiner and Gonik (eds), *High Risk Pregnancy: Management Options* (2nd edn, W B Saunders 1999), p 1131.

probably be titrated to achieve a contraction frequency of four in 10 min each lasting >40 s, provided the FHR pattern is normal. [14]

Fetal distress and oxytocin augmentation

[6.43] It is axiomatic that when abnormalities of the cardiogram appear, oxytocic stimulation should be stopped. The logic is inescapable. If the fetus is distressed (short of oxygen) then increasing stress upon the fetus by increasing the length and strength of uterine contractions is clearly potentially harmful.

[6.44] Even the advocates of 'Active Management of Labour' are careful to limit the effect of oxytocin in increasing uterine activity. They warn against the effects of hypertonic uterine action:

> The rules that govern the use of oxytocin are quite explicit; furthermore, they are rigidly enforced … The personal nurse – who accompanies everyone in labour – records each contraction as it occurs after oxytocin has started. The partogram is used for this purpose; the timescale is divided into intervals of 15 minutes; the optimum number of contractions in this period is five. To guard against hypertonus the number of contractions is not permitted to exceed seven in 15 minutes under any circumstance.[15]

[6.45] Thus, when oxytocin augmentation is employed it is essential that the oxytocin is turned off when:

- there is any significant abnormality of the cardiogram.

- the contraction frequency exceeds five in 10 minutes.

[6.46] Failure to do so will inevitably lead to hypoxia. Without oxygen the supply of energy will fail and cells will be lost – particularly in the brain. The fetus has significant reserves of energy production in the form of anaerobic respiration, a facility that is not available after birth, However without oxygen the breakdown of the energy reserve (glycogen) is incomplete and the products of the intermediate breakdown (chiefly lactic acid) are acidic – hence the value of pH in assessing fetal wellbeing.

---

14. Chua and Arulkumaran, 'Chapter 63 Poor Progress in Labour Including Augmentation, Malpositions and Malpresentations' in James, Steer, Weiner and Gonik (eds), *High Risk Pregnancy: Management Options* (2nd edn, W B Saunders 1999), p 1111.
15. O'Driscoll, Meagher and Robson, *Active Management of Labour: The Dublin Experience* (4th edn, Bailliere Tindall, 2003), pp 49, 50.

[6.47] If the warning signs of fetal heart abnormality and increasing fetal acidaemia are ignored there will be brain damage and cerebral palsy – and eventually death.

CORD PROBLEMS

[6.48] Since the fetus depends entirely upon the placenta for its oxygen and nutrient supply it follows that any obstruction of the umbilical cord, the structure linking the placenta with the fetus, threatens fetal wellbeing. Such problems include:

- obstruction (intermittent, complete);

- abnormalities of the cord (knots, tumours);

- prolapse.

Obstruction to the umbilical cord

[6.49] The average length of the umbilical cord is about 50 cms, but some are much longer. Long cords may become entangled with the fetus, and may become wrapped around the neck or body of the fetus or become knotted. Cords of any length may become trapped between the baby's body and the mother's bony pelvis. This is particularly likely to happen if there is a reduction in the volume of liquor amnii (oligohydramnios). A cord trapped between the baby's body and the mother's pelvis will become obstructed, to a greater or lesser extent, when the uterus contracts and increases the pressure between baby and mother. Such occurrences are common and give rise to a particular pattern of CTG abnormality, the variable deceleration. Such cord compression, occurring only at the height of a contraction, is usually harmless and does not involve the fetus in any significant oxygen lack. A healthy term fetus will withstand such intermittent cord compression for many hours without showing evidence of compromise.

[6.50] If however the contractions are unusually prolonged or abnormally frequent the incidence of compression may begin to interfere with oxygen supply. The characteristic changes on the CTG then become 'complex' variable decelerations.

[6.51] In these circumstances fetal hypoxia will lead to acidaemia in the fetus and eventually, when compensation mechanisms have been exhausted, in damage. Complex variable decelerations require delivery.

[6.52] Occasionally intermittent cord compression may become complete. Once complete the cord transmits no blood in either direction and an acute near-total hypoxic injury will follow and, if not relieved, fetal death.

[6.53] The most common circumstance in which complete occlusion of the cord occurs is in 'cord round the neck'. Many babies are born with the umbilical cord loosely around the neck and no harm results. The cord can be lifted over the baby's head at the time of birth. Occasionally it is necessary to divide the cord if it cannot be looped over the head. Only when the cord is pulled tight around the baby's neck is there likely to be hypoxia. In such cases intermittent occlusion of the cord is commonly seen in the latter stages of labour and intermittent obstruction becomes progressively more profound leading to increasingly complex variable deceleration on the CTG. As, at the very end of labour, the baby descends rapidly though the birth canal the cord may be stretched so tightly that the vessels within it are completely occluded. In the more extreme cases there may be, in addition, obstruction to the great vessels in the baby's neck. In these circumstances, an acute near-total hypoxic injury will result unless the baby is rescued within a few minutes.

[6.54] Once complex variable decelerations begin to appear on the CTG the attendants should be aware that complete occlusion of the umbilical cord is a possibility; the baby needs to be delivered.

Abnormalities of the cord

[6.55] Although rare, structural abnormalities occasionally produce similar obstruction and contribute to fetal hypoxic injury. Bruising (haematoma) or a collection of abnormal vessels may produce a swelling in the cord that, on initial inspection looks like a knot. Such 'false' knots may cause problems if they are sufficiently tense to obstruct the vessels within the cord. True knots in the cord, caused by fetal movements involving the passage of a baby through a loop of its own cord, are rare but will have a similar potential for causing hypoxia.

[6.56] Such abnormalities produce changes on the CTG comparable to those produced by external compression.

Prolapse and presentation of the cord

[6.57] Where a loop of umbilical cord is discovered in front of the baby and with the membranes intact it is referred to as presentation of the cord. In those circumstance the membranes must not be ruptured and every care taken to deliver the baby before spontaneous rupture occurs. Caesarean section is the method of choice.

[6.58] Once the membranes are ruptured the circumstance is referred to as prolapse of the umbilical cord even though the cord remains entirely within the uterus and is not, in the normal sense of the word, prolapsed. The cord is however at risk since with the membranes ruptured the baby's head is likely to descend and obstruct the cord, squeezing it between the baby's head and the mother's pelvis.

[6.59] The diagnosis is usually made on vaginal examination. Because of the danger of cord prolapse it is appropriate, in most circumstances, for the midwife to conduct a vaginal examination whenever membranes rupture spontaneously.

[6.60] Once discovered management is aimed at reducing the risk of compression whilst waiting emergency delivery.

[6.61] The avoidance of compression is usually achieved by two means. The midwife, discovering the prolapse, keeps her hand in the vagina and pressure on the presenting part so as to keep it off the cord. At the same time the mother's position is changed so that gravity assists. Traditionally the mother was moved into the knee-chest position, so that her buttocks were higher than her shoulders. This is not only undignified but uncomfortable and the same effect can be achieved by placing her in the left lateral positon with a large wedge under her buttocks, the exaggerated Sims' position. Once achieved immediate arrangements are put in place for delivery. If the mother is not in labour these manoeuvres are usually sufficient to prevent cord compression and to allow time for safe delivery. If cord prolapse is discovered at full dilatation and with the baby's head in a position from which it can be delivered easily, operative vaginal delivery may be preferable for although it will produce a temporary cord occlusion, it is generally much quicker than complex arrangements necessary to achieve safe Caesarean section.

[6.62] If the cord remains within the uterus, circulation will usually be maintained. Handling may cause spasm of the vessels within the cord and should be avoided as far as possible. Because the temperature in the vagina is marginally lower than inside the uterus, descent of the cord into the vagina will also lead to spasm. Should the cord prolapse outside the vagina, circulation is likely to cease; the cord should be wrapped in a warm damp cloth and replaced gently inside.

[6.63] Provided that cord prolapse happens within the delivery unit, the baby can usually be rescued quickly and hypoxic injury prevented. If cord prolapse is discovered in the patient's home immediate arrangements must be made to transport her rapidly to a consultant unit. During this time it may be necessary to administer tocolytic agents, so as to inhibit uterine contractions.

[6.64] With the appropriate response cord prolapse need not necessarily be followed by fetal injury. In series of reported cases intervals of up to eight hours have elapsed before safe delivery can be achieved.

[6.65] The circumstances in which prolapse of the cord is more likely to happen include:

- unstable lie of the fetus where there is no presenting part forming a 'plug' in the pelvis;

- breech presentation, where the presenting part fills the pelvis less efficiently than the fetal head;

- excessive quantities of liquor amnii (hydramnios);

- a low lying placenta;

- twins.

[6.66] Deliberately to rupture the fetal membranes when there is no presenting part in the pelvis is to invite disaster. The fetal membranes should be preserved if at all possible until the presenting part is safely acting as a plug to prevent a loop of cord escaping.

[6.67] Prolapse of the umbilical cord is not only potentially dangerous for the fetus but often involves the mother in a most dramatic and uncomfortable experience with significant psychological sequelae.

PLACENTAL MALFUNCTION

[6.68] The placenta is the sole support for the baby in the womb. It combines the function of kidney and lung. It provides the baby with gas exchange (oxygen in and carbon dioxide out) and supplies all of the necessary nutrients. Transfer is effected by the pool of maternal blood (the intervillous space) into which chorionic villi are suspended. Mother and baby are separated only by a semi-permeable membrane so that gases and small molecules can diffuse in both directions.

[6.69] If the placenta fails then the baby's wellbeing is at risk. Failure of the placenta may be:

- chronic;

- acute.

Chronic placental failure

[6.70] A small unhealthy placenta fails adequately to supply the baby's needs. Often the reason for the poverty of the placenta is a systemic illness in the mother such as hypertension or diabetes. Whilst many babies of diabetic mothers are exceptionally large (macrosomic) an equal number are unusually small. Occasionally the placenta becomes inadequate for no obvious extrinsic reason.

[6.71] Whatever the cause of chronic placental failure, it is manifested by failure of fetal growth. Intrauterine growth restriction is of two types:

* symmetric;

* asymmetric.

[6.72] In recent times these terms have been replaced by early onset (symmetrical) and late onset (asymmetrical). Symmetric or early onset growth restriction is usually due to genetic factors, a small baby in a small mother; rarely it is the result of some global insult to the baby (such as a virus infection) early in the pregnancy.

[6.73] Of more relevance to litigation is asymmetric or late onset growth restriction. Late onset growth restriction of a structurally normal fetus after 32 weeks' gestation usually results from placental dysfunction. The fetus is slender with normal head circumference and body length. What is lacking is the fat deposits normally seen in a healthy fetus. Thus the head circumference continues to grow, because of differential preference or 'head sparing', whilst the abdominal circumference lags behind because the liver and the omentum are deprived of nutrient stores.

[6.74] Growth restriction can be identified by serial ultrasound measurements provided only that the dates against which progress is being measured are secure. Thus it is essential at the first antenatal visit to be certain about gestation. If the menstrual dates are unclear, or appear to be wrong, then a revised expected date should be constructed by detailed ultrasound, remembering that ultrasound is no more reliable than a good menstrual history and therefore discrepancies of a week or less are probably irrelevant.

[6.75] Once serial ultrasound has identified an 'asymmetric' pattern of growth restriction it becomes important to identify just how serious the placental failure has become. Doppler blood flow studies are essential and can provide accurate information concerning not only placental blood flow but flow through the umbilical and great vessels of the fetus. If circulation becomes sluggish in these vessels a decision will need to be made concerning early delivery. There is a careful balance to be drawn between prematurity and placental failure. As neonatal support improves with time, the balance shifts gradually in favour of early delivery.

[6.76] Once labour starts intense fetal monitoring is essential. For the well grown fetus with a healthy placenta the secondary pump action of the uterus, squeezing the intervillous space empty, to allow refilling with fresh blood, is an advantage to the fetus but if the placenta is unhealthy the onset of uterine contractions constitutes a serious risk. If the CTG suggests fetal distress immediate delivery is the only safe option.

Acute placental failure

[6.77] Premature separation of the unhealthy placenta is sometimes referred to as abruptio placentae or accidental haemorrhage. Such premature separation is usually associated with intense maternal pain and may or may not be associated with visible bleeding. Revealed accidental haemorrhage alerts the attendants to the crisis but the more sinister 'concealed' haemorrhage may go unnoticed. Blood instead of flowing out of the uterus becomes trapped behind the placenta and invades the uterine wall so as to damage the muscle. The absorption into the maternal circulation of the breakdown products cause widespread intravascular coagulopathy, a life-threatening condition for the mother. The priority, once accidental haemorrhage is identified, is resuscitation of the mother followed by swift rescue of the fetus, if the baby is still alive.

[6.78] Whilst the appropriate care is seldom in dispute the issue of causation is much more complicated. Progression of accidental haemorrhage is not necessarily linear. It is often difficult to establish just how much of fetal injury would have been avoided with earlier delivery.

RUPTURE OF THE UTERUS

[6.79] The pregnant uterus is a large muscular tube. Contraction of the uterine muscle changes the shape of the organ and pushes the baby into the pelvis and through the birth canal to effect delivery. Functionally the uterus is in two parts, the upper active part becomes progressively thicker as labour progresses. The neck (cervix) will dilate, as does the 'lower segment' of the uterus which expands and thins out. It is through this 'lower segment' that Caesarean sections are normally performed. The thinner muscle of the lower segment heals much more efficiently and is less likely to rupture in a subsequent labour.

[6.80] When the uterus ruptures, from whatever cause, rhythmic contractions cease, to be replaced by a continuous (tetanic) contraction. The effect of this contraction is to prevent circulation of blood through the placenta causing an immediate risk to the welfare and the life of the fetus. Such contraction will often expel the fetus from the uterus into the abdominal cavity sometimes 'clamping down' on the fetal neck so that one part of the fetus (usually the head) is retained within the uterus and the remainder (usually the body) is expelled. In any event, expelled or not, the fetus will die unless rescued within a few minutes.

[6.81] Rupture of the uterus can occur in four principal circumstances:

- obstructed labour;
- oxytocin abuse;
- direct injury;
- the scarred uterus.

Obstructed labour

[6.82] Obstructed labour is not seen in the developed world. However in developing countries there may be absolute disproportion, circumstances in which the baby is absolutely too big to pass through the maternal pelvis. If the mother is multiparous (having had a previous birth), tumultuous activity of the uterus may be sufficient to cause a rupture in obstructed labour.

Oxytocin abuse

[6.83] Slow labour is frequently managed by the intravenous infusion of a drug, oxytocin, capable of increasing the intensity and frequency of uterine contractions. In response to such management there is a major difference between primigravid (pregnant for the first time) and the multiparous patient. It is commonly said that the primigravid uterus cannot be ruptured by excessive activity and there are indeed no convincing cases of that happening in the world literature. The multiparous patient, on the other hand, reacts much more vigorously to oxytocin particularly where the baby is large and some form of disproportion exists. The multiparous uterus most certainly can be ruptured by the abuse of oxytocin although such a dramatic consequence is fortunately rare.

Direct injury

[6.84] Operative vaginal delivery (see further paras **[6.99]** and **[8.66]**) involves the use of metal instruments which can, if inappropriately employed, cause direct injury to the uterus; examples in the developed world are rare.

The scarred uterus

[6.85] The uterus may be scarred in one of two ways. On some previous occasion, and sometimes unknown to operator or patient, the uterus may have been perforated in the process of dilatation and curettage, hysteroscopy or evacuation of retained products of conception. Such injuries may be both inadvertent and unnoticed; the small hole will close but will be replaced by scar tissue and, in a subsequent vigorous labour may initiate a rupture.

[6.86] By far the commonest cause of uterine rupture in the developed world is a rupture through a previous Caesarean section scar. The classical operation, no longer employed except in very rare circumstances, involved incision through the full thickness of the upper segment, and the scar resulting was often of very poor quality. Such Caesarean section scars would occasionally rupture in pregnancy, before the onset of labour.

[6.87] The lower segment scar, on the other hand, does not rupture, save only in labour. However the first pain of labour can on occasion be the pain of rupture.

[6.88] In addition to overt rupture (bursting asunder) the scar of the lower segment Caesarean section may quietly separate without pain and without any other symptoms so that the only surviving layer is the peritoneum on the surface. This process is usually referred to as 'dehiscence' and may be discovered only at subsequent repeat Caesarean section or other laparotomy.

[6.89] The potential for full scale rupture of the Caesarean section scar raises the difficult problem of vaginal birth after Caesarean section (VBAC). Several aspects need to be discussed:

- the incidence of scar rupture;
- the decision to allow vaginal delivery and the taking of consent;
- the place of induction/augmentation of labour.

The incidence of scar rupture

[6.90] It is not easy to ascertain the incidence of scar rupture. Reliance on published series is not appropriate, for only the best centres voluntarily publish their figures. It used to be said that the incidence of scar rupture was less than

0.5 per cent but current teaching is that the true incidence is probably somewhere around 0.7 per cent.[16] More important than the incidence of scar rupture is the consequence of it. Rupture in labour will usually mean that the woman is in hospital. If rupture of the uterus is diagnosed quickly then her life will not be in danger for laparotomy can be performed in a timely fashion so as to prevent excessive haemorrhage. Not so the baby. Once the uterus has ruptured there will be no effective blood flow through the placenta and unless it is salvaged by laparotomy within a few minutes, the baby is likely to suffer severe hypoxic-ischaemic injury and will probably die. The timescale, even in the best departments, for laparotomy following rupture is seldom soon enough to prevent injury to the fetus.

The decision to allow VBAC and consent for it

[6.91] The woman who has undergone a previous Caesarean section has, like all other pregnant women, only two options, abdominal or vaginal delivery. There has been a tendency in the past to emphasise to such patients the risks of Caesarean section, an experience they have already survived. There has been little appetite for spelling out the risks of the alternative, VBAC.

[6.92] It is a sad reflection on the practice of obtaining consent that, whereas every surgeon requires fully documented consent, with the patient's signature for anything involving a knife, the non-surgical alternative, if there is one, does not apparently require such attention. If the risks of the two alternatives are fully compared and exchanged, this practice can be seen to be flawed.

[6.93] The risk of a repeat Caesarean section as a planned elective procedure, on a routine list with the A-team present is minimal. The difficulty about determining risk of Caesarean section is that figures usually relate to Caesarean section in general and include all sorts of emergency circumstances including those done in the middle of the night in extreme haste and with a very sick patient. In reality planning the operation well in advance when there is no emergency or pathology has zero risk for the fetus. It is sometimes said that the baby born by Caesarean section will have breathing difficulties (tachypnoea of the newborn) but those breathing difficulties, if they occur, are transient and unimportant. The risk for the mother? Not significantly greater than risks of a normal birth (without a Caesarean scar).

[6.94] The risk on the other hand of VBAC is, as explained above, catastrophic for the baby. In addition to these well defined risks there is of course also the

16.   Smith, 'Chapter 73 Delivery after Previous Cesarean Section' in James et al (eds), *High Risk Pregnancy: Management Options* (4th edn, Saunders Elsevier, 2011).

risk to be considered of the attempt at VBAC which ends in an emergency Caesarean section, an altogether more dangerous experience than the elective alternative.

[6.95] It is unacceptable that mothers should be asked to undertake VBAC without full discussion of the risks and without their willing consent and cooperation.

[6.96] There are no reliable premonitory signs of rupture. Much is made of 'scar tenderness' but it is neither specific nor exclusive. The uterus will often rupture without tenderness being reported – and tenderness seldom presages rupture. Variable decelerations are sometimes a feature of the CTG in the minutes before rupture occurs.

The place of induction/augmentation of labour

[6.97] There is significant controversy[17] about the use of prostaglandins for the induction of labour in the circumstances of VBAC. It is however contrary to the manufacturer's advice. If the cervix is unfavourable and induction of labour desired, a safer alternative is a synthetic, sterile, hygroscopic dilator (Dialapan).

[6.98] Other means of induction of labour such as artificial rupture of the membranes do not appear to carry any increased risk save only that induction of labour is often inefficient and requires augmentation. It has traditionally been taught that augmentation, with oxytocin, is acceptable in the context of VBAC. Indeed it probably is with the single proviso that the oxytocin is carefully monitored. That would seem to be an obvious and self-evident condition. However, oxytocin abuse is such a common cause of litigation that one hesitates to sanction the use of a drug which seems so often to be abused. The cautious obstetrician should take the view that VBAC may well be appropriate and permissible, if the mother wants it having been appropriately counselled, but that any failure of the labour should probably be dealt with by a repeat Caesarean section sooner, rather than later.

OPERATIVE VAGINAL DELIVERY

[6.99] In modern obstetrics the only permissible manoeuvres to assist a baby at a vaginal birth are:

- forceps or ventouse delivery from the mid-pelvis or outlet;
- breech delivery.

---

17. Smith, 'Chapter 73 Delivery after Previous Cesarean Section' in James et al (eds), *High Risk Pregnancy: Management Options* (4th edn, Saunders Elsevier, 2011).

[6.100] No attempt at operative vaginal delivery can be undertaken safely without a thorough understanding of the mechanics of labour and the relationship between the fetal head and the maternal bony pelvis. Although much information can now be obtained on the size of the fetus (by ultrasonography) and the size of the pelvis (by modern x-ray and other methods), this information is of little help in forecasting the outcome of labour. In the developed world, the difference between success and failure in achieving safe vaginal delivery is not usually determined by the absolute size of the baby or the mother – but rather by the degree of extension or flexion of the fetal head. The attitude of the baby in turn determines rotation within the pelvis and most occasions of cephalopelvic disproportion are the result of mal-rotation and deflexion. These are important considerations when contemplating operative vaginal delivery.

[6.101] Position is determined by reference to the sutures and fontanelles of the baby's head. It is distressingly frequent to find four or five vaginal examinations recorded in the obstetric records with no indication of fetal position.

[6.102] Descent of the fetal head should be described by both abdominal palpation (head level) and by vaginal examination (station).

[6.103] Head level is determined, on abdominal examination, by an estimate of the proportion of the head that is still palpable above the pelvic brim. The head is notionally divided into fifths. As the term fetal head is approximately the same width as a human hand, the number of fifths still palpable abdominally can be estimated by the observer according to the number of fingers required to cover it.

[6.104] Engagement is the point at which the largest diameter has passed through the pelvic brim, the point at which less than three-fifths of the head remains palpable.

[6.105] Station, on the other hand, is obtained by vaginal examination. The midwife or doctor estimates the level of the leading part of the fetal head in relation to a notional plane between the two ischial spines. The spines are prominent projections into the side wall of the vagina and can easily be identified. The observer then imagines the plane between them and makes an estimate of the leading part of the head above or below the planes.

[6.106] During the course of labour swelling of the fetal scalp (caput) and change in shape of the fetal head (moulding) may distort the findings on vaginal examination, exaggerating the extent to which the head appears to have descended. Abdominal examination to determine the fifths palpable is the more reliable observation since it is not subject to these changes. Maternal obesity and distress may make the observation difficult but an epidural block in preparation for an operative delivery will usually facilitate the observation. In general, station and head level have a constant relationship. In the absence of caput and moulding in an average sized baby with an average sized pelvic the plane of the brim (judged abdominally) corresponds to the plane of the ischial spines (judged vaginally): 'If the lowest point of the head is at the ischial spinal level, the largest diameter is probably just through the pelvic brim, provided there is no marked moulding or caput formation.'[18]

[6.107] Moulding and caput will suggest a lower station than is appropriate for the level of the head as felt abdominally.

[6.108] Assistance provided by forceps or ventouse is defined according to the descent of the fetal head and its rotation. The American classification is reproduced in Table 1. If the fetal head is above +1 (1 cm below the ischial spines) or more than one-fifth palpable abdominally, operative vaginal delivery is not permitted.

Classification of forceps delivery according to station and rotation

[6.109] Outlet forceps – scalp is visible at the introitus without separating the labia, fetal skull has reached the pelvic floor, the sagittal suture is in the antero-posterior diameter or right or left occiput anterior or posterior position, fetal head is at or on the perineum, rotation does not exceed 45°.

Low forceps – leading point of fetal skull is at station ≥ + 2 cm, and not on the pelvic floor; rotation ≤ 45° (left or right occiput anterior to occiput anterior, or left or right occiput posterior to occiput posterior) rotation > 45°.

Mid forceps – station above 2 cm but head engaged.

The obstetric forceps

[6.110] The instrument is of two main types, only one of which is in current use in Ireland. The classical (Simpson) variety forceps has both a cephalic curve (so that it fits the baby's head) and a pelvic curve, to allow for the shape of the maternal pelvis, the curve of Carus. These forceps can only properly be applied

---

18. Ritchie, 'Obstetric Operations and Procedures' in Whitfield (ed), *Dewhurst's Textbook of Obstetrics and Gynaecology for Postgraduates* (5th edn, Oxford Blackwell Science, 1995) 390.

to the head which is facing backwards (occiput anterior) or fully forwards (occiput posterior). They cannot be used to rotate the head from a 90° position where the head is facing directly sideways. Unless the operator is certain of the position (rotation) of the fetal head and the precise level (as judged by both abdominal and vaginal examination), operative vaginal delivery with forceps should never be undertaken. The penalties for the mis-application of the forceps blade are high for both mother and baby. Provided the instrument is properly placed and provided the traction is not excessive the forceps protect the baby's head and there is no danger of injury. There is however danger of injury to the mother and forceps delivery should always be associated with the performance of an episiotomy, a cut, made with scissors, to enlarge the introitus. The cut begins at the fourchette and proceeds at the angle of 45° towards the buttock, deflecting any extension well away from the anal sphincter. With such an incision, damage to the anal sphincter is most unlikely.[19]

[6.111] Misapplication of the forceps blades may cause injury to the baby; the application to be safe must be bi-parietal, each blade being placed against the parietal bone of the baby's skull. So placed, the blade will not encroach upon the orbit and will grip the mandible. Injury to the eye is a distinct hazard if the blade strays inside the orbit. Application and traction before full dilatation risks injury to the maternal cervix; rarely the operator may insert the blade forcibly into the uterus to injure the lower segment.

The ventouse

[6.112] On most of the occasions listed in Table 1 the ventouse may be used as an alternative to the obstetric forceps. As an instrument for traction it is of course much less efficient since it tends to pull off with anything other than modest traction. Because the ventouse does not occupy any additional volume, being applied to the fetal scalp, well away from the vagina, there is less need for episiotomy although, with a large baby or a need for rotation, episiotomy is a wise precaution.

[6.113] Before applying suction the operator must carefully check with a finger that no vaginal wall has been accidentally included, lest traction with the trapped vagina results in avulsion of the vaginal wall and massive haemorrhage.

---

19. De Leeuw, Stuijk, Vierhout and Wallenburg, 'Risk Factors for Third Degree Perineal Ruptures During Delivery' (2001) 108 British Journal of Obstetrics and Gynaecology 383–387. Eogan, Daly, O'Connell and O'Herlihy, 'Does the Angle of Episiotomy Affect the Incidence of Anal Sphincter Injury?' (2006) BJOG: An International Journal of Obstetrics and Gynaecology, DOI: 10.1111/j.1471-0528.2005.00835.x.

The mal-rotated head

[6.114] In the occiput posterior position the head is mal-rotated by 180 degrees and the occiput (back of the head) was towards the back of the pelvis (OP) rather than to the front (OA). In other words instead of the baby coming out facing downwards, towards his mother's sacrum, she will be facing upwards, towards the front of her body. Posterior positions of the occiput are invariably associated with deflexion. That is to say the baby's head is tilted backwards so as to present a somewhat larger diameter to the birth canal than in the occipito anterior position.

[6.115] The diameter of the fetal skull which engages with the birth canal is, in the occiput anterior position, the suboccipito-bregmatic and measures only 9.5 cms (Figure 6.11). By contrast, the occipito-posterior position the larger occipito-frontal diameter measuring 11.5 cms is involved. Greater traction is required to deliver the head in this disadvantageous position.

Figure 6.11

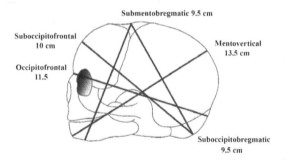

The diameters of the fetal skull

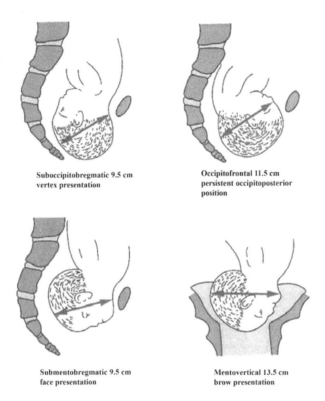

Suboccipitobregmatic 9.5 cm
vertex presentation

Occipitofrontal 11.5 cm
persistent occipitoposterior
position

Submentobregmatic 9.5 cm
face presentation

Mentovertical 13.5 cm
brow presentation

The diameters of the fetal head in relation to the maternal pelvis

[6.116] There are consequent risks for both baby and mother. In particular the risk for the mother is that the birth canal will be over-stretched, will rupture and the rupture will include the anal sphincter. Whilst a generous episiotomy, properly placed, tends to protect the anal sphincter the protection is not absolute.

[6.117] It is not of course ever necessary to deliver a baby in the occiput-posterior position. The operator has the option to turn the baby's head into the more favourable occipito-anterior position, with accompanying flexion, so as to reduce the trauma to both mother and baby.

[6.118] There are three principal ways in which the position of the occiput can be changed:

- special forceps;
- manual rotation;
- the ventouse.

[6.119] Special forceps (Kjelland) are now seldom employed in Irish practice. The technique of using this wonderful instrument takes time to acquire and, in the 21st century, junior doctors, hampered by the European Working Time Directive, spend so little time in the labour ward they cannot acquire the manual dexterity for more complex obstetric manoeuvres.

[6.120] A second alternative is for the operator to put his hand into the vagina (under suitable regional block) grasp the fetal head and simply turn it around through 90°, making sure that the direction of travel (left or right) is properly coordinated with the position of the fetal back. Manual rotation is not a difficult art to learn. The difficulty usually encountered is that the fetal head tends to rotate away as soon as the operator takes his hand off the head. An assistant may be necessary in order to preserve the position whilst the operator assembles the instrument required for delivery. Once rotated, the head can be delivered with conventional forceps or with the ventouse.

[6.121] Rotation with the ventouse is not always easy. It is, for all practical purposes, impossible with a deflexed head and a 'normal' ventouse cup. A special posterior cup is required, a cup that allows traction to be applied to the rim of the cup rather than to the centre. Provided that the posterior cup is applied correctly to the flexion point (a point approximately 3 cms in front of the posterior fontanelle, figure 6.12) traction will cause spontaneous rotation as the head descends through the birth canal.

Figure 6.12

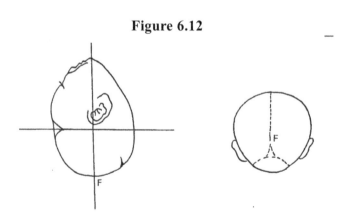

[6.122] In occiput lateral positions of the fetal head, the mal-rotation is 90 degrees so that the occiput is on the left or right of the pelvis. These positions are often referred to as ROT (right occiput transverse) or LOT (left occiput transverse) although, strictly speaking, it is not the occiput but rather the sagittal suture that is transverse. With a terms fetus, such a position (unlike the OP position) is absolutely undeliverable and rotation must be achieved before birth can occur. Since rotation is only 90 degrees it is much easier to achieve and the same three alternative methods are available.

Trial of operative delivery

[6.123] The only circumstance in which it is permissible to attempt forceps or ventouse delivery, remove the instruments and proceed to Caesarean section is in the context of a trial of operative delivery. If the operator has any doubt about the outcome he should not embark upon a forceps or ventouse delivery without full preparation for Caesarean section. That means that the operation should begin in a fully equipped operating theatre with sufficient anaesthesia to proceed directly to Caesarean section with the theatre staff and the anaesthetist prepared to proceed immediately to Caesarean section. The mother must also be informed that, in the event of failure, Caesarean section will immediately be performed. There will be no time for explanations or consent when the attempt at operative vaginal delivery fails. The operator who embarks upon a forceps delivery without these precautions may be tempted, in the event of difficulties, to have 'one last pull' rather than admit defeat. Mature judgment is required; the inexperienced operator must err on the side of caution. In the words of the late Ian Donald: 'Trial of forceps is like lion taming; it is not the sort of exercise one would willingly undertake in expectation of failure.'[20]

Breech delivery

[6.124] Vaginal breech delivery is fast becoming a lost art. There is however no escape. Certain babies presenting as a breech will need to be delivered by the breech no matter how clinicians may plan otherwise. The patient who refuses Caesarean section with a breech delivery, the woman who attends for the first time with the breech on the perineum, the second twin presenting as a breech are all examples of the 'unavoidable' breech delivery. There are essentially two types of breech delivery:

- assisted breech delivery;

- breech extraction.

[6.125] Save only in the case of a second twin, breech extraction (where the operator pulls the baby down the birth canal by the feet) is no longer permissible. Assisted breech delivery is however an entirely reasonable

---

20. Clements, 'Trial of Forceps' (2008) 14 Clinical Risk 49–53; Spencer, 'Trial of Forceps: Legal Aspects' (2008) 14 Clinical Risk 54–58.

undertaking provided only that the operator has sufficient skill. The essential rules are:

• proper antenatal screening of both mother and baby;

• presence at the second stage of labour of a doctor with appropriate experience;

• preparedness for emergency Caesarean section in the event of complications.

[6.126] The size of the baby, the size of the mother's pelvis and the attitude of the fetus are all essential elements of antenatal screening. The attitude of the baby is every bit as important as its weight, and extension of the head, demonstrated on ultrasound, is a clear contraindication to vaginal breech delivery. A footling breech (where the knees are flexed and the feet proceed before the body of the baby) is also unsuitable for vaginal breech delivery because of the very high risk of prolapse of the umbilical cord.

[6.127] There is clear evidence that the external cephalic version at term substantially reduces the incidence of both breech birth and Caesarean section. The success rate for external cephalic version at term is in the order of 60 per cent and the risks are negligible if properly conducted.

[6.128] If version is unsuccessful and conditions are appropriate for breech delivery labour is permitted to proceed normally. Full dilatation of the cervix must be confirmed by a vaginal examination (and not assumed by external signs) for the penalty for delivering the baby's body through an undilated cervix, trapping the head within the uterus, is almost always severe fetal injury. Once the decision has been made to proceed with vaginal delivery, the less the operator interferes with the process the safer it becomes. There must be no traction on any part of the baby at any time. Not until the umbilicus is born should the operator touch the baby and then only to assist the descent of the legs by flexion of the knee joints. The fetal condition may at this time conveniently be checked by palpation of the cord. It is essential that, in the succeeding phases of the delivery of the baby's body, the fetal back should be uppermost. If it is not, the operator should gently hold the body of the baby in a towel and turn the baby, but without exerting traction. When the tip of the scapula is delivered, it is permissible to search for the arms which will usually be found flexed in front of the baby's body. The arms are then readily disengaged with a finger. Only in the rare circumstances of nuchal displacement (arms behind the head) is it necessary to perform the Løvset manoeuvre. Nuchal displacement is almost always a consequence of traction upon the body of the breech and in spontaneous breech delivery will rarely be encountered.

[6.129] Once the arms are delivered, the baby should be allowed to hang by its own weight until the hairs on the nape of the neck are visible. At that point the operator is called upon to intervene. The safest method of delivery of the head is a combination of the Burns-Marshall manoeuvre and the application of obstetric forceps. The Mauriceau-Smellie-Veit manoeuvre is inferior and unsafe. In this manoeuvre, the operator passes his right hand along the ventral surface of the baby and places his middle finger in the baby's mouth. His index and ring finger grasp the baby's shoulder. The left hand is passed along the dorsal surface of the baby and the middle finger presses upon the occiput, so as to flex it, the index and ring fingers grasping the shoulders. In this way, the head may be brought down flexed but the procedure is inferior to the obstetric forceps because:

- the operator has less control;

- the manoeuvre carries with it the risk of cervical spine and brachial plexus injury.

[6.130] The interval from the moment the umbilicus is born (and the cord therefore obstructed) until delivery of the mouth and nose should not exceed ten minutes. During this time, the fetus will be severely short of oxygen but provided there has been no previous compromise, the baby should be capable of resuscitation to normality.

[6.131] If the fetal head does not descend and the obstetric forceps cannot be applied easily, disaster is imminent. The fetal head will usually be arrested at or above the pelvic brim and probably still in the transverse position. The obstetric forceps are at this point of no use and should be abandoned. Unless the fetal head can be brought down quickly into the pelvis and the mouth and nose made available for resuscitation, the baby will die of asphyxia. While this situation should never be encountered with proper antenatal screening it is the one circumstance in which the Mauriceau-Smellie-Veit manoeuvre combined with suprapubic pressure and the McRoberts position may be of assistance. With a generous episiotomy it may be possible for the operator to draw the baby's head into the pelvis whilst still in the transverse position and to rotate it with traction and achieve safe delivery.

Twin delivery

[6.132] The first stage of twin delivery is managed much as any other labour. It is because the position of the second twin, following delivery of the first, is unpredictable that special precautions are necessary. The position of the second twin, whilst the first is still in utero is irrelevant for, with delivery, the second twin previously longitudinal and cephalic may suddenly become transverse and undeliverable.

[6.133] In the second stage of twin delivery therefore there must be present in the labour ward:

- an obstetrician capable of all forms of operative delivery;
- an anaesthetist;
- at least one paediatrician, preferably two.

[6.134] Even if an epidural block is not in place, there should be an intravenous infusion already running before the start of the second stage, so that oxytocin can be introduced if necessary without delay; and so that in the event of Caesarean section the anaesthetist will have immediate intravenous access.

[6.135] Once the first twin is delivered (usually by a midwife) and erogmetrine withheld, the doctor must immediately palpate the mother's abdomen so as to determine the lie of the second twin. An ultrasound machine should be available in the room and, if there is any difficulty in identifying the lie and presentation of the baby, ultrasound should be employed. If the lie of the second twin is not longitudinal the doctor should gently perform external version; it matters little whether the baby is turned to a cephalic or breech presentation. Once longitudinal, uterine activity is awaited. During this time it is essential that the fetal heart is monitored. Provided that the fetal heart is satisfactory, there is no immediate hurry. Once the uterus is contracting the presenting part will usually descend and delivery will occur spontaneously.

[6.136] If the membranes rupture spontaneously, vaginal examination should immediately be performed to exclude cord prolapse. If monitoring of the fetal heart indicates the need to intervene, it will be necessary to rupture the membranes and expedite delivery. Under these circumstances breech extraction may be permissible; if the head presents and is too high for the obstetric forceps, the ventouse may be applied in the reasonable certainty that there is no mechanical obstruction to the delivery. It may be necessary to correct the lie by internal version but the manoeuvre requires general anaesthesia. The alternative is Caesarean section. It is for this reasons that an anaesthetist must be present for every twin delivery and facilities must be appropriate for the rapid induction of general anaesthesia. There is little point in having an obstetrician capable of intervention and an anaesthetist ready to administer a general anaesthetic if the delivery is conducted in a place where such manoeuvres are inappropriate.

Chapter 7

NEONATAL RESUSCITATION[1]

Dr Simon Newell

DOING SIMPLE THINGS WELL SAVES LIVES AND OFFERS LIFELONG HEALTH

[7.01] In the UK, over 700,000 infants are born each year. Almost 95 per cent are born at term. It is estimated that 10 per cent will need some help when they are born to establish breathing and to make the transition from fetal to neonatal life. One to two percent will go on to need advanced resuscitation.

Risk factors for need of resuscitation:

- prematurity;

- intrauterine growth restriction;

- macrosomia;

- thick meconium staining;

- difficult delivery;

- fetal compromise eg hypoxia, infection, antepartum haemorrhage, fetal anaemia, etc;

- fetal malformation.

[7.02] Assessment of risk during pregnancy or delivery alerts the healthcare team to the possible need for resuscitation. In these circumstances, preparation

---

1. References: Dawes et al, 'The treatment of asphyxiated, mature foetal lambs and rhesus monkeys with intravenous glucose and sodium carbonate' (1963) 169 J Physiol 167–184; Neonatal Life Support, Resuscitation Council (UK) 2010. www.resus.org.uk [essential information]; O'Donnell et al, 'Interobserver variability of the 5 minute Apgar score' (2006) 149 J Pediatr 486–489; O'Donnell et al, 'Resuscitation and transport of the newborn' in Rennie and Roberton's *Textbook of Neonatology* (5th edn, Churchill Livingstone 2012) 223–229 [recommended additional resource]; Wilkinson et al, 'Don't stop now? How long should resuscitation continue at birth in the absence of a detectable heartbeat?' (2015) Arch Dis Child (Online first 03.08.15); Wood et al, 'Improved techniques reduce face mask leak during simulated neonatal resuscitation: study 2' (2008) Arch Dis Child Fetal Neonatal 93:F230–F234.

should be made: the right people; the right equipment; and good information for the team and family.

[7.03] Unfortunately, in some infants the need for resuscitation cannot be predicted. This prompts the UK textbook of neonatology to state: about 25 per cent of depressed babies are undiagnosed before birth. This is why everybody who has the responsibility of caring for a neonate must be trained in basic resuscitation techniques.

[7.04] Central to the safe delivery of infants is a continuing programme of training for those who may need to resuscitate and the maintenance and availability of appropriate equipment.

THE UNDERLYING PHYSIOLOGY

[7.05] Babies are not small adults. Current advice for the collapsed adult is the immediate use of cardiac compressions (external cardiac massage). In the adult, a primary cardiac event is the most likely cause. In contrast, newborns have normal hearts. If the baby bradycardic (heart rate < 100 bpm), this almost always reflects the effects of hypoxia and acidosis on the cardiac muscle. In the neonate, a good airway and adequate ventilation of the lungs will almost always result in recovery.

[7.06] If Airway and Breathing manoeuvres do not result in a rise in heart rate, it is most likely that the airway and ventilation have not been achieved.

ABC   Airway   Breathing   Circulation

In the newborn the key to resuscitation is airway and breathing.

Figure 7.1

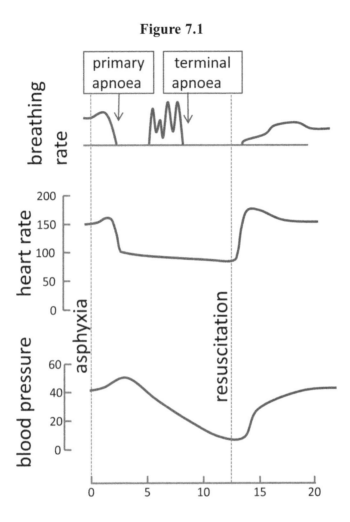

[7.07] The science underpinning resuscitation protocols dates back to animal experiments.[2] With the onset of hypoxia, the fetus rapidly becomes bradycardic. Breathing movements are seen and then followed by primary apnoea. At this stage, delivered and provided with stimulation, an infant will probably recover. Gasping movements precede terminal apnoea. Recovery now demands resuscitation to restore oxygenation and circulation. As hypoxia is relieved, the heart rate usually rises rapidly, circulation is restored and breathing recovers.

---

2.   Dawes et al, 'The treatment of asphyxiated, mature foetal lambs and rhesus monkeys with intravenous glucose and sodium carbonate' (1963) 169 J Physiol 167–184.

[7.08] The inverted triangle demonstrates the steps that may be taken but also reflects the fact that very few infants will require drugs during resuscitation.

Figure 7.2

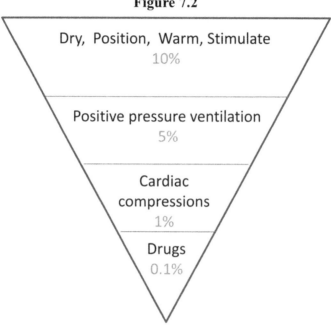

[7.09] Mackay J noted in his 2007 judgment in *Antoniades v East Sussex Hospitals*,[3] 'that to have carried on with CPR [cardiac compressions] and drugs in this case was at best useless and at worst a distraction for the team member with the vital job of A [Airway]'.

ASSESSMENT OF THE NEWBORN

[7.10] At delivery, all newborns are assessed. Virginia Apgar's scoring system (1953) is used routinely and almost universally. The score is usually recorded after delivery and resuscitation. A score of 0, 1, 2 is given for each observation. These same observations are used to evaluate the need for resuscitation.

Score	2	1	0
Heart rate	>100 bpm	<100 bpm	No heart rate
Respiration	Regular breathing	Irregular/slow breathing	No breathing
Tone	Active	Some limb tone	Limp
Responsiveness	Cry	Grimace only	None
Colour (central)	Pink	Blue	Pale

---

3. *Antoniades v East Sussex Hospitals* [2007] EWHC 517 (QB).

[7.11] Most infants are active with flexed limbs, normal tone and show regular breathing and a heart rate over 100 bpm in the first minute. They need no resuscitation. (Apgar score 8–10.)

[7.12] In contrast, the infant who is limp or floppy, inactive, pale, with no respiratory effort and a slow pulse immediately demands attention: division of the cord, transfer to the resuscitation platform and immediate assessment. (Apgar score 0–4.)

[7.13] For the infant who would attract an initial Apgar score of 5–7, whether resuscitation commences immediately or not, the vital necessity is repeated assessment recommended at 30 second intervals, and intervention unless the baby is improving.

[7.14] In the UK, Apgar scores are usually recorded at one and five minutes with additional scores at five-minute intervals if resuscitation continues. It is important to be aware that those present have a tendency to overestimate Apgar scores compared with those reviewing video recordings of resuscitation.[4]

[7.15] UK guidelines now suggest oxygen saturation monitoring during resuscitation. This determines the percentage of oxygenated haemoglobin by shining a red light through the right hand. The device is quickly attached, providing oxygen saturation and pulse rate. By five minutes, saturation should be >80 per cent and by 10 minutes >90 per cent.

RESUSCITATION

[7.16] Infant resuscitation should be performed by those trained to do so: trained paediatricians, trainees in paediatrics, midwives and paediatric nurses. Advanced nurse practitioners may lead advanced resuscitation and are often responsible for teaching trainee doctors.

---

4. O'Donnell et al, 'Interobserver variability of the 5 minute Apgar score' (2006) 149 J Pediatr 486–489.

Figure 7.3

Newborn Life Support

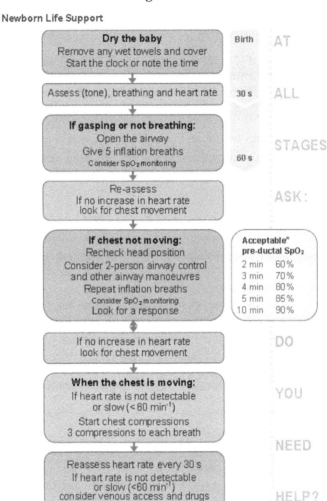

[7.17] Resuscitation guidelines for all age groups including the neonate are agreed by the International Liaison Committee on Resuscitation (ILCOR) and published by the Resuscitation Council (UK). Guidelines are reviewed at five yearly intervals and are freely available on the Council website.[5]

---

5.   (www.resus.org.uk) (Newborn Life Support, 2010).

A – Airway

[7.18] The airway refers to a clear open passage through which air may pass into the lungs. The infant is placed supine on a flat surface. Suction is used to clear blood, mucus, etc, that is present.

[7.19] If an infant has a slow heart rate which is not improving or is not showing regular breathing, positive pressure ventilation is needed. This is first provided through a face mask over the baby's nose and mouth. Positive pressure is provided most commonly through a T-piece. Gas flows up the tube which forms the vertical part of T. One side of the T is attached to the mask and the other is open. Occlusion of the open end applies pressure through the mask. The pressure is usually set on a gauge. Alternatively, the mask is attached to a self-inflating resuscitation bag. This fills with gas when released and when squeezed pushes gas through a valve into the mask.

Figure 7.4

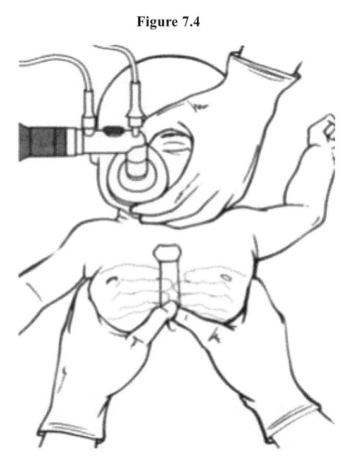

[7.20] If the airway is good, the chest will rise, and almost always heart rate will improve and recovery will follow. If the chest does not rise, the airway is not adequate. This requires adjustment of the head position, aspiration of material in the airway, or better application of the mask.[6] There is a current training focus on improving mask ventilation technique. All providing resuscitation should be familiar with mask ventilation.[7]

[7.21] If initial resuscitation is ineffective and the heart rate remains below 100 bpm, after two to five minutes, tracheal intubation, if available, should be performed. This skilled procedure is not available in all birthing centres. It is expected of more senior trainees in paediatrics, consultant paediatricians and most advanced nurse practitioners.

Figure 7.5

---

6.   Wood et al, 'Improved techniques reduce face mask leak during simulated neonatal resuscitation: study 2' (2008) Arch Dis Child Fetal Neonatal 93:F230–F234.

7.   (Neonatal Life Support, 2010).

Front

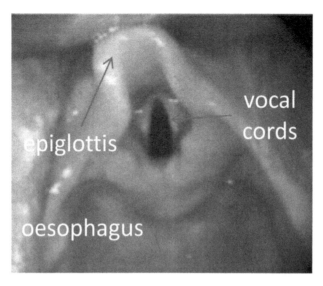

vocal cords

epiglottis

oesophagus

[7.22] A specially designed and marked plastic tube of a size appropriate to the infant, is passed through the vocal cords. This requires direct vision of the cords with a laryngoscope. This device has a blade which lifts the tongue and allows visualisation of the larynx behind the epiglottis.

[7.23] It is important that the tube is in the right place. Recovery of the baby is the best indicator of successful intubation. Air entry is heard on both sides of the chest with a stethoscope. Gastric distension suggests an oesophageal tube. Capnography is now recommended. The infant is ventilated through a small plastic device containing a carbon dioxide sensitive colour indicator which changes colour with exhaled breath. Capnography is helpful and reliable but may not show colour change if the heart rate is absent or in the small preterm infant.

[7.24] If resuscitation is not effective with the tracheal tube, think:

D displacement, is tube in the oesophagus or not at the right level?

O obstruction, is the tube blocked or the trachea blocked below it?

P pneumothorax, rarely air leaks out of the lungs inside the rib cage preventing expansion of the lungs;

E equipment failure, is everything connected and working?

B – Breathing

[7.25] Bradycardia, poor spontaneous breathing, limp tone or poor colour without recovery indicates a need for positive pressure ventilation through the airway. Five inflation breaths with a relatively long period of inflation (2–3 seconds) are given using air. The practitioner looks for a rise in the chest and an improvement in the pulse. Often the five inflation breaths are repeated. This should be effective and if it is not, it is likely that the lungs are not being aerated.

[7.26] If ineffective, the airway should be reviewed, equipment checked, the pressure adjusted (in general up to 30 cm H2O) and increased oxygen concentration used.

[7.27] Continuing ventilation may be required, given at 60 breaths per minute each lasting around 0.5 seconds. If the infant improves in pulse and colour but remains apnoeic (not breathing), the airway is better maintained by trachea intubation if available.

[7.28] The first marker of restoration of oxygenation and circulation is a rise in the heart rate above 100 bpm, typically followed by improvement in central colour of the baby's trunk and then regular breathing.

C – Circulation

[7.29] A small proportion of infants, despite a good airway and effective breathing with chest rise do not show improvement in heart rate. A pulse below 60 bpm, when those present are confident that the lungs are aerated, indicates need for cardiac compressions (external cardiac massage).

[7.30] This entails compression of the chest on the sternum just below a line between the nipples so that the chest is compressed by 1/3 of its diameter, at around 100/minute. In the newborn, cardiac compression is provided with positive pressure ventilation at a ratio of 3:1. Three cardiac compressions are provided for each ventilation breath.

D – Drugs

[7.31] If the infant remains bradycardic or asystolic (no heart rate), adrenaline is given. Adrenaline is best given through an umbilical venous catheter, thin plastic tube passed into the umbilical vein in the cord stump. It may also be given through an intravenous line, or into a tibial intra-osseous line (needle inserted into shin bone). An increased dose may be given into a tracheal tube. Occasionally intravenous bicarbonate, volume expansion with saline or dextrose may be administered.

[7.32] In the infant who requires adrenaline, the prognosis is much less favourable.

Post-resuscitation care

[7.33] An infant who recovers should remain with her mother and family. A plan for observations and review should be established with the midwife who is caring for the mother and baby.

[7.34] If continuing respiratory support is required, the infant will usually be transferred to the baby unit receiving ventilation, most commonly through a tracheal tube. This must be performed by someone trained to deal with any deterioration in transit.

[7.35] Therapeutic hypothermia (cooling) offers considerable advantage in the prevention of permanent brain injury following intrapartum asphyxia. Assessment during resuscitation, including the infant's condition, the need for ventilatory support or Apgar score <5 at 10 minutes or severe acidosis should prompt consideration of early passive cooling. Simply this means turning off heaters, allowing the infants temperature to fall and most importantly carefully monitoring of core temperature to ensure that it does not fall below 33°C.

[7.36] If an infant is asystolic (no heart rate) despite resuscitation, a decision may be made to cease resuscitation. Current UK guidelines indicate that cessation of resuscitation should be considered after 10 minutes of established asystole on the basis of poor survival rates and risk of brain injury. This view has recently been challenged, suggesting continued resuscitation until 20 minutes.[8] In current practice, most continue until 15 minutes. There remains no evidence to continue beyond 20 minutes.

Special considerations

[7.37]

- Thick meconium in the liquor raises the risk of aspiration of this fetal stool into the lungs. Suction of meconium from the upper airway and, if it is present, from below the vocal cords is generally performed in the infant who is quiet and not breathing. This does not prevent all meconium aspiration syndrome.

---

8. Wilkinson et al, 'Don't stop now? How long should resuscitation continue at birth in the absence of a detectable heartbeat?' (2015) Arch Dis Child (Online first 03.08.15).

- Fetal blood loss may occur with antepartum haemorrhage, tearing of fetal blood vessels with rupture of membranes or through bleeding from the fetus into the maternal circulation. The diagnosis is not usually made before delivery. If intensely pale even when the pulse improves with resuscitation, anaemia is considered. Immediate vascular access and administration of saline followed by emergency uncross matched blood transfusion is needed.

- The child with congenital abnormalities particularly where these may threaten the airway should be delivered in an appropriate setting with available expertise. If fetal diagnosis allows, a plan should be in place.

- Preterm infants, especially those below 32 weeks' gestation are more likely to need intervention at birth. Extremely preterm infants often require tracheal intubation. Avoidance of hypothermia by immediately placing the infant into a polythene bag is important. At less than 25 weeks' gestation, ethical considerations and discussion with the family may determine that resuscitation is not in an infant's best interests.

Common errors in resuscitation

[7.38] Investigation of resuscitation is most likely when an infant has an adverse outcome with stillbirth, neonatal death, or long-term neurodisability. Those present should record, with times in minutes after birth, the steps taken and the infant's response. Key information includes the intervention and the effect this has on the heart rate. Notes should include observation of chest rise indicating lung expansion if A and B are effective.

[7.39] The commonest problem is failure to achieve a good airway and adequate breathing. This may reflect problems with equipment, resuscitation technique or staff training but occasionally an infant is unable to respond even to good resuscitation. If recovery follows rapidly upon different intervention or involvement of another practitioner, this raises questions about the previous resuscitation and whether it was appropriate care in the hands of those who were present.

Chapter 8

THE LAW

[8.01] Cerebral palsy claims are the most complex, most time-consuming and most expensive to prepare of all childbirth-related medical negligence claims. The stakes are high and when successfully litigated, these claims have the highest associated damages. Because of the large sums of money involved, these claims are usually vigorously defended.

BREACH OF DUTY

[8.02] The expert who addresses breach of duty is usually an obstetrician, with a midwife sometimes also being required. It is necessary to show that signs of fetal compromise should have been detected and that delivery should have been expedited. The principal errors of obstetric management associated with claims for cerebral palsy are as follows:[1]

Antenatal

[8.03] Failure to detect or to take account of:

- fetal abnormality;
- intra-uterine infection;
- maternal hypertension including pre-eclampsia;
- maternal diabetes;
- special investigations including ultrasound scans;
- intra-uterine growth restriction;
- twins;
- abnormal and/or unstable presentations;
- cephalopelvic disproportion;
- placental abruption;
- placenta praevia;
- the need to monitor fetal wellbeing;
- preterm labour.

---

1. Adapted from Clements and Rosenbloom, 'Medico-legal issues: the United Kingdom perspective' in Levene, Chervenak and Whittle (eds), *Fetal and Neonatal Neurology and Neurosurgery* (3rd edn, Churchill Livingstone, 2001).

Labour

[8.04] Failure to detect or to take account of:

- CTG abnormalities;
- the abuse of oxytocin;
- malpresentation;
- disproportion;
- umbilical cord complications;
- fetal scalp blood samples;
- dysfunctional labour and the secondary arrest of labour;
- the need to avoid difficult vaginal delivery especially in the presence of fetal distress;
- trial of operative vaginal delivery;
- previous injury to the uterus (VBAC);
- use of the ventouse;
- the conduct and timing of Caesarean section;
- the need to conduct delivery in an appropriate environment;
- the need to have the necessary paediatric and anaesthetic assistance available;
- the management of shoulder dystocia.

Postnatal

[8.05] Failure to detect or to take account of:

- the need to reverse the effects on the fetus of narcotic drugs given to the mother;
- the need to have the necessary paediatric assistance available;
- the need to intubate or otherwise effectively resuscitate and provide proper respiratory support for the baby;
- the appropriate surroundings and expertise required and necessary for the further care of the baby.

CAUSATION

[8.06] Causation is often the point on which cerebral palsy claims are lost. There will often be those cases where, notwithstanding that there has been breach of duty, the outcome for the baby would probably have been the same without it. It is important to recall that only 10 to 15 per cent of cerebral palsy is related to birth events. There are many causes of cerebral palsy and whilst the cause of the majority of cases remains unknown, the most common allegations in litigation surround hypoxia during labour. In litigation, attention focuses on detection of intra-partum asphyxia and its prevention. Most actions which come before the courts alleging hypoxic cause for cerebral palsy relate to intrapartum events. In making a rational decision about causation, lawyers should ask the following questions:

1.   was there evidence of marked and severe asphyxia during labour?

2.   did the baby show signs of hypoxic-ischaemic encephalopathy in the newborn period with evidence also of asphyxial injury to other organ systems?

3.   is the child's disability one which birth asphyxia could explain?

4.   has the work-up been sufficient to rule out other conditions?[2]

[8.07] If all of the 'markers'[3] are present, the court may be persuaded that asphyxia during labour caused the cerebral palsy.

[8.08] Experts in neonatology, paediatric neurology and neuroradiology, if there has been neuroimaging, are commonly relied on to address issues of causation. By assessing the clinical condition of the child immediately after birth and subsequently, it is possible for the experts to express an opinion on whether, on the balance of probabilities, the cerebral palsy was caused by hypoxic-ischaemic damage during labour. Consideration and identification of the timing of irreversible brain damage is necessary in order to establish what the child's condition would have been with proper care.[4]

[8.09] Chronic partial hypoxia in labour leading to brain damage occurs where, for a sustained period, the fetus is receiving some oxygen, but less than is needed. It does not necessarily produce severe cardiorespiratory depression with low Apgar scores at delivery, but it does produce hypoxic-ischaemic encephalopathy in the newborn period. Failure of the part of medical staff to understand, interpret and react to an abnormal CTG is probably the most common complaint of the plaintiff. The abuse of oxytocin (Syntocinon) causing

---

2.   Adapted from Freeman and Nelson, 'Intrapartum asphyxia and cerebral palsy' (1988) 82 *Paediatrics* 240–249.

3.   The usual criteria used to assess the likelihood of an individual's cerebral palsy having arisen as a consequence of intrapartum hypoxia.

4.   Westcott and Guthrie, 'Injuries at birth: the basics of a claim' (2003) JPI Law 217–224 (Dec).

excessive uterine activity and intermittent chronic hypoxia is also a recurrent theme. It is so often a part of the picture that it is unsurprising how few cases run – abuse of oxytocin is so self-evidently the result of negligence that most of the cases settle before trial.

[8.10] Acute near total hypoxia in labour leading to brain damage occurs where for a short period, the fetus is almost completely deprived of oxygen. Brief periods of acute near total hypoxia-ischaemia is associated with the disasters of labour such as cord compromise, placental abruption, ruptured uterus, acute maternal hypertension or shoulder dystocia. A plaintiff will likely succeed if she can show that the disaster should never have been allowed to happen.

[8.11] Certain themes recur throughout cerebral palsy cases: communication failure, delay and the cascade of events. There are communication failures both between doctor and patient and amongst staff. Good communication is the key to avoiding litigation. Good practice may provide a reasonable defence to litigation but good communication will often obviate it. Delay is ubiquitous in birth asphyxia claims: delay in making observations and delay in interpreting observations, delay in making decisions to intervene and delay in intervening. Childbirth disasters are not usually achieved by one end-player: they are the result of a series of indecisions or incorrect decisions: a cascade of events. [5]

[8.12] A good starting point in any analysis of cerebral palsy litigation is *Dunne v National Maternity Hospital and Anor*[6] which was our first reported case on the subject. Difficult as it is to comprehend, in cases of twin pregnancies it was the practice of the National Maternity Hospital to seek to identify only one fetal heartbeat. The obstetrician in *Dunne* did not direct an alteration of this daft practice.

[8.13] The case came before the High Court and was the very last jury trial in a personal injuries case in Ireland. The plaintiff succeeded and was awarded an unprecedented amount in damages. The defendants appealed, submitting 33 grounds of appeal each, and a retrial was ordered. The Supreme Court found that a misdirection had been given to the jury on the issue of whether the hospital's policy of only monitoring one twin's fetal heartbeat was a 'general and approved practice' within the profession. The case ultimately settled and judgment was entered against the first defendant hospital only.

---

5.   Clements, 'Medico-Legal Aspects' in Chamberlain and Steer (eds), *Turnbull's Obstetrics* (3rd edn, Harcourt, 2001) and Edozien, 'Obstetrics and gynaecology' in Powers and Barton (eds), *Clinical Negligence* (5th edn, Bloomsbury Professional, 2015), 1261.

6.   *Dunne v National Maternity Hospital and Jackson* [1989] IR 91.

[8.14] The plaintiff's mother had been in labour with twins which was slow to progress. Grade I meconium was discovered when the membranes were ruptured, upon auscultation a fetal heartbeat was found and dilatation was 3 cm.

[8.15] Labour continued to progress very slowly and oxytocin was commenced. Meconium Grade II deposit was discovered. A fetal blood sample on the scalp of the leading twin was carried out which was normal. A continuous electronic monitor was attached to the scalp of the leading twin. The second defendant was informed by telephone that the cervix was fully dilated and that the plaintiff was being delivered. The plaintiff was born naturally and the second defendant arrived within minutes of his birth. Fifteen minutes later, the second twin was stillborn and showing signs of maceration. This had not been detected by the defendants prior to delivery. The plaintiff was in a poor condition and it became clear that he had sustained severe brain damage.

[8.16] The plaintiff's case was that injury arose from severe oxygen deprivation due to placental dysfunction which impeded oxygen access especially during the late stages of labour when contractions were greatest; that this should have been detected earlier and delivery performed by Caesarean section. The plaintiff argued that in twin pregnancies, it was unacceptable to simply monitor one fetal heartbeat and that the general and approved practice was to attempt to identify and monitor both fetal heartbeats. One of his experts stated that the practice of the hospital in the case of a known twin pregnancy not to seek to identify two fetal hearts was one of which he had never heard being adopted anywhere else. He said it was clearly wrong, and that to look for two fetal hearts was something basic, which he compared to putting on the lights of a vehicle when it became dark. In his opinion, to seek to identify one only was absurd.

[8.17] The defendants' response was that injury was caused by oxygen deprivation owing to massive twin-to-twin blood transfusion in the 12 to 24 hours before commencement of labour. They considered that monitoring two fetal heartbeats was notoriously unreliable and that the longstanding practice in the hospital of seeking to identify a single fetal heartbeat was adequate.

[8.18] Importantly, Finlay CJ in the Supreme Court stated that the principles already laid down by the court[7] related to issues raised in *Dunne*. There was no argument submitted on the hearing of the appeal which constituted any form of

---

7. In *O'Donovan v Cork County Council* [1967] IR 173 which adopted and followed the decision of the former Supreme Court in *Daniels v Heskin* [1954] IR 73. The reasoning in *O'Donovan* was expressly followed by the Supreme Court in *Reeves v Carthy and O'Kelly* [1984] IR 348. It was again approved and applied to a case of professional negligence by a solicitor in *Roche v Peilow* [1985] IR 232.

challenge to the correctness of the statements of principle laid down, although there was controversy concerning their application to the facts of the case. Finlay CJ, in his judgment, set out the legal principles to be applied by courts in determining whether there has been medical negligence. These '*Dunne* principles', which apply to diagnosis and treatment alike, have remained unaltered ever since. They are:

1. The true test for establishing negligence in diagnosis or treatment on the part of a medical practitioner is whether he has been proved to be guilty of such failure as no medical practitioner of equal specialist or general status and skill would be guilty of if acting with ordinary care.

2. If the allegation of negligence against a medical practitioner is based on proof that he deviated from a general and approved practice, that will not establish negligence unless it is also proved that the course he did take was one which no medical practitioner of like specialisation and skill would have followed had he been taking the ordinary care required from a person of his qualifications.

3. If a medical practitioner charged with negligence defends his conduct by establishing that he followed a practice which was general, and which was approved of by his colleagues of similar specialisation and skill, he cannot escape liability if in reply the plaintiff establishes that such practice has inherent defects which ought to be obvious to any person giving the matter due consideration.

4. An honest difference of opinion between doctors as to which is the better of two ways of treating a patient does not provide any ground for leaving a question to the jury as to whether a person who has followed one course rather than the other has been negligent.

5. It is not for a jury (or for a judge) to decide which of two alternative courses of treatment is in their (or his) opinion preferable, but their (or his) function is merely to decide whether the course of treatment followed, on the evidence, complied with the careful conduct of a medical practitioner of like specialisation and skill to that professed by the defendant.

6. If there is an issue of fact, the determination of which is necessary for the decision as to whether a particular medical practice is or is not general and approved within the meaning of these principles, that issue must in a trial held with a jury be left to the determination of the jury.

[8.19] The defendant's suggestion in *Dunne* that in twin labour only one fetal heartbeat needed monitoring was so clearly a practice with 'inherent defects' that no person giving the matter due consideration could possibly justify it.

[8.20] In the end, the merits of the claim were never determined by a court as the case settled during re-trial for reasons unknown. As a result of this case however, the National Maternity Hospital changed its stated policy and practice which had been to monitor the fetal heartbeat of only one twin (the leading twin) in labour and commenced a policy of monitoring the fetal heartbeat of both twins in labour. The case was 'a principal architect in moving medical cases into the mainstream of legal, and of judicial, thinking ... a landmark case for more than one reason and ultimately... accelerated the process by which barriers, peculiar to this type of action were stood down'.[8]

RESUSCITATION FAILURE

[8.21] Most babies require little support when born and will begin to breathe spontaneously without help. A minority, who have suffered some form of intrauterine stress, will require considerable assistance to support respiration and to provide sufficient oxygen to the vital organs.

[8.22] *Dunne v Coombe Women and Infants University Hospital*[9] was the first Irish cerebral palsy claim to reach court conclusion in which the alleged negligence concerned the failure to perform a timely resuscitation of a baby in need of assistance. Irvine J held that the defendant was negligent in failing to ensure that the plaintiff received an acceptable standard of care in relation to the intubation and ventilation which was required within the first 10 minutes of his life. The disagreement between the parties was as to timing of injury.

[8.23] The plaintiff was born in moderate condition, did not breathe spontaneously and required immediate resuscitative assistance. His condition deteriorated and he required emergency intubation. It was alleged that the defendant was negligent in the care it afforded the plaintiff, in failing to restore his heartbeat until 23 minutes post-birth, during which interval the plaintiff suffered a period of near total acute hypoxia-ischemia. The court had to decide why the plaintiff was born in only moderate condition and why he went on to sustain catastrophic injuries during a period when the defendant maintained he

---

8.   Mr Justice McKechnie, 'Patients' Rights: Access to Justice and the Case for Candour', conference paper dated 4 November 2013.

9.   *Dunne v Coombe Women and Infants University Hospital* [2013] IEHC 58.

was receiving resuscitation of a nature that should have fully protected him from sustaining hypoxic injury.

[8.24] The defendant originally maintained that damage was likely caused by an hypoxic-ischaemic event which occurred in the hours or days before delivery or that something else had happened prior to the plaintiff's birth which would account for the fact that he became brain damaged despite the delivery of competent and timely resuscitation. That hypothesis was later abandoned. Subsequently the defendant maintained that the plaintiff was probably born with an inborn error such that he did not breathe spontaneously at birth or respond normally to timely resuscitative efforts and thereby sustained his present injuries during a period of hypoxia in and about the time of his birth.

[8.25] The plaintiff's experts did not consider the plaintiff's condition or failure to breathe spontaneously at birth to be unique or extraordinary. It certainly did not warrant the defendant seeking to explain it by reference to some sinister underlying genetic or metabolic disorder. The plaintiff was born less well than was expected having regard to his mother's labour, but nonetheless in moderate condition with a valid Apgar score of five at one. Even if the plaintiff had been born with any of the disorders contended for by the defendant, the existence of any such disorder could not have accounted for his failure to respond to timely and effective resuscitation. Several of the experts repeatedly stated that they had never come across such a case in practice and that they knew of no mechanism by which such an inborn error could make it more difficult to resuscitate a baby nor had they ever read about such a case in the medical literature.

[8.26] When the plaintiff fell ill with rhabdomyolysis in February 2012, the proceedings were adjourned to enable the parties to assess the extent to which that illness might impact upon the causation issue in the case. It was not until day 27 of the resumed hearing that the defendant first sought to advance any mechanism to explain how the presence of an inborn error could have adversely impacted on the plaintiff's ability to breathe spontaneously at birth or to respond to timely and effective resuscitation. It was unable to explain how, if the plaintiff had suffered anything which profoundly affected him at the moment of his birth, he had previously behaved normally in the womb in terms of his movements and cardiac activity. Nor could it explain how after the first 30 minutes of the plaintiff's life he appeared to have had no adverse effects from such a disorder from birth in July 2002 until February 2012.

[8.27] The defendant was not in a position adequately to explain why an infant born with an inborn error could not be resuscitated. The court inevitably concluded that the plaintiff was not born with any underlying defect of the nature advised by the defendant's witnesses. The defendant was not able to point to a condition which is known to medical science and for which there is a test that, if carried out, would resolve the causation issue. Even if the plaintiff was subjected to all of the testing advised by the defendant, and even if such testing pointed towards a certain medical condition, none of the defendant's experts was able to explain how the presence of such a condition would have had the effect of temporarily interfering with his ability to respond, like any other baby, to positive pressure ventilation and intubation if delivered in a timely and effective manner.

[8.28] What, then, was likely to have happened to the plaintiff between the time of his birth and the time when the paediatric registrar arrived to assist in his resuscitation? This was in dispute along with the time of his arrival and what happened thereafter.

[8.29] Irvine J was satisfied that the defendant, in failing, having regard to the plaintiff's condition at birth and over the first minute of his life, to have a senior member of its paediatric staff capable of carrying out an intubation of a newborn present and in attendance by the time he was five minutes of age, caused the delay responsible for him sustaining all of his injuries.

[8.30] Having regard to the plaintiff's condition at birth, including his normal blood gases and knowing that he had no cardiac or pulmonary problems, he should have responded to positive pressure ventilation had it been effectively delivered. Having regard to the decline in the plaintiff's Apgar score over the first five minutes of life, the court considered it highly likely that a failure to deliver effective bag and mask ventilation was responsible for this deterioration.

[8.31] Irvine J stated that because positive pressure ventilation is fraught with difficulties, it is incumbent upon a maternity hospital to have its midwifery staff sufficiently trained to identify a baby's potential need for intubation and to have a system in place such that it can ensure that within five minutes of a baby developing respiratory distress, a senior member of the medical staff capable of intubation will be in attendance. In this case, assistance did not arrive to resuscitate the plaintiff until he was something approaching fifteen minutes of age. His heartbeat only started to recover in response to the prompt administration of intravenous adrenalin following reintubation when he was about 23 or 24 minutes of age.

[8.32] If the defendant had acted with reasonable care for the plaintiff's welfare, there was no reason why he should not have been effectively ventilated and had this occurred he would not have gone on to develop the injuries which afflicted him.

CTGS

[8.33] The CTG provides the most reliable evidence of fetal wellbeing during the course of labour. Abnormalities on the CTG should trigger appropriate responses from the attendant staff.

The Supreme Court dismissed the plaintiff's appeal in *O'Mahony v Tyndale and Anor*[10] where the cerebral palsy claim had been made alleging delay in his delivery by between 7 and 12 minutes longer than was reasonable, and inadequate nursing records within the 24-hour nursery. A difficulty was thrown up by the absence of a CTG.

[8.34] Quirke J in the High Court (in a written judgment dated 7 April 2000)[11] found that no case of negligence had been made out against the medical attendant, and further that the system in use by the hospital for the recording of clinical symptoms was in accordance with general and approved practice. Some deficiencies had been highlighted; however, the overall evidence had failed to establish that the system operated by the defendant hospital had caused or contributed to the plaintiff's injuries. On appeal, Keane CJ held that the plaintiff had failed to show that there was evidence relating to his care which could be said to be missing.

[8.35] Counsel for the plaintiff sought to invoke the application of the maxim *omnia praesumunter contra spoliatorem* ('everything is presumed against a wrongdoer') to overcome the difficulty presented by the lack of relevant records, or CTG in the last 26 minutes prior to the plaintiff's delivery, which he submitted the hospital had destroyed or suppressed. At the very least, it was submitted, the onus of proof shifted by the application of the maxim and as at all times the trial judge had treated the onus as resting on the plaintiff, a retrial should be allowed.

[8.36] There was nothing to indicate that a trace which had been taken was in fact destroyed by the defendants, but, altogether apart from that consideration, the maxim was thought to be of no relevance. The trace, if it had been available, might have shown that the condition of bradycardia continued, and even intensified, up to the time of delivery. Alternatively, it might have shown that it settled down. Since, however, the defendants' case, supported as it was by credible evidence, was that if the episode of bradycardia had led to hypoxia, the baby could not possibly have presented the normal and healthy appearance which it did, the missing trace would not have been in any way critical to the

---

10.   *O'Mahony v Tyndale and Anor* [2000] IEHC 43.
11.   *O'Mahony v Tyndale and Anor* [2000] IEHC 43.

issue which had to be resolved. As to the destruction of whatever records were kept by the nurses in the 24-hour observation nursery, there was no evidence of any records of the baby's feeds having been taken or of any abnormal symptoms which the baby was displaying. The criticism, indeed, of the hospital system of record-keeping, accepted by the trial judge, was that routine records were not kept by the nurses in the observation nursery and there was no evidence whatever of any written records recording anything in relation to the plaintiff ever having existed in the case of the observation nursery. Accordingly, the court was satisfied that the maxim had no application.

[8.37] The maxim exists to ensure that no party to a case is disadvantaged by the wrongdoing of his opponent in destroying or suppressing evidence, but Keane CJ found that:

> there is no authority for the proposition that it could be invoked so as to produce a clear injustice, ie an obligation on a court of trial to disregard the weight of the evidence which it has heard because some of the documents, although of no significance in the outcome of the case, have been, for no sinister reason, mislaid or destroyed or because some documents never existed in the first place.

[8.38] *Fitzpatrick v National Maternity Hospital*[12] involved a plaintiff with cerebral palsy successfully concluding his action in a trial on liability only which ran for 55 days in the High Court. This was a case of failure properly to interpret and act on an abnormal CTG trace and resultant delay in delivery. The defendant had delivered a full defence and had specifically pleaded that if there had been any undue delay in delivering the plaintiff, such delay was caused solely by the refusal of the plaintiff's mother to permit an episiotomy and forceps assisted vaginal delivery. That outrageous contributory negligence allegation was, sensibly, abandoned at trial. The failure to adequately inform the parents as to the dangers of not having a particular form of delivery was found to have been negligent. The plaintiff suffered increasing irreversible hypoxic-ischemic injury to his brain and other injuries during a period of about a half an hour and it was held that the defendant's delay materially contributed to his cerebral palsy.

[8.39] A senior midwife at the defendant hospital was negligent in failing to call for the obstetric registrar and in failing to discontinue the use of oxytocin when she should have. The plaintiff was deprived of the opportunity of being delivered without irreversible brain injury. The obstetric registrar should have delivered the plaintiff at or before a certain time thereby sparing the plaintiff all

---

12. *Fitzpatrick v National Maternity Hospital* [2008] IEHC 62.

of his injuries. Herbert J found that the delay on the part of the obstetric registrar in delivering the plaintiff was 'in the circumstances of the dire emergency then prevailing seriously substandard' and that this negligence on his part materially contributed to the amount of irreversible brain damage and other injuries suffered by the plaintiff.

[8.40] All of the expert witnesses were in agreement on the foregoing unless it could, somehow or other, be found that the delay was excusable by reason of an alleged delay on the part of the plaintiff's mother in allowing the ventouse to be used and her alleged complete refusal to allow the use of forceps or an episiotomy. Herbert J found that there was no material or untoward delay on her part in allowing the use of the ventouse. She would not have refused the forceps assisted delivery and the episiotomy had she been informed in straightforward and unequivocal terms that the plaintiff was in distress and unless he was delivered immediately that he would suffer serious injuries. The failure on the part of the defendant so to inform the plaintiffs' parents was substandard. But for the negligence and breach of duty in failing to provide adequate information, the plaintiff's mother would have immediately consented to those procedures or to any other necessary medical procedures at whatever time she might have been asked.

[8.41] The defendant appealed to the Supreme Court and in the interim the case settled for €4.5 million without an admission of liability and the High Court judgment was set aside.

PLACENTAL FAILURE

[8.42] Throughout pregnancy and labour the fetus is totally dependent upon the placenta for nutrients and gas exchange. Failure of the placenta may lead initially to slow growth and ultimately to oxygen lack.

[8.43] In *Quinn v Mid-Western Health Board and North Eastern Health Board*[13] the plaintiff claimed there was an omission to perform a timely ultrasound scan which would have shown asymmetric growth restriction which should have led to early delivery and the avoidance of her brain damage. *Quinn* is an example of breach of duty without causation and the nub of the case was timing of injury.

---

13.   *Quinn v Mid-Western Health Board and North Eastern Health Board* (14 October 2003) HC, O'Sullivan J.

[8.44] At the age of 10 years the plaintiff was diagnosed with cerebral palsy. MRI scan revealed severe generalised periventricular leukomalacia and other brain damage, but no damage to the plaintiff's cortex or sub-cortex.

[8.45] The plaintiff had been delivered by Caesarean section. She was a small baby with little fluid around her. She had exhibited abnormal traces and Apgar scores were low. She required resuscitation and exhibited neurological abnormalities including a convulsion. She was a poor feeder and sleeper. She remained in hospital for 34 days in total.

[8.46] The plaintiff's mother was an insulin-dependent diabetic, which, it was alleged, meant her pregnancy was in the high risk category of pregnancies and that certain scans which should have been conducted were not. The omission, it was alleged, meant that progressive starvation of the fetus and progressive brain damage was not diagnosed. The defendants admitted negligence in failing to perform a scan at around 30 weeks' gestation, however, they contended that it was apparent from two CTs and an MRI that the plaintiff's injuries had already been suffered by that time and that even had ultrasound been carried out at that time it would have been too late to prevent the injuries. Their case was that the plaintiff suffered a single catastrophic insult prior to that point in the pregnancy (at around 28 to 34 weeks' gestation). Timing of injury would be crucial.

[8.47] The plaintiff had a very difficult task: the breach of duty was the failure to perform a scan, and causation is always harder to establish when one is dealing with an omission rather than a positive act. Unfortunately it proved too difficult to establish that if performed, the scan would have shown asymmetric growth restriction sufficient to stimulate the need for delivery at a time before the damaging starvation and oxygen deprivation had injured the fetus. The plaintiff was unable to prove, on the balance of probabilities, that all or a significant part of her injuries occurred after the 35th week of gestation.

[8.48] O'Sullivan J was satisfied that his finding in that regard was sufficient to dispose of the case but 'in case [he was] incorrect' in the conclusion as reached, he also decided to set out findings on the other issue in the case, namely the plaintiff's life expectancy. Having heard evidence from experts for both sides, he concluded that the plaintiff had a life expectancy of 35 years.

[8.49] The plaintiff's appeal to the Supreme Court,[14] on grounds that the particular circumstances of the case called for a modified approach to proof of causation, was dismissed. It was held that the plaintiff was required to discharge the burden of showing that the breach of duty complained of caused her damage

---

14. *Quinn v Mid-Western Health Board and Anor* [2005] 4 IR 1, [2005] 2 ILRM 180.

by showing that but for the breach she would not have suffered the damage. The evidence led on behalf of the defendants was such as to bring about a situation where the plaintiff had not tilted the scales decisively in favour of the case on causation contended for by the plaintiff's experts.

[8.50] It was not enough to show that her condition worsened during the period from the start of difficulties until delivery – it had to be further shown that early intervention would have prevented the damage. This was the long-established 'but for' principle of causation. Kearns J suggested that any approach which had the effect of reversing the onus of proof, or transferring the onus of proof to the defendant, would be one of such importance, even in the few exceptional cases where it might be appropriate, that it would require a full court – or perhaps even legislation – before a change of such magnitude to existing law could take place. Nor did special circumstances arise or exist to bring the claim within the more relaxed requirements for establishing causation which were found to exist in *McGhee v National Coal Board*[15] and *Fairchild v Glenhaven Funeral Services Ltd*[16] whereby causation might be inferred or the onus of proof reversed.

[8.51] Parties to litigation must of course bring forward their whole case at first instance and not seek to do so at a later time. The plaintiff in this 'truly tragic case' had not argued at trial that the normal requirements of proof on the part of the plaintiff did not apply and so unfortunately could not make a new case to that effect on appeal.

[8.52] *Purdy v Lenihan and Ors*[17] is another good example of the causation difficulty. The plaintiff, who suffered cerebral palsy, claimed damages for alleged negligence arising out of his birth at the National Maternity Hospital when his mother was at 33 weeks and three days' gestation. His case was that there was a failure to perform a Caesarean section on his mother and failure adequately to prepare for a possible blood transfusion to her some hours prior to his birth. The case was dismissed in the High Court for failure to establish causation, despite clear breaches of duty. The plaintiff appealed to the Supreme Court where Keane CJ dismissed the appeal and affirmed the order of the High Court that there was credible evidence to support a finding that, on the balance of probabilities, the plaintiff's injury was not caused by negligence on the part of the defendants during the 20 minutes immediately prior to the plaintiff's birth.

[8.53] Because such a length of time had elapsed since the plaintiff's birth (23 years) and because so many of the medical notes and records had been lost,

---

15. *McGhee v National Coal Board* [1973] 1 WLR 1.
16. *Fairchild v Glenhaven Funeral Services Ltd* [2002] UKHL 22, [2003] 1 AC 32.
17. *Purdy v Lenihan and Ors* [2003] IESC 7, Keane CJ.

Johnson J in the High Court acceded to an application by the defendants to strike out parts of the plaintiff's claim on the basis that they would not be in a position properly to defend themselves.

[8.54] The obstetrician had considered that the mother's diagnosis of placenta praevia should be confirmed by ultra sound. (In placenta praevia it is the mother who bleeds. Only if her blood pressure falls to dangerously low levels is circulation through the placenta impaired.) It was not in dispute that, at that stage, he did not order the cross-matching of blood. (The cross-matching of blood would have involved taking a blood sample, analysing the blood type, identifying units of stored blood of the same type and making this blood available in the event that a transfusion became necessary. The significance of cross-matched blood being available in the present case was that it would be essential if a Caesarean section were to be performed.)

[8.55] The notes available recorded the mother as having suffered a further substantial ante-partum haemorrhage. At that stage an IV drip was ordered and four units of blood were directed to be cross-matched. Further, a Caesarean section was to be performed if the bleeding continued. The obstetrician went off duty and was replaced by a registrar. The mother had a further bleed. It was noted that she looked pale and needed blood and it was directed that a Caesarean section be performed as soon as blood became available.

[8.56] The lower segment Caesarean section was performed and the plaintiff was delivered with a forceps with some difficulty, because the placenta was in the left anterior lateral position. Following delivery, the uterus and abdomen were closed in a routine manner. The plaintiff's condition at birth was poor and he was intubated. His Apgar score was one at one and he suffered from respiratory distress syndrome. Subsequently he was diagnosed with cerebral palsy.

[8.57] As for causation, the plaintiff claimed, but failed to establish, that the injury occurred during a continuing substantial haemorrhage in the last 20 minutes or so preceding delivery. There was an absence of notes and records charting the crucial 20-minute timeframe, and whether the haemorrhage did in fact occur.

[8.58] The central issue on appeal was whether there was credible evidence to support a finding that on the balance of probabilities the damage caused to the plaintiff was caused during earlier bleeds and not during the crucial 20 minutes prior to his delivery, or in the alternative, a finding that the plaintiff had not established as a matter of probability that that it had occurred during the latter rather than the former period. Keane CJ was satisfied that there was such credible evidence.

[8.59] There were conflicting views expressed by experts on both sides. The condition of the plaintiff was going to be of critical importance in determining the timing of the damage. Johnson J had taken the view that the defendants' theory of causation was the more favourable, based on the fact that the available notes indicated that the plaintiff had only been intubated for a minute after his birth and the only other reference to a longer period of intubation was in the discharge letter. Keane CJ considered the trial judge entitled to come to the conclusion he did; that the trial judge was entitled to prefer the view of the defendants' expert that the damage occurred during a bleed at a much earlier stage.

[8.60] There was evidence also supportive of the view that to attempt to carry out a Caesarean section at an earlier stage and when cross-matched blood was not available would have exposed the plaintiff's mother to an unjustifiable risk. As for the performance of a vaginal examination in theatre before embarking on a Caesarean section, there was evidence that general and approved practice was adhered to in that regard.

[8.61] The claimant in *Loraine v Wirral University Teaching Hospital NHS Foundation Trust*[18] suffered cerebral palsy as a consequence of fetal asphyxia sustained by him when his mother suffered a profound placental abruption shortly before his birth. In finding for the claimant, Plender J held that the defendant ought to have disclosed to those treating his mother the records of her earlier treatment in the same hospital. Had this been done, the diagnosis of a fibroid in her uterus would have been made at some stage prior to 18 August 2000, she would have been admitted to hospital and the claimant would not have sustained the injury.

[8.62] Fetal asphyxia could have resulted from either profound placental abruption or from cord prolapse. The court had to decide whether the defendant was liable to compensate for the claimant suffering an unforeseeable manifestation (placental abruption) of a foreseeable danger (cord prolapse) arising from a breach of a duty. The defendant denied causation arguing that even if negligence were established, it was not liable because the claimant's injury was not reasonably foreseeable.

---

18. *Loraine v Wirral University Teaching Hospital NHS Foundation Trust* [2008] EWHC 1565 (QB).

[8.63] The practice at the hospital was to rely on the patient to identify potential complications and to retrieve files only if it appeared from the patient's report that these might be material. Plender J found that this was a flawed system; and one that exposed the mother to an avoidable risk. Mistakes may occur which are not due to negligence and breach of duty on the part of individuals, but are due to bad administration or unsafe systems of work and in such circumstances the hospital authority is primarily liable.

[8.64] The proposition that a claimant can recover when the precise manner of the incidence of the damage is not foreseeable is illustrated in *Hughes v Lord Advocate*[19] where Lord Reid stated that 'a defender is liable although the damage may be a good deal greater in extent than was foreseeable. He can only escape liability if the damage can be regarded as differing in kind from what was foreseeable.' That principle has been applied in several medical negligence cases such as *Wisniewski v Central Manchester Health Authority*[20] and *Hepworth v Kerr.*[21]

[8.65] In *Loraine*, the damage suffered by the claimant did not differ in kind from what was foreseeable. The damage foreseeable in the event of a cord prolapse is precisely the same in kind as the damage suffered by reason of placental abruption. That damage is cerebral palsy in consequence of fetal asphyxia. The consequence of the negligence was foreseeable even if the mechanism bringing it about was not and so the claimant succeeded in establishing liability.

OPERATIVE VAGINAL DELIVERY

[8.66] On occasion it becomes necessary to hasten vaginal delivery at the end of labour either because of concern about oxygenation or because of undue delay. A variety of instruments are available to achieve operative vaginal delivery.

[8.67] Most such deliveries are relatively simple. They are performed by doctors in training and succeed easily. Sometimes the prevailing conditions raise serious questions concerning the facility of the procedure and require special precautions.

[8.68] Where an obstetrician attempts a forceps delivery on the labour ward, rather than as a 'trial of instrumental delivery' in theatre with the mother fully

---

19.   *Hughes v Lord Advocate* [1963] AC 837.
20.   *Wisniewski v Central Manchester Health Authority* [1998] PIQR 324.
21.   *Hepworth v Kerr* [1995] Med LR 139.

prepared for Caesarean section, he will have the burden of justifying his actions where he fails to deliver the baby, precipitates an acute bradycardia and is unable to deliver by Caesarean section before permanent brain damage ensues.[22]

[8.69] *Parry v North West Surrey Health Authority*[23] was a classic case of mistaken clinical judgment. The plaintiff was successful in claiming that an attempt by a senior house officer and acting registrar at forceps delivery when he was too high in his mother's pelvis caused an episode of bradycardia which in turn caused acute hypoxia-ischaemia, resulting in his cerebral palsy.

[8.70] The courts's findings were based, to a large extent, on the unreliability of the expert evidence called by the defence. The judge even remarked that one of the witnesses called on their behalf was indeed 'more of an advocate at times'!

[8.71] The plaintiff's mother, at 5'2 was in good health throughout her first pregnancy, which proceeded without any problems. Her pelvis was normal and the plaintiff was a normal-sized baby with a head of an average diameter.

[8.72] The court found for the plaintiff on several grounds. The obstetrician's examination revealed a warning sign, to the acting registrar in particular, of a high head. The delay in the acting registrar seeing the plaintiff's mother deprived him of any first-hand knowledge, effectively leaving her care solely in the hands of the midwives.

[8.73] The more critical period commenced when the plaintiff's mother's cervix became fully dilated but the acting registrar was unaware of this and the obvious risk of an arrested descent which existed and should have been realised.

[8.74] Several breaches of duty were identified. There was an episode of bradycardia which indicated that the plaintiff was in distress but which the acting registrar was unaware of. The midwife omitted all abdominal palpations and relied solely on vaginal examination. When returning after having left a student midwife in charge for 40 minutes, the midwife discounted pushing that had occurred before her return and should have summoned a doctor. A further episode of fetal distress occurred and was a further warning sign which warranted consideration. The acting registrar ordered an epidural top-up without examining the plaintiff's mother – he failed to seek all the available information and was negligent in failing to palpate abdominally the plaintiff's mother – he failed to seek all the available information and failed to conduct an abdominal palpation.

---

22.   Spencer, 'Trial of forceps – legal aspects' (2008) 14 Clinical Risk 54–58.
23.   *Parry v North West Surrey Health Authority* [1994] 5 Med LR 259.

[8.75] The failed extraction with Kielland's forceps (after attempted ventouse extraction) was done at an unacceptably high level, the acting registrar should have proceeded to Caesarean section which would have spared the plaintiff coming to harm. The attempt at delivery by forceps when the plaintiff was too high in his mother's pelvis at least materially contributed to, if it did not solely cause, the episode of bradycardia which in turn caused the acute hypoxia-ischaemia.

[8.76] The defendant had attempted to advance an alternative causation theory, that there was a very severe cord compression. An expert gave an aided demonstration of the different ways in which this can happen but the judge was unconvinced. Had this occurred, he considered that the acting registrar would have noticed this set of affairs, explaining as it would have done, the sudden bradycardia.

[8.77] There are cases where the so-called '10-minute rule' applied, such as *Kingsberry v Greater Manchester Strategic Health Authority.*[24] The claimant therein succeeded in an action for negligence resulting from the failure to carry out a trial of instrumental delivery at the time of his birth in 1985 which, had it been performed would, it was found, have avoided all of the damage which resulted in his cerebral palsy.

[8.78] There was transverse arrest and no progress during the second stage of the mother's labour. It was the claimant's case that there was clear evidence of fetal distress from the CTG, a registrar should not have proceeded to attempt a forceps delivery on the ward, but should have called the senior registrar to attend sooner, or a Caesarean section should have been undertaken, or a trial of forceps should have been carried out in theatre with the senior registrar in attendance. Had this happened, the true head position would have been identified and the claimant's delivery would have occurred within 10 minutes of the onset of bradycardia, sparing him from injury.

[8.79] Experts on both sides were unanimous that trial of forceps was an accepted obstetric management technique by the time of the plaintiff's birth and was to be employed when the operator recognised or ought to have recognised that the prospects of successful delivery were uncertain. The judge was convinced that there were a half a dozen relevant factors in this claimant's case which should have led to the conclusion that such uncertainty did exist and that trial of forceps was warranted. Failure to undertake a trial of forceps was not in

---

24. *Kingsberry v Greater Manchester Strategic Health Authority* [2005] EWHC 2253 (QB), [2006] 87 BMLR 73, [2011] LS Law Med 334.

accordance with a practice accepted as proper in 1985, nor did it withstand logical analysis.

[8.80] As to causation, McKinnon J found that it is possible for a fetus to survive, but suffering brain damage, if not revived after 10 minutes of bradycardia. He was of the view that had there been a trial of forceps, the so-called '10-minute rule'[25] would have applied and the plaintiff would have been delivered safely within 10 minutes of the application of forceps and well within 10 minutes from the onset of bradycardia.

[8.81] McKinnon J's finding was subsequently applied in *Purver v Winchester and Eastleigh Healthcare NHS Trust*,[26] a case where the brain damage occurred despite delivery having been carried out as a trial of forceps.

[8.82] The claimant's mother was admitted to the defendant hospital overdue and was induced. A senior registrar decided to proceed to a trial of forceps. The CTG was a critical piece of evidence. The experts were in agreement that between 19.43 and 19.53 there were four decelerations.

[8.83] There were four attempts at forceps before proceeding to operate, which decision was recorded at 19:50 on the trace. The claimant was born in poor condition, had hypoxic-ischaemic encephalopathy and went on to develop cerebral palsy. The claimant's case was that the decision to proceed to operate should have been taken sooner.

[8.84] It was agreed on the basis of the obstetricians' agreement that the start of the collapse of fetal circulation was at 19.48 and delivery at 19.56 would, on balance, have meant sparing the claimant all of the damage he went on to suffer. There was, in effect, eight minutes to get the baby out and if the team had been fully prepared, knew what the objective was and worked expeditiously towards it, the court believed there was no reason why the eight-minute decision-to-delivery time could not have been achieved, stating that 'with the right preparations and the right mind-set on the parts of everyone involved this could and should have been achieved'.

[8.85] The objective of a reasonably competent and well-informed obstetrician carrying out trial of forceps in 1997 would be to deliver the baby well within the period of 10 minutes from the time that he or she had identified either the onset

---

25. The 10-minute rule derives its name from the rationale that once a severe bradycardia sets in, permanent injury will occur if perfusion to the brain is not restored within 10 minutes.

26. *Purver v Winchester and Eastleigh Healthcare NHS Trust* [2007] EWHC 34 (QB).

of, or serious risk of the onset of, a significant fetal bradycardia, provided that to do so would not expose the mother to untoward risk. A reasonably efficient and competent obstetric team could have achieved a decision to delivery time of less than 10 minutes if full preparations for the Caesarean section had been made in advance of the use of forceps.

[8.86] In the New South Wales case of *Simpson v Diamond and Anor (No 2)*[27] the plaintiff, who had been born in 1979 by emergency Caesarean section after the defendant obstetrician[28] made several attempts at a forceps delivery, suffered serious bradycardia due to the repeated forceps attempts and her injury resulted in cerebral palsy. It is another example of a claim based on failure to perform trial of forceps succeeding, albeit liability was admitted and the reported appeal dealt solely with quantum.

QUANTUM

[8.87] Cerebral palsy is a portmanteau term covering a myriad of different abnormalities of movement and posture. In the most severe forms the child will require 24-hour care every single day of their life. The damages awarded must reflect this huge financial burden.

[8.88] Although the sums awarded in general damages are reasonably stable, lawyers must be meticulous in the compilation of schedules of special damages. Details of the sums of money which will be required adequately to provide for the plaintiff's future will have to be very carefully collected in consultation with numerous experts who will assess in the greatest detail what equipment, nursing, medical and other care the plaintiff will need. Technologies are constantly developing which are leading to the provision of ever more sophisticated and expensive equipment. This adds to the expense but more importantly, enables injured plaintiffs to communicate their needs and to have a better quality of life.[29]

[8.89] Quantum experts regularly engaged in cerebral palsy cases include: experts on life expectancy, care experts, speech and language therapists, physiotherapists, dental experts, rehabilitation consultants, neuropsychologists,

---

27. *Simpson v Diamond and Anor (No 2)* [2001] NSWSC 1048.
28. Shortly before the hearing, the obstetrician admitted liability, prompting the claimant to discontinue proceedings against the hospital. He subsequently cross-claimed against the hospital but was unsuccessful.
29. 'Large awards in cerebral palsy cases' (1998) 5(11) Medical Law Monitor 1–2.

educational psychologists, architects, quantity surveyors, actuaries and accountants.

Chapter 9

TIMING FETAL BRAIN DAMAGE CAUSED BY ACUTE NEAR TOTAL ASPHYXIA

Dr Ben Lloyd

INTRODUCTION

[9.01] There are two main patterns of brain damage following birth asphyxia (impaired circulation and oxygenation around the time of delivery).

[9.02] A baby can show one or both patterns:

- damage caused by a chronic partial hypoxic-ischaemic insult;

- damage caused by an acute near total hypoxic-ischaemic insult.

This chapter concerns the second of these patterns. In this chapter, I shall review the two main ways of determining the time of onset of a baby's brain damage caused by an acute near total hypoxic ischaemic insult – the working forward method and the working backward method.

[9.03] The working forward method relies on identifying the start of a significant bradycardia (slow heart rate). The time of onset of damage is determined by adding 10 to 15 minutes to that time – in recognition of the evidence that the first 10 to 15 minutes after the onset of the insult are non-damaging.

[9.04] The working backward method relies on determining the severity of the child's impairments and then making a judgment about the duration of the brain damaging element of the acute near total hypoxic-ischaemic insult. The time of onset of damage is then determined by working back from the time that the brain damaging insult ended – which is usually the time that the heart rate reaches 100 beats per minute.

[9.05] It is often the case that both the working forward method and the working backward method are useful when determining the likely time of onset of a baby's brain damage.

[9.06] In any case where a baby's brain has been damaged by a severe hypoxic-ischaemic insult at the end of labour other relevant pieces of evidence should be considered when determining the likely start of the damage – notably:

- the underlying pathological process;

- whether or not there has been any reduction in fetal movements;

- the extent to which there has been a chronic partial hypoxic-ischaemic insult before the onset of the acute insult;

- the results of any blood gas analysis – fetal scalp sampling during labour, cord gas sampling, the first neonatal gas;

- the condition of the baby at birth;

- the newborn course – including the timing of the encephalopathy;

- the neuroradiology.

In my experience, however, these matters are generally of lesser importance when considering the time of onset of damage caused by an acute near total hypoxic-ischaemic insult than they are when considering the time of onset of damage caused by a chronic partial hypoxic-ischaemic insult.

[9.07] My review of the methods for determining the likely time of onset of brain damage caused by an acute near total hypoxic-ischaemic insult consists of the following elements:

(a) what is meant by a bradycardia?

(b) when does damage occur after onset of an acute near total hypoxic-ischaemic insult?

(c) review of the working forward method for determining timing of brain damage (the 10–25 minute principle);

(d) review of the working backward method for determining timing of brain damage;

(e) is it reasonable to consider units of time less than five minutes when reviewing the timing of a baby's brain damage by an acute, near total, hypoxic-ischaemic insult?

(f) the implications of the introduction of therapeutic cooling;

(g) summary.

(A) WHAT IS MEANT BY A BRADYCARDIA?

[9.08] Bradycardias can be severe or less severe.

In the most clear cut case a baby's heart rate drops suddenly to a rate of less than about 60 beats per minute as a result of a catastrophic event such as acute cord compression or uterine rupture. Such an episode is serious and, according to animal experiments, brain damage will start probably within about 10 minutes of its start.

In real life, however, bradycardias are often less severe than this.

[9.09] The NICE classification of CTG abnormalities defines a normal fetal heart rate as being greater than 110 beats per minute – and anything less than 110 beats per minute represents a bradycardia. Although a fetal heart rate of 105 beats per minute is concerning it will not lead to damage of the type associated with a more severe bradycardia.

[9.10] Indeed, as discussed in the Appendix there is evidence that a prolonged bradycardia of 80 beats per minute or even slower may not be damaging. In line with this view is the observation that it is not uncommon to see perfectly healthy newborn term babies who in the first days of life can have a heart-rate well below 100 beats per minute – sometimes for hours – without there being damaging hypoxia-ischaemia.

The more severe the bradycardia is then the more likely it is to be damaging – and the more quickly brain damage will supervene.

(B) WHEN DOES DAMAGE OCCUR AFTER THE ONSET OF AN ACUTE NEAR TOTAL HYPOXIC-ISCHAEMIC INSULT?

[9.11] Many experts (deriving support from animal experiments) consider that the period needed to damage the brain after the onset of a severe acute near total hypoxic-ischaemic (as manifested by a bradycardia – slow heart rate) is typically about 10 minutes.

[9.12] Thereafter, as time passes, the severity of the brain damage worsens (along with the severity of the consequent impairments) until up to about 25 minutes after the onset of the insult – by which time the baby is likely to be unresuscitatable.

[9.13] There are, however, two reasons why animal experiments probably do not apply exactly to real life and babies.

Firstly, there are likely to be differences between baby monkeys and babies – with babies probably being more tolerant of severe hypoxia-ischaemia than monkeys. Secondly, in laboratory experiments, the hypoxic-ischaemic insults that were applied were total rather than near-total – as they almost always are in real life labours/deliveries.

[9.14] As just discussed, an important explanation for why fetuses can be exposed to a prolonged bradycardia and yet later demonstrate relatively little or even no brain damage is that a less severe bradycardia is not always associated with damagingly reduced perfusion of the brain.

[9.15] It is my view that when there is a severe bradycardia (with heart rate less than about 60 beats per minute) brain damage is likely to start about 10 to 15 minutes after the onset of an acute near total hypoxic-ischaemic insult. Thereafter the damage worsens until the fetus becomes unresuscitatable – about 25 minutes after the onset of an acute near total hypoxic-ischaemic insult.

[9.16] When the bradycardia is less severe (with a fetal heart rate that is greater than about 60 beats per minute) judging the likely time of onset of brain damage following the onset of five the bradycardia becomes increasingly uncertain – depending on the relative mildness of the bradycardia. This uncertainty limits the value of the working forward method – and is an important reason why I consider that the working backward method is usually to be preferred when there are lesser degrees of bradycardia.

(C) REVIEW OF THE WORKING FORWARD METHOD FOR DETERMINING TIMING OF BRAIN DAMAGE (THE 10–25 MINUTE PRINCIPLE)

[9.17] It has been standard practice for many years to time a baby's brain damage in relation to an acute near total hypoxic-ischaemic insult by working forward from the time that a bradycardia starts – using the 10–25 minute principle.

[9.18] The 10–25 minute principle is simple. It leads to the following guidance for the courts:

- if the bradycardia lasts less than 10 minutes the baby will probably be undamaged;

- if the bradycardia lasts more than 25 minutes the baby will probably be unresuscitatable;

- there will be increasing amounts of brain damage as the length of the bradycardia persists beyond 10 minutes and up to 25 minutes.

[9.19] I consider that there are two main problems with the working forward method. The first problem is a practical one; the second problem is more fundamental.

[9.20] The first (and practical) problem with the working forward method is that it is often the case that it is not known when the bradycardia started. In such cases this important timepoint (which it is essential to determine if the working forward method is to be applied) has to be the subject of surmise.

[9.21] The second and more fundamental problem with the working forward method is that, as discussed above (and set out in detail in the Appendix), there is evidence that a baby can suffer a prolonged bradycardia (beyond 10 minutes) that is not brain damaging if the bradycardia is not very severe – that is greater than about 60 beats per minute.

[9.22] Nevertheless, I consider that the working forward method is useful when:

- the time of onset of the bradycardia is known;

- the bradycardia is severe – less than about 60 beats per minute.

Under those circumstances it is my view that it is likely that brain damage will probably supervene within 10–15 minutes of the onset of the bradycardia.

[9.23] Whether the time of onset is closer to 10 minutes after the start of the bradycardia or closer to 15 minutes after the start of the bradycardia depends on consideration of the factors set out in the introduction above – including, particularly:

- the severity of the bradycardia;

- whether or not there had a significant chronic partial hypoxic-ischaemic insult before the bradycardia started.

(D) REVIEW OF THE WORKING BACKWARD METHOD FOR DETERMINING TIMING OF BRAIN DAMAGE

[9.24] Given the limitations of the working forward method as set out above, it is my view that it is often the case that the more useful way to examine timing in a baby who has suffered brain damage due to an acute, near total hypoxic-ischaemic insult is to use the severity of the child's impairments to work out the likely duration of the brain-damaging element of the hypoxic-ischaemic insult that the baby was exposed to.

[9.25] The next step is to determine when the brain-damaging element of the hypoxic-ischaemic insult ended – that is when resuscitation led to the baby's heart rate reaching 100 beats per minute.

[9.26] This can be described as the working-backward method of determining when a baby's brain was damaged.

[9.27] The working-backward method relies on the fact that it is generally agreed that, however long it takes for brain damage to supervene after the start of an acute near total hypoxic-ischaemic insult (traditionally 10 minutes), there is a period of about 15 minutes between the time of onset of brain damage and the time of death (traditionally 25 minutes after the start of the acute near total insult).

[9.28] This figure of 15 minutes derives from animal experiments. In fact, I consider that, on occasion, a fetus can survive an insult whose brain damaging element lasts as long as 20 minutes.

[9.29] Thus, in cases of brain damage due to an acute near total hypoxic-ischaemic insult, the duration of the brain damaging element of the insult ranges from less than a minute to about 15 or (at the most) 20 minutes.

[9.30] Put another way, there is about a 15 to 20 minute difference between the duration of the insult that causes the mildest discernible neurological impairments and the duration of the insult that causes the worst possible neurological impairments that are still compatible with ongoing survival.

Some considerations limiting the accuracy of the working backwards method

[9.31] I consider that it is important to bear in mind the important principle of biological variability. Thus:

- different babies will have differing degrees of resilience in relation to tolerating an acute, near total, hypoxic-ischaemic insult.
- the completeness of the acute, near total, hypoxic-ischaemic insult will also vary from situation to situation.

[9.32] In the following scheme for timing the duration of an acute near total hypoxic-ischaemic insult, I have relied on the generally held view that there is a 15–20 minute interval between the time of onset of the brain damage (which conventionally starts 10 minutes after the start of the insult) and the time when the baby becomes unresuscitatable (which is conventionally considered to be 25–30 minutes after the time of onset of the insult). I consider that this principle that all the damage always happens over 15–20 minutes is likely to be something of an approximation – particularly when the duration of the insult is markedly prolonged.

[9.33] Nevertheless, I consider that the scheme I set out below is likely to represent a reasonable guide to the duration of insults associated with different levels of impairment – on the balance of probabilities.

[9.34] Another assumption involved in the working backward method, which is likely to be somewhat simplistic, is that damage occurs in a more or less linear fashion.

[9.35] It is my view that the assumption of linearity is more reasonable than two alternative possibilities:

- most/all of the damage occurs at the beginning of the period when damage first starts – with little or no damage thereafter;
- most/all of the damage occurs at the end of the damaging period – with little or no damage before that.

[9.36] A significant shortcoming of the working backward method is that, in some cases, at least some of a child's impairments were caused by a process other than an acute near total hypoxic-ischaemic insult. The commonest such insult is a chronic partial hypoxic-ischaemic insult. Another common complicating insult is hypoglycaemia.

[9.37] When there are two causes of a child's impairments the determination of the duration of the damaging element of the acute near total hypoxic-ischaemic insult is complicated because that determination depends on an assessment of the severity of a child's impairments.

[9.38] In such cases an allowance must be made for the fact that some of a child's impairments were caused by a process other than an acute near total hypoxic-ischaemic insult.

How to time the onset of brain damage using the working backward method

[9.39] An important step in timing the onset of brain damage when using the working backward method is to determine when the brain-damaging element of the insult ended. This is usually considered to be the point during resuscitation at which the baby's heart rate reaches 100 beats per minute.

[9.40] The time of onset of the brain damage is then calculated by working backward from the time the brain-damaging insult ended – using the determination of the duration of the brain-damaging element of the insult as set out in the scheme below.

[9.41] It is my view that a child who has suffered about five minutes of a brain-damaging acute, near total, hypoxic-ischaemic insult around the time of birth is likely to:

- be fully ambulant – but with significantly impaired walking and running;

- have only mildly impaired hand function;

- be significantly dysarthric – but be readily comprehensible;

- be no more than mildly impaired in relation to learning difficulties.

[9.42] In my view, a child who has suffered about 10 minutes of a brain-damaging acute, near total, hypoxic-ischaemic insult is likely to:

- be just about able to sit;

- have only a little useful hand function;

- be so dysarthric that speech will be more or less unintelligible;

- have definite learning difficulties.

[9.43] In my view, a child who has suffered 15 minutes of a brain-damaging acute, near total, hypoxic-ischaemic insult is likely to:

- be unable to lift their head;

- have no useful hand function;

- have no speech;

- have severe learning difficulties.

[9.44] The child who has survived an insult whose brain damaging insult lasted the maximum possible time of 20 minutes will be even more disabled than this.

[9.45] For reasons set out above, there must be significant doubt about the accuracy of the clinical features that I have attributed to the three different durations of damaging insults – 5, 10 and 15 minutes. Furthermore, many children will not fit well into the categories. Thus, some children will have, for instance, remarkably preserved intellect and yet not be able to sit.

[9.46] Furthermore, I know of no published evidence to support the use of these descriptions of impairments after insults of differing durations. These descriptions are based on my own experience of examining more than 190 children who have suffered a brain-damaging acute near total hypoxic-ischaemic insult and whose perinatal periods I have analysed (with others – notably obstetricians) while preparing a causation report.

[9.47] In some of these children the impairments were very subtle – to the point that they were barely detectable on examination. In other children the impairments were lifethreateningly severe. Most of the children had impairments between these extremes.

[9.48] I consider that my scheme setting out the likely clinical features after different periods of damaging insult represents a reasonable approximation – on the balance of probabilities.

[9.49] At least some neuroradiologists will attempt to undertake a similar estimation of the duration of an insult by review of the severity/pattern of the damage identified by MR scanning.

(E) IS IT REASONABLE TO CONSIDER UNITS OF TIME LESS THAN FIVE MINUTES WHEN REVIEWING THE TIMING OF A BABY'S BRAIN DAMAGE BY AN ACUTE, NEAR TOTAL, HYPOXIC-ISCHAEMIC INSULT?

[9.50] I consider that there is general agreement that it is reasonable to consider the duration of a brain-damaging insult in units of five minutes. I am aware that many experts consider that scientific knowledge about these matters is sufficiently limited that it is not reasonable to make judgments about shorter periods of time.

[9.51] I fully accept the lack of published data – but in my view (as discussed above) this is more of a problem for the accuracy of my account of the typical clinical features seen after 5/10/15 minutes set out above than it is for my view that it is reasonable, in some cases, to define the insult as having lasted midway between two of the four times in my scheme (0, 5, 10, 15 minutes).

[9.52] I would observe that the considerable differences between the impairments seen after 0/5/10/15 minutes means that a considerable number of children do not fit the overall picture of the clinical features at 0/5/10/15 minutes – and would (in my view) clearly be better placed roughly midway between two of those times.

[9.53] Thus, I consider that using aliquots of time of less than five minutes is helpful because of the very considerable difference between the levels of impairment that I have described as being typical after brain damaging insults lasting 5, 10 and 15 minutes.

[9.54] In my view it is at least sometimes reasonable/necessary to make an estimate of the level of impairments at the following further times – that is:

- the midpoint between 0 and 5 minutes;

- the midpoint between 5 and 10 minutes;

- the midpoint between 10 and 15 minutes.

[9.55] Thus, I consider it is reasonable, in cases where the pattern of impairments is approximately midway between the pattern of impairments that I have described after 12 insults, whose brain-damaging element lasted 5, 10 or 15 minutes, to conclude in such cases that it is probable that the brain-damaging element of the acute, near total, hypoxic-ischaemic insult lasted:

- 2 to 3 minutes (the midpoint between 0 and 5 minutes);

- 7 to 8 minutes (the midpoint between 5 and 10 minutes);

- 12 to 13 minutes (the midpoint between 10 and 15 minutes).

[9.56] I am sympathetic to the view that uncertainty about the various assumptions underlying my scheme means that the scheme's foundations are too uncertain to allow judgments to be made about periods of time less than five minutes. Nevertheless, the very considerable difference between the levels of impairment that I have described as being typical after brain damaging insults lasting 5, 10 and 15 minutes means that in my view such judgments are reasonable – on the balance of probabilities.

[9.57] I would observe that these finer judgments are of limited relevance unless they result in the conclusion that shortening the insult the child suffered would lead to the determination that a child's care needs would have been significantly less than they are.

(F) THE IMPLICATIONS OF THE INTRODUCTION OF THERAPEUTIC COOLING

[9.58] The situation in relation to timing the onset of brain damage has been complicated by the introduction of the technique of therapeutic cooling, after delivery – when a baby has been exposed to potentially brain-damaging hypoxia-ischaemia.

[9.59] This is because there is now powerful evidence that the brain-damaging effects of a hypoxic-ischaemic insult can be lessened, or even abolished, as a result of therapeutic cooling.

[9.60] This beneficial effect of cooling adds further uncertainty to the already uncertain task of timing a baby's brain damage – whether using the working forward method, or the working backward method.

[9.61] The timings set out in the scheme set out above will be shorter when a baby is exposed to cooling. With the current state of knowledge about the benefits of cooling I know of no way to quantify this shortening.

[9.62] Given that in a typical case of brain damaging birth asphyxia, it is the case that whenever the baby was delivered, cooling (if it was subsequently used as treatment) would still have been used, regardless of when the child was born (unless earlier delivery means that the baby would have avoided a significant hypoxic-ischaemic insult), I consider that it is reasonable to continue to use the same scheme set out above when attempting to time the onset of a baby's brain damage, either using the working forward method, or the working backward method.

[9.63] Nevertheless, when making judgments about either the likely time of onset of the brain damage or the benefits of somewhat earlier delivery, it may well be necessary to incorporate an adjustment to allow for the beneficial effects of cooling.

(G) SUMMARY

[9.64] There is still much to be learnt about timing the onset of brain damage when a fetus is damaged by an acute near total hypoxic-ischaemic insult – and about how to quantify the benefits of cooling.

[9.65] The working forward method is useful when the bradycardia is severe and when its time of onset is known. When the bradycardia is less severe and/or when its time of onset is uncertain, then in my view the working backward approach is more useful.

[9.66] I have set out a scheme for arriving at an estimate of the timing of the insult based on the severity of the child's impairments – that is the working backwards method.

[9.67] There are a considerable number of uncertainties about the assumptions underlying this scheme – which have been somewhat increased as a result of the introduction of therapeutic cooling. Nevertheless, I consider that this scheme setting out the likely clinical features after different periods of damaging insult represents a reasonable approximation – on the balance of probabilities.

[9.68] It is my view that, in some cases, a combination of both the working forward method and the working backward method may help to offset somewhat the uncertainties that accompany each of the two individual methods.

REVIEW OF EVIDENCE THAT BRAIN DAMAGE CAN ENSUE WELL AFTER A BRADYCARDIA LASTING LONGER THAN 10 MINUTES

[9.69] I shall now present evidence that challenges the conventional view that after the onset of an acute near total hypoxic-ischaemic insult:

- brain damage typically supervenes after about 10 minutes;

- the baby will typically be unresuscitatable after about 25-30 minutes.

As will be seen this work often concerns insults where the bradycardia was greater than 60–70 beats per minute.

Evidence from work by Kayani and colleagues[1] – 2003

[9.70] It is important to note that this study concerned babies exposed to severe placental abruption – a very specific cause of an acute near total hypoxic-ischaemic insult. It is likely that fetal heart rate patterns will differ from other causes of an acute near total hypoxic-ischaemic insult.

[9.71] Kayani and her co-workers examined the relationship between the duration of the terminal bradycardia and the outcome in a series of babies who had suffered a placental abruption.

[9.72] The authors studied 33 babies. The authors divided the outcome of the babies into 'good' or 'poor'. A good outcome meant that at the age of at least a year, there was no evidence of a developmental problem. A poor outcome was defined by death of the baby or survival with cerebral palsy.

[9.73] Importantly the definition of bradycardia was 90 beats per minute.

[9.74] There were only 33 babies in the study. Eleven had a poor outcome (eight deaths, three cerebral palsy) and 22 had a good outcome.

[9.75] The authors reported that the duration of the bradycardia for fetuses with a good outcome ranged from six minutes to 65 minutes. More usefully, the figures for the 25th centile and the 75th centile in relation to the length of bradycardia in the fetuses in the good outcome group were 16.5 minutes to 33.5 minutes respectively.

---

1. Kayani and colleagues published a paper entitled 'Pregnancy outcome in severe placental abruption' in (2003) 110 British Journal of Obstetrics and Gynaecology 679–683.

[9.76] To put this last observation into plain English, it means that 25 per cent of the fetuses (which was only five or six fetuses) with a good outcome had had a bradycardia lasting at least 33.5 minutes. This is far longer than the 10 minutes by which those who espouse the working forward method would say the fetus should typically have been damaged.

[9.77] I consider that the explanation for this is that in at least some cases the bradycardia will not have been relatively mild – greater than 60 beats per minute. As discussed in the accompanying chapter less severe bradycardias may well be less damaging – or even not damaging at all.

[9.78] In any event, 75 per cent of the fetuses with a good outcome had a bradycardia lasting longer than 16.5 minutes.

[9.79] Apart from the use of a relatively mild definition of bradycardia, there are significant shortcomings to this study. Thus:

- the study is small;

- the study includes seven babies of less than 32 weeks' gestation;

- there are also a number of babies (it is not clear from the paper how many) in whom the bradycardia was present at the time of admission. This last observation means that some of the times in Table 1 can be extended even further;

- the follow up process was not very satisfactory. If staff in the hospital were not following up with the baby's progress then information was gained from the primary care team. It is not clear how often this was the case;

- there are no neonatal details presented;

- all the hypoxic-ischaemic insults in this study were as a result of placental abruption (separation of the placenta from the uterine wall).

This last shortcoming is important because it may be the case that abruptions are particularly likely to be associated with a non-damaging bradycardia than other causes of an acute near total insult such as cord occlusion.

[9.80] Despite these shortcomings, I consider that the results of this paper support the view that is common for fetuses to survive a bradycardia before delivery for considerably more than 10 minutes – without being brain damaged.

[9.81] As discussed above, this phenomenon is probably because the bradycardia was often not very severe.

Evidence from Naeye and Shaffer[2] – 2005

[9.82] The authors set out to investigate useful ways of timing brain damage caused by an acute near total hypoxic-ischaemic insult.

[9.83] I note this passage in the 'Methods' section: 'Clinical, laboratory, brain imaging and placental findings were reviewed from 608 pregnancies that had produced full term neonates with cerebral palsy and possible antenatal, hypoxic-ischemic origin.'

[9.84] The aspects of each child's case that were studied included:

- duration of the bradycardia;

- serial full blood counts, studying particularly normoblasts, platelets and lymphocytes;

- differences at birth between base excess values in umbilical arterial and venous bloods;

- brain damage patterns.

[9.85] The authors set out their sources thus:

> Medical records from these pregnancies, along with slides having placental tissues for microscopic review came from parties in malpractice claims, our medical center's medical records, treating physicians at other institutions and parents who wanted explanations for their child's cerebral palsy.[3]

[9.86] One problem with the fact that details of the children were obtained from multiple sources (notably those who were the subject of malpractice claims) is that the children studied may well not have been representative of children who suffered brain damage as a result of an acute near total hypoxic-ischemic insult as a whole.

[9.87] I would also observe that, although the authors started with 608 possible pregnancies, by the time their various exclusion criteria had been applied, they were left with just 92 children.

---

2.   Naeye and Shaffer's work was published in a paper entitled 'Postnatal laboratory timers of antenatal hypoxic-ischemic brain damage' published in (2005) 25 Journal of Perinatology 664–668.
3.   Naeye and Shaffer, 'Postnatal laboratory timers of antenatal hypoxic-ischemic brain damage' (2005) 25 Journal of Perinatology 664.

[9.88] On the other hand, it is my view that collecting 92 children who had suffered brain damage as the result of an acute near total hypoxic-ischemic insult is a considerable achievement.

[9.89] I would observe that the authors took steps to exclude children with 'non-hypoxicischemic causes' for their brain damage.

[9.90] The exclusions from the study were generally uncontroversial. Thus, exclusions from the study (in a bid to exclude children whose cerebral palsy was caused by something other than hypoxia-ischemia) included:

    b.   children with recognised malformations;

    c.   children with a known genetic disorder.[4]

However, there is one exclusion criterion which, in my view, must have excluded many children whose cerebral palsy was, nevertheless caused by an acute near total hypoxic-ischemic insult at the end of labour:

> Children who might have experienced earlier hypoxemia before birth because of some recognised chronic placental, fetal or maternal disorder were excluded from the analyses.[5]

[9.91] The authors observed that apart from the blood gas findings,[6] most of the 92 children did not have complete enough data sets to be included in every subsequent analysis. Inherent shortcomings in retrospective studies of this sort mean that this is not at all surprising.

Nevertheless, the incompleteness of the data available for some children is a further weakness of this study.

[9.92] One striking aspect of this case is that the authors only included children who:

> Had electronic fetal heart rate monitoring (EFM) documentation of the sudden unexpected onset of fetal bradycardia (less than 70 beats per minute) that continued for twenty or more minutes until birth.[7]

---

4.   Naeye and Shaffer, 'Postnatal laboratory timers of antenatal hypoxic-ischemic brain damage' (2005) 25 Journal of Perinatology, 664 after the heading 'materials and methods'.

5.   Naeye and Shaffer, 'Postnatal laboratory timers of antenatal hypoxic-ischemic brain damage' (2005) 25 Journal of Perinatology 665.

6.   Naeye and Shaffer, 'Postnatal laboratory timers of antenatal hypoxic-ischemic brain damage' (2005) 25 Journal of Perinatology 665.

7.   Naeye and Shaffer, 'Postnatal laboratory timers of antenatal hypoxic-ischemic brain damage' (2005) 25 Journal of Perinatology 664.

[9.93] A little later in the method section, the authors state:

> In primate studies, the onset of fetal bradycardia has closely coincided with the start of hypoxic-ischemic brain damage (two references are cited). On this basis the present studies used bradycardia's onset time as the baseline to determine if other clinical, laboratory and brain image findings had value as timers of the brain damage's start. Neonates whose antenatal bradycardia was less than or equal to fifteen minutes in duration were not included in the analyses because hypoxiaischemia of this short duration rarely produces brain damage.[8]

I do not understand why in this passage the authors state that they excluded children with bradycardia less than or equal to 15 minutes in duration, whilst their original criteria for at least screening the records was that the duration of the bradycardia had to be 20 minutes or more.

[9.94] I would further observe that despite the authors' contention that they excluded all children whose fetal bradycardia had lasted less than 15 minutes (0.25 hours), 9 of 52 children depicted had had a fetal bradycardia which had lasted less than 0.25 hours.

[9.95] I am also struck by the fact that the following sentence contains no references to published literature to support its contention: 'Neonates whose antenatal bradycardia was less than or equal to fifteen minutes in duration were not included in the analyses because hypoxemia-ischemia of this short duration rarely produces brain damage.'

[9.96] An obvious shortcoming in this study is that it included no children without brain damage. Thus, these data cannot be used to determine when (after the onset of a terminal bradycardia) damage is more likely than not to occur. Nevertheless, I consider that the data presented in this paper do provide information about the likely time of onset of brain damage after a fetal bradycardia.

[9.97] Given the importance of the question of how long the bradycardia needs to be before brain damage is likely to supervene, it is striking that the authors excluded all children whose bradycardia was less than 15 minutes, on the grounds that so few of them will have suffered brain damage.

[9.98] As discussed earlier, there were no data about children who survived a prolonged bradycardia, and who did not suffer brain damage – beyond the

---

8.   Naeye and Shaffer, 'Postnatal laboratory timers of antenatal hypoxic-ischemic brain damage' (2005) 25 Journal of Perinatology 665.

statement that such damage was rare until the bradycardia had lasted at least 15 minutes.

[9.99] Of the 52 children depicted, about half had suffered a bradycardia lasting longer than 0.4 hours (24 minutes). Indeed, five brain-damaged children had survived despite a fetal bradycardia lasting longer than 0.7 hours (42 minutes).

[9.100] In summary, I consider this paper has a number of flaws.

In relation to the purpose of this review of the likely time of brain damage after the start of a bradycardia, the most striking statement is, unfortunately, unsupported by any presented data: 'Neonates whose antenatal bradycardia was less than or equal to fifteen minutes in duration were not included in the analyses because hypoxia-ischemia of this short duration rarely produces brain damage.'

This statement is at odds with the contention of those who espouse the working forward method who rely on the assumption that damage is likely to start after 10 minutes.

[9.101] Naeye and Shaffer however do present data to challenge the other widely held principle – that is a baby exposed to more than 25 to 30 minutes of a terminal bradycardia is very likely to be unresuscitatable, or to die in the first days of life.

[9.102] I would observe that the definition of bradycardia is stricter than that used by Kayani and co-workers – less than 70 beats per minute rather than 90 beats per minute. Nevertheless, this definition is greater than the figure of 60 beats per minute that I cited as being a reasonable basis for using the working forward method.

[9.103] In summary, despite its shortcomings, it is my view that this paper challenges the conventional wisdom both that after the onset of a fetal bradycardia, brain damage is likely after 10 minutes and, more convincingly, that death is likely/inevitable after a bradycardia has lasted 25 to 30 minutes.

Chapter 10

TIMING FETAL BRAIN DAMAGE CAUSED BY CHRONIC PARTIAL ASPHYXIA[1]

Dr Peter Dear

[10.01] There are several mechanisms by which fetal brain damage can occur around the time of birth. These include focal or widespread arterial ischaemia, intracranial haemorrhage, venous thrombosis, direct trauma and infection/inflammation.

[10.02] What follows deals with the specific issue of the timing of fetal brain damage occurring as a result of progressively worsening intrapartum hypoxia, ultimately leading to acidaemia, impaired cardiac output and diminished cerebral flow (ischaemia). This is commonly referred to as chronic partial asphyxia to acknowledge the fact that progressive hypoxia is almost invariably accompanied by carbon dioxide retention and the formation of lactic acid leading to a mixed (respiratory/metabolic) acidosis.

[10.03] It is worth stating at the outset that it is brain ischaemia that causes the damage. As long as the flow of blood to the brain is maintained, low blood oxygen content is unlikely to cause damage.

INTRODUCTION

[10.04] The human fetus is well adapted to cope with a shortage of oxygen without sustaining injury to its tissues and organs, and this is just as well as

---

1. References: Jensen, Hohmann and Künzel, 'Redistribution of fetal circulation during repeated asphyxia in sheep: Effects on skin blood flow, transcutaneous PO2, and plasma catecholamines' (1987) 9(1) J Dev Physiol 41–55; Stewart, 'Blood flow and metabolism in the developing brain' (1987) 11(2) Semin Perinatol 112–6. Cowan, Rutherford Groenendaal, Eken, Mercuri, Bydder, Meiners, Dubowitz and de Vries, 'Origin and timing of brain lesions in term infants with neonatal encephalopathy' (2003) 361 Lancet 736–742; de Haan, Gunn and Gluckman 'Fetal heart rate changes do not reflect cardiovascular deterioration during brief repeated umbilical cord occlusions in near-term fetal lambs' (1997) 176 Am J Obstet Gynecol 8–17; de Haan, Gunn, Williams and Gluckman, 'Brief repeated umbilical cord occlusions cause sustained cytotoxic cerebral edema and focal infarcts in near-term fetal lambs' (1997) 41(1) Pediatric Research 96–104; Parer, King, Flanders, Fox and Kilpatrick, 'Fetal acidemia and electronic fetal heart rate patterns: Is there evidence of an association?' (2006) 19(5) J Matern Fetal Neonatal Med 289–294.

some shortage of oxygen is almost inevitable during the course of labour and delivery. There are, though, many potential complications of labour and delivery that can overwhelm fetal defences and threaten the integrity of the brain and other organs.

[10.05] Broadly speaking, there are complications that lead to an abrupt cessation in oxygen delivery to the fetus (such as placental abruption, umbilical cord occlusion or uterine rupture) and complications that lead to a gradual reduction in fetal oxygenation over time (such as excessive uterine activity or intermittent cord compression).

[10.06] An abrupt cessation of oxygen delivery to the fetus soon overwhelms any compensatory mechanisms and within five minutes or so there is a drastic fall in blood pressure and blood flow to the brain. Damage occurs within the most vulnerable brain regions and if the situation is not resolved the fetus soon dies. Fetuses who are delivered after the onset of brain damage but before death show a characteristic pattern of damage involving the basal ganglia, thalami, hippocampi, cerebellar vermis and the grey and white matter adjacent to the central sulci of the cerebral hemispheres. This pattern of damage is shown by an MRI scan and can often be inferred from the pattern of disability. In a medico legal context these are cases of 'acute profound asphyxia' and are discussed elsewhere in this book.

[10.07] Sometimes, a fetus sustains brain damage from a combination of chronic partial asphyxia and acute profound asphyxia. In almost every instance of this, the acute asphyxia occurs at the end of a period of partial asphyxia. It is important to recognise that in these circumstances the damage to the parts of the brain affected by partial asphyxia (see later) continues to occur throughout the period of profound asphyxia.

[10.08] When fetal hypoxia is of more gradual onset and more modest in severity, the fetus has the opportunity to protect its brain by the implementation of changes within its circulation. The flow of blood to the carcass and systemic organs is reduced by the constriction of the blood vessels supplying them, while the flow of blood to the brain, heart and adrenal glands is increased. The peripheral vasoconstriction is mainly the result of adrenaline release and the resulting increase in the blood pressure favours perfusion of the brain.[2]

[10.09] Within the brain there is a further redistribution of the circulation. The flow of blood to the brainstem, thalami, basal ganglia and cerebellum

---

2. Jensen et al, 'Redistribution of fetal circulation during repeated asphyxia in sheep: Effects on skin blood flow, transcutaneous PO2, and plasma catecholamines' (1987) 9(1) J Dev Physiol 41–55.

(hindbrain) is preserved or increased to a much greater extent than that to the cerebral hemispheres (forebrain). This is partly because the blood vessels supplying the brain stem are more sensitive to the dilating effect of carbon dioxide than those in the cerebral hemispheres and partly because the vessels supplying the hemispheres are supplied with more sympathetic nerve fibres and so take part in the general vasoconstriction mediated by adrenaline.

[10.10] The reduction in blood supply to systemic organs such as the liver and kidneys accounts for the damage to these organs (almost invariably transient) that is often seen in association with brain damage from chronic partial asphyxia.

[10.11] Another consequence of persistent fetal hypoxia is the gradual accumulation of acid in the tissues and blood. This begins to develop when the supply of oxygen to the tissues is insufficient for the complete conversion of glucose into energy (aerobic glycolysis) and the process stops at the production of lactic acid (anaerobic glycolysis). Anaerobic glycolysis provides much less energy but, nonetheless, some useful energy. The concentration of lactic acid in the blood can be measured directly on a sample of fetal scalp blood or on umbilical cord blood after birth but can also be estimated indirectly by calculation of the base deficit. It is axiomatic that chronic partial asphyxia will not cause fetal brain damage unless a significant metabolic acidaemia has developed.

[10.12] So, during persisting modest fetal hypoxia there is a circulatory redistribution in favour of the more primitive parts of the brain essential for survival and the gradual development of a metabolic acidaemia. Up to a point, these adaptations allow intact survival (or at least survival) if delivery occurs soon enough. They do not, though, have an infinite capacity to protect the fetal brain and at some point in time the effects of hypoxia and acidaemia on the heart will prevent it from pumping well enough to maintain the blood pressure, and the blood supply to the least protected parts of the brain will fall to levels that can no longer support the requirement of brain cells for glucose and oxygen. When the energy supply to brain cells becomes insufficient, a host of biochemical changes occurs which lead to both immediate and delayed cell death.

[10.13] This situation is made worse by the loss of the normal autoregulation of brain blood flow brought about by hypoxia. Autoregulation is a mechanism by which brain blood vessels alter their calibre in order to maintain a constant flow of blood over quite a range of blood pressure. The loss of autoregulation means that brain blood flow becomes pressure passive.

[10.14] When the blood pressure falls, the most vulnerable region of the cerebral hemispheres to ischaemic damage is that which lies at the outer reaches of the cerebral circulation. This is the so-called 'watershed' or 'borderzone' region. In common with fluid flow in any pipe, such as a garden hose, there is a pressure drop-off along the pipe (mainly due to frictional forces). As the driving pressure for blood flow falls (due to the decrease in blood pressure) the tissue perfused by the blood vessels furthest from the heart becomes ischaemic first. If the heart were to stop all brain tissue would be equally ischaemic, as is the case with acute profound asphyxia.

[10.15] The watershed region of the cerebral hemispheres lies between the end-distributions of the anterior, middle and posterior cerebral arteries, in a long strip either side of the midline. Damage to this region is the hallmark of fetal brain damage from chronic partial asphyxia and is generally easily seen on the MRI scan.

TIMING THE DAMAGE FROM CHRONIC PARTIAL ASPHYXIA

[10.16] In the great majority of cases of parasagittal watershed damage the damage has been acquired during labour, and this is almost certainly the case when the baby suffers from an encephalopathic illness during the first few days of life. In fact, in over 90 per cent of cases of neonatal hypoxic-ischaemic encephalopathy there is evidence of a perinatally-acquired insult and neuroimaging evidence of brain damage acquired before birth is very rare.[3] In my own experience, it is exquisitely unusual to see watershed damage in association with an acute hypoxic-ischaemic encephalopathy in a baby born by Caesarean section prior to the onset of labour. This is probably because a fetus in such an adverse hypoxic intrauterine environment as to be critically hypotensive and unable to perfuse its brain is likely to succumb and present as a stillbirth.

[10.17] In the medico legal context the typical situation is that of an acidaemic baby born in poor condition who then suffers from an acute encephalopathy and has an MRI scan which shows watershed damage. The causation question is, when did the damage occur and how could it have been avoided by a different course of obstetric/midwifery management?

---

3.   Cowan, 'Origin and timing of brain lesions in term infants with neonatal encephalopathy' (2003) 361 Lancet 736–742.

[10.18] We know that the damage will not have begun to occur until the fetus had suffered from a sufficient severity and duration of hypoxia to have caused its blood pressure to drop below the level required to perfuse the watershed regions of the cerebral hemispheres. We know that by that time a metabolic acidosis will have developed and cerebral blood flow autoregulation will have been compromised or lost. This is a pretty critical state of affairs and if the hypoxia is sustained or worsens it is likely to prove lethal.

[10.19] Once perfusion is critically compromised it is likely that brain damage will follow within about 30 minutes, although this time cannot be verified in the case of the human fetus. We do know, though, that 20 minutes of acute profound asphyxia does not usually cause damage to brain tissue within the watershed regions, apart from a localised area around the central sulci, whereas 30 minutes of profound asphyxia causes widespread brain damage or death.

[10.20] What is not generally known is the duration of partial asphyxia necessary to reach the point of critically reduced perfusion of the watershed regions. That appears to vary greatly from case to case and will be determined mainly by the pace at which hypoxia and acidaemia develop. In the case of fetal hypoxia caused by uterine contractions, the pre-existing state of the utero-placental vascular unit and the contraction frequency, particularly the interval between contractions when fetal oxygenation improves, will be the major determinants and fetal hypoxia can progress very gradually over several hours and hardly ever within less than one hour. On the other hand, when placental abruption causes modest fetal hypoxia, as it may do on occasion, the progress to critically reduced brain perfusion is likely to be quicker as there is no respite from impaired feto-maternal gas exchange.

[10.21] Unfortunately, there is currently no means of monitoring fetal blood pressure or brain blood flow and so we have to rely on indirect methods such as CTG monitoring and fetal blood gas analysis.

[10.22] Some insights into the likely timescale of events leading to parasagittal damage derive from animal experiments. Perhaps the best evidence arises from studies involving brief repeated umbilical cord occlusions in the fetal sheep.[4] This mimics the effect of uterine contractions on fetal oxygenation and the animals sustain mainly parasagittal damage similar to those seen in the human fetus. When the cord is occluded for either 1 out of every 2.5 minutes or 2 out of every 5 minutes it takes at least 30 minutes before any fetus develops a fall in

---

4.   DeHann et al, 'Brief repeated umbilical cord occlusions cause sustained cytotoxic cerebral edema and focal infarcts in near-term fetal lambs' (1997) 41(1) Pediatric Research 96–104.

blood pressure during occlusion that is below baseline values. Thereafter, individual blood pressure responses vary in timing but there are increasingly longer episodes of hypotension during and following cord occlusions which cumulatively compromise blood flow to the watershed regions causing damage. Eventually, sustained hypotension develops and the animals die. In the case of the animals who developed parasagittal damage the total time that the blood pressure was below the baseline value was around 60 minutes, albeit with considerable variation between individuals. During every cord occlusion there was a bradycardia for the duration of the occlusion but neither the depth nor duration of the deceleration changed during the series of occlusions, giving no clue as to what was happening to the blood pressure. Metabolic acidaemia developed, and after approximately one hour the fetal pH was about 7 with a base deficit of 14 to 18mmol/L.

[10.23] It seems clear from these experiments that repeated, frequent episodes of hypotension can cause watershed damage, and that fetal heart rate changes do not reliably indicate when hypotension is occurring. As a result, the CTG cannot be used to determine the point at which the cerebral circulation becomes compromised.

[10.24] The CTG is, nevertheless, useful from a medico legal causation point of view as a means of identifying a point in time prior to which it is unlikely that brain damage from chronic partial asphyxia has begun to occur. The common sequence of fetal heart rate changes during the development of progressive fetal asphyxia in the previously healthy fetus is as follows. The first abnormality in the presence of uterine contractions is the appearances of fetal heart rate decelerations. These are followed by an increase in the baseline heart rate and, as acidaemia develops, a diminution in baseline variability. If hypoxia is unrelieved or worsens the fetal heart rate will eventually fall and become unstable or else a persistent bradycardia will develop leading to death.

[10.25] The presence of normal or near normal baseline variability is good evidence that the pH of fetal blood is above 7.15mmol/L[5] and it is unlikely that brain damage will occur until the pH has fallen to lower levels than that. Once baseline variability has become persistently absent it is possible that the fetal heart rate decelerations are accompanied by hypotension which threatens the viability of brain tissue within the watershed regions of the cerebral hemispheres.

---

5.   Parer et al, 'Fetal acidemia and electronic fetal heart rate patterns: Is there evidence of an association?' (2006) 19(5) J Matern Fetal Neonatal Med 289–294.

[10.26] It is only when there is continuous fetal heart rate monitoring that the sequence of changes outlined above can be seen and the latest time for safe delivery can be stated with a fair degree of confidence. Unfortunately, continuous CTG monitoring is not always employed. Intermittent CTG monitoring may also give enough information about the progress of fetal heart rate abnormalities to allow a reasonable opinion on the timing of damage to be reached.

[10.27] In the absence of CTG monitoring it is often very difficult to time damage from chronic partial asphyxia. If a baby with watershed damage was born with a significant metabolic acidaemia (pH <7 and base deficit >14mmol/L) and was in poor condition, needing resuscitation, it is reasonable to believe that the asphyxia continued until birth but saying when it started to cause damage is often impossible. In those circumstances, though, it is likely that delivery, say, 30 minutes earlier would probably have had a significantly beneficial effect on the severity of the damage.

[10.28] It is sometimes the case that damaging asphyxia has remitted prior to birth, such that the baby is born in reasonable condition with no great severity of acidaemia in cord blood. This is unusual but can happen if Syntocinon has been discontinued or movement of the fetus has relieved a compressed umbilical cord. In the absence of CTG monitoring it would be very difficult to time the damage in such cases.

[10.29] Intermittent fetal heart rate observations may offer some help if they are performed properly and at appropriate times. When the uterus is contracting, the absence of decelerations denotes an absence of fetal hypoxia but baseline variability cannot reliably be assessed. During the second stage of labour the maternal heartbeat may be mistaken for the fetal heartbeat and provide false reassurance as to the fetal condition. This is more common than is generally recognised and should always be considered when the condition of a baby at birth is far worse than would be suggested by the heart rate observations.

PART IV
OTHER INJURIES

Chapter 11

FAILED PREGNANCY

INTRODUCTION

[11.01] Pregnancies fail for two principal reasons:

- the early stages of development go seriously wrong so that the fetus is grossly abnormal, or in some cases does not develop at all (an anembryonic pregnancy). In such cases the conceptus consists entirely of trophoblast (miscarriage);

- the pregnancy implants in the wrong place (ectopic).

Rarely there is a third explanation: pregnancy is normal but the uterus is incapable of retaining the fetus to the point of viability (incompetent cervix).

MISCARRIAGE

[11.02] The nomenclature of a failing pregnancy is often confusing for the lay person. The terms 'miscarriage' and 'abortion' are often assumed to have different meanings whereas, to the professional, the terms are interchangeable. Abortion, whilst to some carries connotations of intent, is equally applicable to the spontaneous event.

[11.03] The difference between miscarriage and stillbirth is a matter of gestation. The definition of stillbirth is the birth of a dead baby after 24 weeks' gestation; in Ireland there is in addition a weight definition of 500 grams. Delivery of a live baby at any gestation is of course treated as the birth of any other live baby. It is only when pregnancy fails that the definition applies.

[11.04] The adjectives used to refine the term miscarriage need explanation:

- **threatened** miscarriage is vaginal bleeding in the presence of early intrauterine pregnancy;

- **inevitable** miscarriage is bleeding associated with dilatation of the cervix and/or rupture of the fetal membranes but without the passage of any solid material;

- **incomplete** miscarriage refers to the passage of some products of conception, but not all;

- **complete** miscarriage refers to the passage of all products of conception;

- **spontaneous** miscarriage indicates that the process is unaided;

- **induced/therapeutic** miscarriage are terms used to describe medical intervention so as deliberately to terminate the pregnancy;

- **missed** miscarriage is a dead pregnancy completely retained within the uterus.

[11.05] The cause of miscarriage is almost always a failure of the reproductive process. Major genetic errors are usually miscarried within the first trimester. It is however a continuum. A few lethal malformations are not inconsistent with intrauterine life and may allow the fetus to survive well into the second, or even third trimester. Non-lethal malformations frequently persist until term and may only be diagnosed after birth. With one notable exception all miscarriages seem to have this same aetiology. It follows therefore that nothing the doctor can do is likely to alter the outcome. If the fetus is miscarried because its genetic makeup is incompatible with even intrauterine life, efforts to change the outcome are necessarily fruitless. Even if there was negligence in the treatment, that could not have caused the miscarriage.

[11.06] The one exception is the fetus that 'falls out' of a uterus because the cervix no longer remains closed until term. The 'incompetent cervix' is treatable for, unlike all other forms of spontaneous miscarriage it is not the fetus that is abnormal, only the uterus. Occasionally incompetent cervix may occur without prior surgery/conception, the cervix having apparently been incompetent from the beginning. More frequently there is a history either of cervical surgery (for instance for the treatment of cervical pre-cancer) or of a term delivery. In both cases the cervix is damaged and unable to withstand the pressure of the growing uterus, allows the membranes to prolapse and eventually to rupture.

[11.07] This type of miscarriage is of course treatable by a stitch (cerclage) in the cervix. Several types of cerclage are described. They are best performed in the early weeks of pregnancy once a major genetic malformation has been excluded by ultrasound. Where the cervix has been so extensively removed by previous surgery that too little of it persists to allow cerclage to be performed through the vagina, the alternative of abdominal cerclage is available. Although the procedure is at least as effective as vaginal cerclage it is more difficult to perform and does of course mean opening the abdomen of the pregnant woman at about 10–12 weeks.

DIAGNOSIS

[11.08] When a patient presents with bleeding in early pregnancy it is essential that a proper diagnosis is made. It is not acceptable to delegate such investigations to a junior doctor in training who may have little expertise at the detailed ultrasound examination required. It is not an examination to be undertaken lightly for the result of it is of the greatest importance to the patient. If the pregnancy is dead, then the sooner the conceptus is evacuated the better for the mother. If the fetus is alive and inside the uterus it is essential that that fact is established early on so that the appropriate management can be provided. Misdiagnosis of miscarriage should be a 'never' event. 'The death of an embryo should be regarded as of equal significance to that occurring at a later stage'.[1]

[11.09] If, discovering that the fetus is no longer alive, there is considerable material remaining in the uterus then the options for treatment are:

- expectant (doing nothing); and

- surgical.

[11.10] Most early miscarriages will complete themselves without assistance but it may take time and the experience is not one that most women would wish to prolong. The alternative of evacuation of retained products of conception is both simple and safe, provided only that it is performed with modern instruments. Metal instruments such as dilators, curettes and forceps were all too capable of perforating the pregnant uterus and in the past the operation has consequently had a significant morbidity. With the introduction of suction evacuation it is no longer necessary to introduce metal instruments into the uterus. The suction curette (which comes in a range of sizes) can be introduced into the cervix without dilatation and is itself flexible and incapable of perforating the uterus. It is not even necessary to use a general anaesthetic and the procedure can readily be performed in the outpatient department with little distress to the mother.[2]

[11.11] If instead the operation is delegated to a doctor who uses 19th century instruments and perforates the pregnant uterus, there can be little defence.

---

1. Hately, Case and Campbell, 'Establishing the Death of an Embryo by Ultrasound; Report of a Public Inquiry with Recommendations' (1995) Ultrasound Obstet Gynaecol 5.353–7.
2. Sharma, 'Manual Vacuum Aspiration: An Outpatient Alternative for Surgical Management of Miscarriage' (2015) 17 The Obstetrician and Gynaecologist 157–161.

[11.12] On those rare occasions where the pregnancy fails in the second trimester (after 13 weeks) a different technique is required to empty the uterus. The surgical procedure (D & E), which requires special training, involves dilatation of the cervix (safely achieved by a synthetic, sterile hygroscopic cervical dilator – Dilapan-S) and removal piecemeal of the fetal parts (D & E), completed by suction. It is essential that immediately after the evacuation the surgeon personally checks that all major bony parts of the fetus have been evacuated and identified. If the considerable skills required for this procedure are not available, alternative non-surgical means, involving drugs to stimulate the uterus, will usually be effective in time.

ECTOPIC PREGNANCY

[11.13] An ectopic pregnancy is one in which the fertilised ovum implants in a site other than the normal uterine cavity. The possible sites are the ovary, the Fallopian tube, broad ligament, a rudimentary horn of an abnormal (bicornuate) uterus and the uterine cervix. By far the commonest site is the Fallopian tube. Since the isthmus of the Fallopian tube is its narrowest portion, ectopic pregnancies are more likely in this part of the tube than in the wider ampulla or fimbrial end. With twins, there is the possibility of a simultaneous intrauterine and extrauterine pregnancy as well as simultaneous bilateral tubal pregnancies.

[11.14] Ectopic pregnancy is doomed to failure. Whilst the vast majority die without treatment and are absorbed without trace, a minority will precipitate a grave emergency by rupturing the structure (such as the Fallopian tube) into which they implant, with torrential haemorrhage.

[11.15] The diagnosis of ectopic pregnancy may be difficult. The presenting symptoms are usually a combination of amenorrhoea, abdominal pain and vaginal bleeding – the same symptoms that accompany a threatened miscarriage. In the later stages there may be episodes of fainting and signs of intra-abdominal bleeding such as shoulder-tip pain (because blood in the peritoneal cavity irritates the diaphragm). Differential diagnosis in the early phases can only be made by expert ultrasound examination. Even more important than is the case with miscarriage, it is essential that ultrasonography for a suspected ectopic pregnancy is carried out by a sonographer with appropriate expertise and experience. Accurate and rapid estimations of the hormone βHCG is also an invaluable aid.

[11.16] If on ultrasound examination there is an intrauterine sac then the patient can be reassured. Save only in the rare combination of a heterotopic and simultaneous ectopic pregnancy is there any danger. If the pregnancy sac is clearly extrauterine then βHCG estimation becomes critical for management. If the βHCG level is falling expectant management is appropriate. If the βHCG is rising slowly there is a possibility of medical treatment, involving the drug methotrexate which destroys trophoblast. Clinical treatment is only acceptable where there is no fetal heart beat and the βHCG level is less than 5,000 international units, the patient is asymptomatic and is willing to have serial βHCG estimations. With rising levels of βHCG and a high probability of extrauterine pregnancy, surgery becomes a necessary choice.

[11.17] Laparoscopy is acceptable if there is no significant intrauterine bleeding and the definitive surgery to remove the ectopic pregnancy is often possible through the laparoscope. With intraperitoneal bleeding or pathology that makes laparoscopy unsafe or unusually difficult, laparotomy is the necessary alternative. The evidence is that salpingectomy (removal of the Fallopian tube) is marginally better than salpingostomy (opening the tube, removal of the pregnancy and closure) for the subsequent fertility rates are no better with salpingostomy and it avoids the risk of a second ectopic pregnancy in the same tube.

[11.18] Molar pregnancy in which the trophoblast (the fetal contribution to the placenta) becomes neoplastic (a hydatidiform mole) or malignant (chorioncarcinoma) is seldom associated with a surviving fetus and is, in any event, exceptionally rare in Western Europe. It is characterised by concentrations of βHCG many times greater than is seen in a normal pregnancy.

THE LAW

[11.19] Miscarriage litigation is usually about misdiagnosis: either failing to diagnose a miscarriage or making an incorrect diagnosis of miscarriage where the diagnosis should be of something else. Occasionally litigation is about perforation of the uterus when evacuation is performed using the wrong instruments.

[11.20] The plaintiff in *Griffin v Patton and Tyndale*[3] was awarded €100,000[4] in damages by O'Donovan J for her pain and suffering due to the first defendant's negligence in the carrying out of a surgical procedure for evacuation of retained products of conception (ERPC) at the Bon Secours Hospital in Cork. The action against the hospital was dismissed.

---

3. *Griffin v Patton and Tyndale* (21 March 2003) HC, O'Donovan J.
4. The plaintiff was awarded €75,000 for five years of past pain and suffering and €25,000 for future pain and suffering.

[11.21] During the 17th week of the plaintiff's pregnancy and through no fault of anyone, her unborn child died. She was referred to the first defendant consultant obstetrician and gynaecologist, who arranged for an ultrasound scan which confirmed the heart-breaking news that her baby had died. It was hoped that the dead fetus could be evacuated from the uterus as soon as possible and for this purpose the plaintiff was prescribed dosages of prostaglandins orally, then per vaginam and, laterally, intravenously. Unfortunately, they did not work.

[11.22] Interestingly, O'Donovan J was satisfied that the first defendant did not advise the plaintiff that she had the option of doing nothing in hope that nature would take its course and that, ultimately, the fetus would be delivered naturally and, in particular, that she was not told that that was the safest option insofar as her wellbeing was concerned and, particularly, that it was the option which would not inhibit her prospects for having more children which might be the case insofar as exercising any one of the other possible options was concerned.

[11.23] When the plaintiff awoke from the general anaesthetic following surgery, she said that she saw both the first defendant and a night sister crying and that she, herself, was on an operating table, at the side of which she could see baby parts on a sheet. Thereafter, following a short service in the hospital, the plaintiff was given the remains in a white box which she arranged to have buried. At that stage, she was of course satisfied that her dead baby had been removed from her body.

[11.24] The first defendant maintained that she satisfied herself that she had removed the complete fetus from the uterus. Unsurprisingly, all the doctors agreed in evidence that it is incumbent on the doctor carrying out this surgical procedure to satisfy himself or herself that all parts of the fetus are removed. It was common case also among the medical experts who gave evidence that without negligence, small pieces of soft tissue can be accidentally left behind. That normally presents no problem because within days they are passed out of the body in the normal way. What was in issue however was whether a piece of bone of 5.5 centimetres in length (and probably a lower limb of the baby) could be accidentally left behind in the uterus without there being negligence on the part of the surgeon. The question arose not only whether it could ever happen without negligence but also whether even if it could, the defendant was in fact guilty of negligence on this occasion.

[11.25] Following the ERPC procedure to which she was subjected, the plaintiff was discharged on antibiotics. However, as time passed, she was not healing properly. The plaintiff sought help with regard to an ulcer which had troubled her over the years and was subjected to a pelvic ultrasound scan which disclosed that there was a piece of bone some 5.5 cm in length located in her uterus.

[11.26] The plaintiff complained of a smell and said she had pain and passed pieces of bone and flesh in the toilet. She succeeded in retrieving one piece of bone which she wrapped in tinfoil and gave to the first defendant, who arranged for another scan, following which she told her that there was some bony matter from the baby still inside her and the plaintiff was readmitted to hospital where she underwent an evacuation through the vagina. Following that operation, the pain which the plaintiff had been experiencing up to then began to ease and it gradually abated but it was some months before it was gone altogether.

[11.27] The first defendant had not carried out a visual check of the pieces of fetus which she had removed which was sufficient to identify the major bony structures of the fetus, much less to satisfy herself that the entire fetus had been removed. She 'made no mention whatsoever of major bony structures'. Rather she referred to 'bits of tissue ... bits of body ... bits of bone ... bits of everything.., a jingle-jangle of bits'. She said that you look at those bits and the volume involved and assess it.

[11.28] O'Donovan J accepted that the plaintiff had an element of grief on account of the loss of her unborn child and that this had been exacerbated somewhat by her failure in the meantime to become pregnant. She continued to grieve for her lost baby but that grief was aggravated by the fact that she believed her baby was spread around; down the sewer, partly in the Bon Secours hospital and partly in the box. There was no doubt but that the negligent failure to complete the ERPC procedure caused great distress and that as a result, she experienced the vast majority, if not all, of the psychological problems of which she complained. Moreover, while no doubt grief persisted over that period of time and still persisted, the judge was equally satisfied that it was relatively insignificant when compared with the symptoms of the post-traumatic stress disorder condition which she claimed she developed as a result of the failed ERPC procedure which had a hugely disruptive effect on way of life and her capacity to look after her husband and children. It was accepted that her ongoing psychological problems would abate but this would take some time and the probabilities were that she would continue to have to attend a psychiatrist for at least another year.

[11.29] The case was unsuccessfully appealed to the Supreme Court on liability only[5] where it was held that the weighing of the expert evidence was a matter for the trial judge.

---

5.   *Griffin v Patton and Tyndale* [2004] IESC 46.

[11.30] The plaintiff in *Maguire v Randles and Ors*[6] claimed damages for alleged negligence of the defendants in inserting a contraceptive coil into her womb at a time when she was in fact pregnant as a result of which, she alleged that she suffered a miscarriage causing to her great distress and upset.

[11.31] Following the birth of her ninth child, the plaintiff decided that she would like a rest from childbearing for a time and she therefore asked the second defendant to arrange with the first defendant, a general medical practitioner with a special interest in family planning, to have a contraceptive coil inserted in her womb. The required arrangements were made and the coil was inserted. On the date of insertion however, the plaintiff unknown to herself was in fact pregnant and the fact of such pregnancy was not detected by the first defendant.

[11.32] Lynch J found, of course, that it was not good medical practice to fit a coil in a pregnant woman and therefore those facts called for an explanation from the first defendant. He was, however, satisfied on the balance of probabilities that the plaintiff, who had had the coil fitted in the past and knew the requirements, knew that she should be menstruating if the first defendant were to fit the coil. She had in fact informed the second defendant that she had started to menstruate and was not pregnant.

[11.33] On the date of the impugned treatment, the plaintiff attended at the first defendant's rooms where she was interviewed and examined. She was bleeding in a manner identical to and indistinguishable from menstruation and she told the first defendant that this was her menstrual period. The first defendant carried out all the usual procedures before fitting the coil and nothing appeared which might reasonably have indicated to the first defendant that the plaintiff was in fact pregnant.

[11.34] In fact the plaintiff was pregnant but the pregnancy was an anembryonic pregnancy. There was no fetus present in the womb and the plaintiff was never going to produce a child from that pregnancy. A miscarriage was inevitable and the bleeding with which the plaintiff presented at examination by the first defendant was in fact the commencement of the miscarriage process although it had been indistinguishable from menstrual bleeding. The coil which was fitted by the first defendant had no material effect on the progress towards the ultimate miscarriage and so there was no causation of injury. Accordingly the plaintiff's claim failed.

[11.35] Litigation for ectopic pregnancy usually centres around delay in diagnosis, particularly if the patient is sent home and subsequently suffers a

---

6.   *Maguire v Randles and Ors* (21 June 1991) HC, Lynch J.

traumatic rupture with major intraperitoneal bleeding. Whilst the distress and subsequent psychiatric condition may attract damages, it is seldom possible to argue that the end result would have been any different. The fact that the tube has ruptured almost certainly means that it would have been lost in any event. The usual explanation for such error leading to delay is that the ultrasound examination has been delegated to a doctor/midwife with inadequate training and experience.

[11.36] The plaintiff in *English v South Eastern Health Board and Howard*[7] was awarded €75,000 in damages by Ryan J arising out of delayed diagnosis and treatment of her ectopic pregnancy. The defendants were concurrent wrongdoers and considering their respective degrees of fault, the first defendant was ordered to make a contribution of 60 per cent and the second defendant of 40 per cent.

[11.37] The plaintiff was admitted to hospital in Clonmel suffering from an ectopic pregnancy but was erroneously thought to be suffering from molar pregnancy, which is a far more unusual condition. The second defendant, a consultant obstetrician and gynaecologist, directed that she be transferred to hospital in Cashel for a surgical opinion and noted the possibility that she might be suffering from acute retrocecal appendicitis, a diagnosis described by one of the plaintiff's experts as 'bizarre', the indicators of same such as fever and high white blood cell count not being present.

[11.38] The plaintiff was transferred by ambulance to Cashel and was recorded as suffering severe pain on that journey. There it was realised that she did not in fact have retrocecal appendicitis or indeed any surgical problem. She was kept overnight for observation and was transferred back to Clonmel the next day, although she was bleeding intra-abdominally. Upon her arrival back at the hospital in Clonmel the second defendant performed a laparotomy and the plaintiff's ruptured fallopian tube was excised with three litres of blood being removed from her peritoneal cavity.

[11.39] The plaintiff made a satisfactory physical recovery from the operation but claimed she was severely psychologically damaged by the incident and that her suffering was ongoing. She had serious psychiatric problems before the events in question and had suffered from depression.

[11.40] The plaintiff claimed that the second defendant was negligent in failing to diagnose and treat the ectopic pregnancy and further that his decision to transfer the plaintiff to Cashel for a surgical opinion was unjustified. She also

---

7.   *English v South Eastern Health Board and Howard* [2011] IEHC 362.

claimed that the decision by Cashel to transfer the plaintiff back to Clonmel was inexcusable.

[11.41] The relevant medical witnesses were almost unanimous in their condemnation of the decision made at Cashel to send the plaintiff back to Clonmel when she was so critically ill. Both experts called on behalf of the plaintiff and Cashel supported the argument that the second defendant should have considered the possibility of ectopic pregnancy and taken appropriate action and there was no reasonable basis for thinking there might be a separate and coincidental pathology that warranted general surgery. Although the procedure which the plaintiff ultimately underwent to remove the ectopic pregnancy would have been necessary regardless of any negligence on the part of the defendants, the severity of it would have been less pronounced. She would in all likelihood have avoided a vertical abdominal incision and instead have had a transverse suprapubic incision, and she would not have needed large-scale blood transfusion.

[11.42] The second defendant did not make a diagnosis before transferring the plaintiff but merely went along with the diagnosis which had previously been mentioned, which was of an extremely rare condition, without recording or addressing the possibility of one that was 10 times more probable. Under cross-examination the second defendant agreed that ectopic pregnancies were far more common than molar pregnancies. The occurrence of the former is one in 300 and the occurrence of the latter is one in 3,000. The positive pregnancy test, the absence of a fever, the other symptoms the plaintiff had developed – in particular the pleuritic pain which was indicative of intra-abdominal bleeding – meant that the possibility of an ectopic pregnancy should have been excluded before arranging her transfer to Cashel for a surgical opinion. The plaintiff's pregnancy hormone levels were not consistent with a molar pregnancy because the figure was not high enough, strongly pointing towards an ectopic pregnancy. This should have been entertained as a differential diagnosis but it was not mentioned anywhere in the notes. Another of the plaintiff's experts described as 'inexplicable' and 'astonishing' the failure to perform a laparoscopy when it was noted that the plaintiff had pleuritic chest pain, indicating that she had blood in her peritoneal cavity which was irritating her diaphragm. Laparoscopy was 'an essential diagnostic tool' at this point and would have led to the ectopic pregnancy being identified and the fallopian tube where the ectopic was located could have been removed.

[11.43] The second defendant's failure to exclude the diagnosis of ectopic pregnancy was negligent. Furthermore, the decision to transfer the plaintiff to Cashel had more to do with his own anxieties than with medical analysis and he was negligent in that regard also. The plaintiff was subjected to a terrifying ordeal and put in a near-death situation. The transfer and return caused real distress to the plaintiff and contributed to the overall psychological impact of the ectopic pregnancy and the loss of a baby. The return to Clonmel by ambulance was described by Ryan J as the nadir of the plaintiff's traumatic experience.

[11.44] The plaintiff was entitled to damages to compensate for the physical and psychological injury she sustained during and because of the journey to Cashel, the time she was there and the return to Clonmel.

[11.45] The plaintiff had serious psychological problems prior to her ectopic pregnancy and consequently only part of her psychological difficulties could be attributed to the medical events surrounding her ectopic pregnancy and a smaller element of that was attributable to the added trauma caused by the defendants' negligence.

[11.46] The plaintiff in *Laycock v Gaughan and Others*[8] unsuccessfully made two separate and distinct claims against the defendants. She claimed that there was a failure to adequately monitor the plaintiff's symptoms and condition, and that she was wrongly advised that she was routinely pregnant when her pregnancy was ectopic and, thereafter there was a negligent and unnecessary delay in appropriate investigation and treatment thereby exposing her to the risk of serious and life threatening injury.

[11.47] She claimed she suffered an initial injury arising out of the performance by the first defendant of a diagnostic laparoscopy, that the first defendant incorrectly located a secondary port in her abdomen which punctured her right inferior epigastric blood vessel, thereby causing her bleeding and consequent bruising to her abdomen. Her expert witness gave evidence that he was of the opinion that bruising as extensive as that described by the plaintiff at the location where he found scarring was consistent with the puncture of the plaintiff's right inferior epigastric blood vessel. The first defendant stated in evidence that if he had punctured the epigastric vessel as alleged it would have been inconceivable that he would have failed to notice and further that a puncture of such a major artery would have resulted in extensive and very noticeable bleeding with substantial risks to the patient. He stated that it was possible he might have damaged a small vessel which would have resulted in bruising, that such damage was not necessarily consistent with negligence on his part, but that it was not satisfactory from a patient's point of view. He said that, if he became aware of some bruising at a later stage, he might have apologised to the plaintiff for any additional discomfort or distress which she suffered. The

---

8. *Laycock v Gaughan and Ors* [2011] IEHC 52.

expert evidence adduced on behalf of the first defendant was consistent with the defendant's evidence. Quirke J found that the plaintiff did not establish by way of evidence on the balance of probabilities that the first defendant performed the laparoscopic procedure negligently. In particular, it was not established on the evidence, as a matter of probability, that the first defendant incorrectly located a secondary port in her abdomen which punctured her right inferior epigastric blood vessel.

[11.48] The plaintiff's second claim related to the performance of a right salpingectomy by the first defendant. She claimed that this procedure, which was carried out to remove an ectopic pregnancy, should have been performed by way of laparoscopy rather than open surgery and that as a consequence of the open surgery she has an unnecessary abdominal scar and suffered unnecessary post-operative pain, discomfort and distress. The first defendant gave evidence that he started a laparoscopy on the plaintiff but due to the volume of blood present within the plaintiff's peritoneal cavity he was unable to see the right fallopian tube clearly so he proceeded to laparotomy because he was more comfortable operating that way. The evidence adduced on behalf of the first defendant confirmed that surgery by laparotomy was the appropriate treatment for the plaintiff in the circumstances of this case.

[11.49] With regard to the second procedure also, the plaintiff failed to prove that the course taken by the first defendant was one which no medical practitioner of like specialisation and skill would have followed had he been taking the ordinary care required from a person of like qualification.

CONCLUSION

[11.50] Miscarriage litigation arises in the context of misdiagnosis (both ways) or injury when incorrect instruments are used to evacuate the uterus of retained products of conception. Ectopic litigation arises where there has been delay in diagnosis where the distress and subsequent psychiatric condition may be compensable. Both miscarriage and ectopic claims generally attract relatively modest damages.

Chapter 12

OBSTETRIC BRACHIAL PLEXUS INJURY

DEFINITIONS

Shoulder dystocia

[12.01] The definition of shoulder dystocia is simple and requires only the translation of the Greek work 'dystocia' into English. The prefix 'dys' means difficult, impaired or abnormal and the Greek 'dustokia' is defined (OED) as 'difficult or abnormally painful childbirth'. The older textbooks identified many kinds of dystocia, cervical dystocia, dystocia from defaults in the forces, dystocia from faults in the parturian canal, dystocia from faults in the fetus, etc. Munro Kerr[1] initially had an opening chapter on eutocia (normal childbirth) and dystocia (difficult labour).

[12.02] The word simply means difficult delivery of the shoulders. Unfortunately there are those who seek to define shoulder dystocia in a way that distorts both the meaning of the phrase and the litigation arising from it. The RCOG guideline[2] defines shoulder dystocia as 'a vaginal cephalic delivery that requires additional obstetric manoeuvres to deliver the fetus after the head has delivered and gentle traction has failed'. But of course that is to define the condition by the treatment required to address it. It is as if we define appendicitis as a condition requiring appendicectomy. However, such a definition is a defendant's charter for what it really means is that if no 'additional manoeuvres' are recorded then shoulder dystocia (no matter how difficult it was to deliver the shoulders) did not occur.

OBPI

[12.03] Brachial plexus injury at the time of birth describes damage (permanent or temporary) to the nerves of the brachial plexus (5th, 6th, 7th and 8th cervical and the 1st thoracic). The commonest variety of brachial plexus injury, involving the 5th and 6th cervical nerve roots was first described by the great William Smellie in 1763. Over 100 years later it was described by Duchenne and in 1873 by Erb. For many years it was known as the Erb-Duchenne paralysis. It involves a deformity in which the arm is held in adduction and is internally rotated, the forearm being extended and pronated. The muscles affected are the deltoid, the supra and intra-spinatae, the terres minor, the biceps, the brachialis

---

1. Moir, *Munro Kerr's Operative Obstetrics* (7th edn, Tindall and Cox, 1964).
2. RCOG Guidelines, *No 42 Shoulder Dystocia* (2nd edn, 2012).

and the brachio-radialis. The arm adopts a position similar to that of a waiter expecting a tip. There is no loss of sensation.

[12.04] Such are the vagaries of eponymy that the condition has for many years been described as Erb's palsy, a term which is now applied to all brachial plexus injuries irrespective of the nerve roots involved. It was Augusta Klumpke who described the rarer form of brachial plexus injury in which the lower roots, C8 and T1, are involved. She published her description in 1885. To avoid eponymous confusion the condition is best referred to as obstetric brachial plexus injury.

THE ANATOMY

[12.05] Five nerve roots (figure 12.1) form the main nerve supply to the upper limb. In order to reach the arm they travel from the spine through the web of the neck and amongst the muscles. The upper trunk of the brachial plexus (C5 and 6) has the longest route into the arm and is most at risk if a distraction force is applied across the plexus. Such distraction forces are encountered in road traffic accidents where casualties, particularly motor cyclists, strike the road or a fixed object with considerable force so that the head and the tip of the shoulder are forcibly separated. Whilst the skin and muscles will stretch and usually survive intact, nerves have a finite length and are not elastic. Bruising, partial tearing or in some cases complete avulsion from the spinal cord will then follow. Whilst some of the minor injuries to the nerves may 'heal' in time, a major disruption of the fibres and avulsion result in permanent injury since nerves cannot regenerate.

Figure 12.1

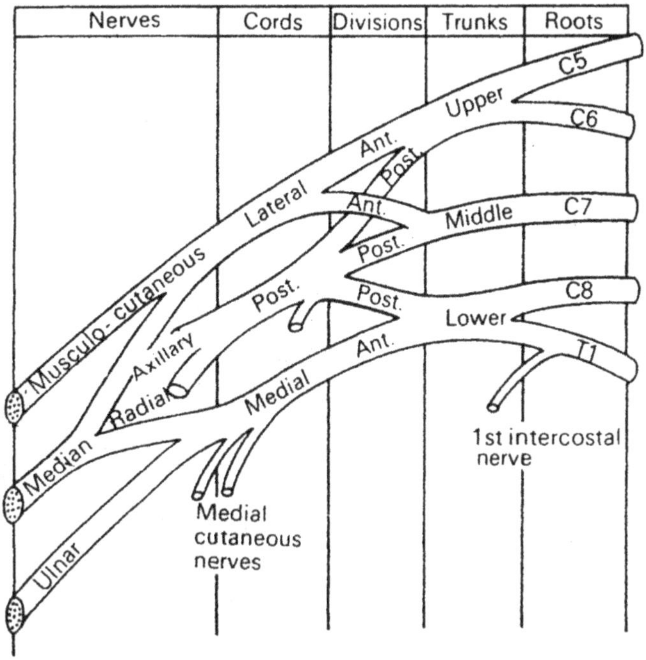

[12.06] Obstetric brachial plexus injury results when, at some time during the birth process, a distraction force across the brachial plexus is sufficient to cause permanent damage to a nerve. OBPI can occur with any presentation of the fetus and with any type of delivery. Injuries at Caesarean section are usually found in small and often premature babies. The operator makes an incision in the uterus sufficient to deliver the baby's head and then finds that the aperture is too small to accommodate the shoulders and the resulting traction causes injury. Similarly in a breech delivery, again particularly with a small baby, the after-coming head may become trapped in an incompletely dilated cervix. Once again the necessary traction to deliver the baby's head results in injury.

[12.07] The majority of brachial plexus injuries, those borne vaginally in cephalic presentation, are associated with large babies. Although the head delivers the chin does not fully clear the perineum and the baby's head tends to retract into the birth canal, the 'turtle' effect. It is once again the distraction force applied across the brachial plexus that results in injury. The single most important risk factor for shoulder dystocia and brachial plexus injury is large size (macrosomia).

[12.08] Macrosomia was traditionally defined as a baby weighing more than 4 kilos but in recent years 4.5 has been the accepted threshold throughout the developed world.[3]

[12.09] The baby born to the diabetic mother is particularly at risk. Such babies are often very large (particularly when the diabetes is poorly controlled) and they are of a different shape being much 'chunkier' with a very broad shoulder girdle. If high birth weight is anticipated then the mother should be carefully counselled as to the risks and invited to express a view as to her preferred method of delivery.

GOOD PRACTICE

[12.10] Since the birth of a large baby carries an increased risk of shoulder dystocia, it is appropriate to consider antenatal counselling in some detail. Much shoulder dystocia occurs without warning and in circumstances where the increased risk is not only unknown, but perhaps unknowable. But for some mothers the risk is all too obvious to the obstetrician – and must be shared with his patient. Babies usually increase in size in birth order; a history of previous big babies necessarily involves the risk that the next will be larger still. A history of previous shoulder dystocia, whether or not mother or baby was injured, increases the risk eight-fold. For the diabetic mother the risk occurs at a lower birth weight than for the non-diabetic mother simply because of the shape of the baby.

[12.11] Shoulder dystocia carries risks for both mother and baby. For the mother the commonest injury is massive soft tissue damage to the pelvic floor which may include anal sphincter injury and lifelong impaired ano-rectal continence. For the baby not only OBPI but asphyxial injury may result if rescue is delayed beyond the baby's tolerance – usually about 10 minutes.

[12.12] These are risks which any reasonable mother would wish to take into account in deciding whether to opt for a vaginal delivery or Caesarean section. Whilst most mothers are prepared to risk injury to themselves, they are usually much less tolerant of risk to their baby. The obstetrician should make an attempt to quantify the risk so as to enable the mother to decide which for her is the preferable route. Consent in these circumstances takes on a peculiar flavour. Once pregnant there are only two possibilities, vaginal birth or Caesarean section. There is no third alternative. Whilst most doctors are meticulous in

---

3. Campbell, 'Fetal Macrosomia: A Problem in Need of a Policy' (2014) 43 Ultrasound Obstetrics Gynaecology 3–10.

obtaining 'consent' for operative intervention they seem to have little appreciation of the need, equally great, for proper consent to the non-surgical alternative. The question needs to raised: what risks of elective Caesarean section could outweigh the known risk in any particular case of vaginal delivery?

[12.13] Advice on safe methods of dealing with shoulder dystocia has evolved slowly since the mid-1990s. Neither obstetric nor midwifery textbooks in the early 1980s were particularly helpful to the doctor or midwife faced with the desperate emergency of shoulder dystocia. Of all labour ward emergencies it was the most feared for the timescale available for dealing with shoulder dystocia is so limited.

[12.14] Advice, such as it was, could be summarised as:

1. Do not pull on the fetal head when the anterior shoulder is obstructed – not until the shoulder is released.

2. A change of maternal position may be all that is necessary to dislodge the obstructed shoulder. The common recommendations were lithotomy and 'all fours'.

3. If change of position does not immediately succeed then the mother should be placed on her back and pressure applied to the suprapubic area to displace the anterior shoulder behind the symphysis pubis (suprapubic pressure – figure 12.2).

[12.15] By the late 1980s the midwifery textbooks contained such clear but limited advice. The watershed, in terms of practice, occurred in the mid-1990s. James O'Leary published an excellent monograph in 1992.[4] The book was, however, not commonly found in circulation here until some years later. In that book O'Leary described, *inter alia*, 'the McRoberts maneuver'. William A McRoberts junior practiced his manoeuvre with great success for more than 40 years. He published it, belatedly, and only in a somewhat obscure journal.[5] The manoeuvre is of the greatest simplicity and involves hyperflexion of the mother's hips and knees, pushing her knees as close to her shoulders as possible. This does nothing to enlarge the inlet of the pelvis but it opens up the pelvic brim to the fetus and removes the sacral promontory as a point of obstruction. It is remarkably successful. The manoeuvre had been advanced by Gonik in an

---

4. O'Leary, *Shoulder Dystocia and Birth Injury: Prevention and Treatment* (McGraw-Hill, 1992).

5. McRoberts, 'Maneuver for Shoulder Dystocia' (1984) 24 Contemporary Obstetrics and Gynaecology 17.

earlier publication.[6] The technique did not reach the textbooks here until 1994. In that year several publications[7] advocated its use.

[12.16] The McRoberts manoeuvre did not arrive in the midwifery textbooks until 1999. By the end of the century the advice given in both obstetrics and midwifery textbooks was that fetal injury could best be avoided in shoulder dystocia with the application of McRoberts manoeuvre and suprapubic pressure.

[12.17] Whilst these manoeuvres will relieve most cases of shoulder dystocia without injury it is sometimes necessary to adopt more complicated manoeuvres such are set out in the HELPERR mnemonic. A similar algorithm is produced in the RCOG Green Top Guideline. In fact the current practice favours delivery of the posterior arm as the 'next manoeuvre' rather than the more complicated and difficult rotational alternatives.[8]

[12.18] It is however important to point out that neither the performance of any of these manoeuvres nor the failure to perform them causes injury. Omission of the recommended manoeuvres may be prejudicial to the definition of the injury – but the injury itself is caused by traction.

[12.19] These manoeuvres are advised as ways of delivering the baby, so as to avoid traction to prevent injury. The plaintiff will only succeed if traction is proved as a means of relieving obstruction, to the detriment of the brachial plexus.

[12.20] To what extent can midwives and junior doctors be trained so as to improve outcome and decrease the incidence of injury? Shoulder dystocia training has been advocated since 1998 but until recently there has been no evidence concerning the best method of training, nor that training improves outcome. A recent study[9] investigated the long-term effect of evidence-based shoulder dystocia training on the management of, and neonatal outcomes

6.   Gonik, Stringer and Held, 'Alternative Maneuver for the Management of Shoulder Dystocia' (1983) 145 American Journal of Obstetrics and Gynecology 882–898.
7.   Roberts, 'Shoulder Dystocia' in Studd (ed), *Progress in Obstetrics and Gynaecology* (Churchill Livingstone, 1994) vol 11; Gibb, 'Operative Delivery' in Clements (ed), *Safe Practice in Obstetrics and Gynaecology* (Churchill Livingstone, 1994).
8.   Ansell et al, 'Shoulder dystocia: A qualitative exploration of what works' (2011) Midwifery DOI:10.1016/j.midw 2011.05.007.
9.   Crofts et al, 'Prevention of brachial plexus injury – 12 years of shoulder dystocia training: an interrupted time-series study' (2015) BJOG 2015: DOI: 10.1111/ 1471-0528.13302.

following, shoulder dystocia. They reviewed the management and outcomes of 1,148 cases of shoulder dystocia cared for within a single UK healthcare institution, now more than a decade after the introduction of training. That no one of the 17,037 babies in the last cohort suffered permanent BPI challenges the commonly held view that permanent injury is largely unavoidable. Permanent brachial plexus injuries must no longer by regarded as an inevitable complication of shoulder dystocia.

[12.21] Continuation of an annual programme of mandatory, multi-professional training for intrapartum emergencies that includes 30 minutes of hands-on shoulder dystocia training, for all maternity staff, is feasible in the long term. This chapter provides further evidence that effective training of staff is key to more effective management of shoulder dystocia.

THE DEFENCE

[12.22] It will come as no surprise that there is seldom a record that significant traction was applied to the fetal head with the shoulder arrested. The plaintiff therefore is put to proof that such traction occurred and the defendants use a number of standard responses to explain how the injury could come about without operator traction.

THE MECHANISM OF LABOUR

[12.23] Before explaining various common defences it is necessary to understand a little about the mechanism of labour. The fetal head is not a sphere, it is an ovoid. Because the inlet of the pelvis is also ovoid (with its widest diameter perpendicular to the maternal spine) the fetal head will almost always engage in the pelvic brim with the sagittal (central longitudinal) suture in the transverse position. However the pelvic outlet is rotated through 90° so that it is ovoid in the opposite plane from the brim. The widest diameter of the outlet is the anteroposterior diameter. The fetal head therefore needs to rotate. The direction of rotation is determined by the attitude of the fetus. The part of the fetal head that arrives on the pelvic floor first will rotate to the front because of the sloping funnel shape of the pelvic floor. If, as it should be, the fetal head is well flexed then the back of the head (occiput) rotates to the front. This means that when born the baby's head is facing backwards, with the occiput to the front.

[12.24] The shoulder girdle must achieve the same rotation, following on the head, so that in an ideal labour the shoulder girdle will engage the pelvic brim in the transverse diameter and will rotate through 90°, just as the head has done before it, to exit in the anteroposterior plane. By this time of course the fetal head has come to face the left or right and, depending upon which way the fetal head turns, the shoulders will be arranged accordingly.

[12.25] In order to achieve shoulder dystocia the shoulders must be attempting entrance to the pelvis in the wrong plane, in the anteroposterior diameter which is much smaller and upon which the shoulders may become arrested. However the posterior shoulder will almost always be within the pelvis at the time when the anterior shoulder becomes arrested. If the fetus can be made to rotate the trunk or if the shoulder can be persuaded to slip behind the symphysis, the problem is overcome.

POSTERIOR SHOULDER INJURY

[12.26] There is very little reliable literature on posterior shoulder injury but there is the occasional anecdote with carefully recorded notes that a baby has been born vaginally with an injury to the posterior shoulder. It is of course the anterior shoulder that becomes arrested behind the symphysis pubis in classical shoulder dystocia. Unless there is coincidental arrest of the anterior shoulder on the symphysis pubis, with posterior shoulder injury there may be no 'dystocia', no delay because the shoulder is arrested.

[12.27] How then does the injury occur? There is at present no convincing answer. The received wisdom is that maternal soft tissues are not sufficiently resistant to cause the injury. In other words, if the baby's head is pulled in an upwards direction the posterior shoulder, if it is in any way arrested by the maternal soft tissues, will usually tear the maternal tissues rather than the baby's brachial plexus. It is of course conceivable that with a very small premature baby such traction against maternal soft tissues could produce an injury and indeed can be observed to do so in Caesarean section when the surgeon makes too small an incision into the lower segment and a relatively large head of a premature baby is then pulled through the incision with damage to one (sometimes both) brachial plexus. So if the maternal soft tissues cannot do it, what causes the posterior shoulder injury in a vaginal birth? The theory (and it is no more than that) is that at some stage during the birth, the posterior shoulder is arrested on the sacral promontory. The sacral promontory is no more than a 'bump' on the top of the sacrum and is certainly not an obstacle of the same magnitude as the symphysis pubis. But that is the theory. It is not conceivable that maternal force from above could cause the injury so it must be some force exerted from below. For the theory to be credible the birth must therefore involve an operative vaginal delivery with forceps. It is doubtful whether the ventouse could exert sufficient traction since it is designed to fall off when pulled against resistance.

[12.28] The operator cannot possibly know that obstruction of the posterior shoulder is occurring and therefore cannot be blamed if there is a posterior shoulder injury, even if it is caused by this hypothetical mechanism involving the obstetric forceps. It follows therefore that if the judge finds that the injured shoulder is posterior, the plaintiff cannot succeed.

[12.29] In order to determine which shoulder is anterior and which posterior at the time of birth, it is necessary to have a reliable record of the position of the fetal head. When describing position the denominator is the occiput (the back of the head). If the occiput is on the left then it is the right shoulder that will be anterior and vice versa. Alternatively the position of the fetal back must be noted by abdominal examination. Unfortunately it is by no means uncommon to find that neither the position of the fetal back nor the position of the occiput is recorded at all, at any stage. Both observations are of course liable to error.

[12.30] It follows therefore that every retrospective series which purports to show that posterior shoulder injury is common is hostage to the deficiencies of note keeping. The majority opinion both of doctors and judges is that posterior shoulder injury, if it occurs at all, is rare.

[12.31] The solution to the problem for the plaintiff is to have an eye-witness. The mother is usually in no position to know to which side the baby's head turns after birth and therefore the side of the occiput. She cannot see. Her birth partner however can and on occasion the birth partner will have a clear memory of seeing the baby (almost always born facing downwards) turns his or her head to the right or left, thus demonstrating which shoulder is anterior.

MATERNAL PROPULSION

[12.32] The most common defence offered to an allegation of excessive traction is that there was no traction at all (or hardly any) and the injury to the baby is entirely due to maternal propulsion from above. Here the literature is confusing. We know from countless publications that the incidence of brachial plexus injury is quite small. The great majority of shoulder dystocia is managed without causing the baby any harm. Even for very large babies the overall risk of permanent OBPI is of the order of 4 to 8 per cent. The majority of brachial plexus injury is of course temporary and, because it is only associated with bruising, the effect is limited to the first few months of life.

[12.33] It must follow therefore that if properly recorded the incidence of shoulder dystocia would greatly exceed the incidence of permanent brachial plexus injury.

[12.34] It comes as something of a surprise therefore to discover that there was a flood of American literature in the 1980s and 1990s suggesting that obstetric brachial plexus injury was a great deal more common than shoulder dystocia. The argument was advanced therefore that much brachial plexus injury did not follow shoulder dystocia but occurred without any apparent difficulty being appreciated. How could that be? Even if half of all brachial plexus injury was caused by maternal propulsion that would still not produce figures such as are claimed in the American literature. The answer is the way in which the figures were produced. They were obtained by the interrogation of hospital databases.

[12.35] The International Classification of Disease (ICD) allocates a complex number to all known diagnoses. Shoulder dystocia and OBPI will each have an ICD number. These numbers are not often entered into the hospital database by doctors or by midwives but usually by clerks. The clerk works with the record of each individual hospital admission and allocates the appropriate ICD number to it. The information is only as good as the diligence of the clerks who search the records. It is easy to see why a clerk might pick up OBPI but fail to pick up the shoulder dystocia that caused it. Shoulder dystocia will have been recorded (if at all) only by the midwife or the doctor who conducted the delivery and only in the course of describing the birth. That page of the notes is not one to which the clerks would normally turn, looking for a diagnosis. However, the presence of OBPI is known to midwives, physiotherapists, obstetricians, orthopaedic surgeons, paediatricians, etc. It is 'all over' the notes and could hardly be missed. The production of these figures was claimed by the authors to prove their theory in support of maternal propulsive effort as the causative factor.

[12.36] So is maternal propulsive effort a reality? Indeed it is and there are very well authenticated cases in the literature, eye witness accounts of babies born precipitately (in one case 'shot across the bed'!) where the injury occurs to a baby 'untouched by human hand'. In other words a precipitate delivery may be associated with an injury that is not due to traction. The explanation is not difficult. The mechanism is similar to that observed in whiplash. The fetal head advancing swiftly down the birth canal has a velocity of its own when the shoulder is suddenly arrested. For a few milliseconds therefore there will be a significant distraction force between the head and the shoulder, sufficient to cause injury.

[12.37] Once the head is arrested that cannot happen. The only way that the mother can exert a force upon the baby to deliver the obstructed shoulder is through the baby's spine. Only the spine will transmit the force, for the rest of the baby is floppy and compressible. The birth canal is not a straight tube. It is a canal whose posterior wall is many times longer than the anterior wall. This is the 'curve of Carus'.

Figure 12.2
The curve of Carus and its effect on the maternal force
transmitted through the baby

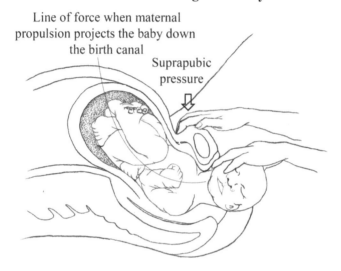

[12.38] Once the head is arrested any force from the mother transmitted through the fetal spine will tend to move the head towards the anterior shoulder, not away from it. 'Labor forces are compressive and expulsive, not traction or stretching'.[10]

[12.39] The theory of maternal effort reaches its apotheosis where there is operative vaginal delivery. There is of course in such cases no effective maternal effort; it does not however deter the defendants from attempting to invoke it.

THE LESSER OF TWO EVILS

[12.40] When the baby's progress down the birth canal is arrested by the anterior shoulder being caught on the symphysis pubis the baby has no oxygen supply. The umbilical cord is by this time compressed by the bones of the maternal pelvis against the fetal body and will not transmit oxygen effectively. The baby,

10. O'Leary, 'In Utero causation of Brachial Plexus Injury: Myth or Mystery?' in *Shoulder Dystocia and Birth Injury* (3rd edn, Humana Press, 2009).

although their head is in air, cannot expand the chest and therefore cannot breathe. Large term infants will withstand such conditions for about ten minutes. After that time there will be increasing hypoxic injury and eventually the baby will die. There are occasions when the accoucheur, midwife or doctor will be able to say to the court that they had tried everything they knew to deliver the baby and were fearful that any further delay would lead to brain damage, cerebral palsy and even death. In those circumstances they felt entitled to pull harder on the fetal head and risk brachial plexus injury as the lesser of two evils. This honest defence is seldom heard but the court would rightly have sympathy for a doctor or midwife caught in this dilemma who made such a decision.

THE LAW

[12.41] A shoulder dystocia claim will ordinarily be made on the following premise: that there was such an injury to a baby's brachial plexus nerves resulting in permanent obstetric brachial plexus injury (wrongly known as Erb's palsy) and that the person delivering the baby must have 'pulled too hard'. The defence routinely advanced in response to such a claim is that only reasonable force was used, and even if a greater force than normal was used, it was used in order to avoid an even more serious consequence, asphyxial injury. The reply to that defence may then be that shoulder dystocia should have been predicted and delivery effected earlier by way of Caesarean section.[11]

[12.42] Inappropriate manoeuvres such as excessive lateral traction and fundal pressure would be impossible to defend in current practice. Hospitals should continually review and revise their management guidelines with reference to changing evidence-based practice.

[12.43] Aside from breach of duty, highly complicated issues arise in the context of causation. The answer of a defendant to the claim that excessive force was applied is that there are alternative causes of brachial plexus injury – causes related to the normal forces of labour and/or no more than normal delivery applied forces.

[12.44] What can be gleaned from the claims that have made it all the way to the point of court determination is that in the presence of macrosomia, anterior shoulder injury and recorded shoulder dystocia, it is likely that the injury was caused by traction. The issue a court will have to decide then is whether the

---

11.   Matthews, 'Birth Injuries: Shouldering the Blame' (2005) PILJ 36 (June) 11–14.

traction applied was necessary and appropriate in the circumstances, or whether it was unreasonable.

[12.45] A defendant will frequently seek to rely on the fact that either there was no recorded shoulder dystocia, or there was but that the injury suffered was one to the baby's *posterior* shoulder. If these arguments are successfully advanced and favoured by a court, the defendant may escape liability for injury.

[12.46] In shoulder dystocia cases as in any other obstetric fault cases, the final moments preceding the child's delivery and birth are critical.

[12.47] Establishing breach of duty will be the responsibility of either an obstetrician or a midwife (occasionally both). The principal causation expert will be an orthopaedic surgeon with a special interest and experience of brachial plexus injury. However, a number of other experts will need to be engaged to assist with quantum.

[12.48] Reports on quantum will have to be procured from a number of experts including from a physiotherapist, an occupational therapist, and a vocational consultant. Much will depend on the plaintiff's ability to earn a living; paradoxically, the higher the standard of education, the less will be the plaintiff's reliance on having two fully functioning arms. Particularly for a girl scars around the neck from previous surgery will also sound in damages. Therapeutic treatment options for the future and their costing will have to be considered.

[12.49] The plaintiff in *O'Sullivan v Kiernan and Bon Secours Health Systems Ltd*[12] suffered a fractured clavicle and stretching injury to her brachial plexus during her delivery which resulted in Erb's Palsy. She was awarded €256,766.02 having established that her injury was caused by the negligence of the first defendant consultant obstetrician, who applied excessive traction to her head during delivery on 20 January 1996, two years after the watershed.[13] It was surprisingly found that the objectives of the McRoberts manoeuvre could be achieved in the left lateral position.

[12.50] Substantial conflict arose between the evidence of those who participated in the labour process and those who had a recollection of it: between the evidence of the first defendant and that of the plaintiff's parents.

[12.51] O'Neill J concluded that the version of events given by the parents was to be preferred to that of the first defendant. He was satisfied that in the detailed

---

12.   *O'Sullivan v Kiernan and Bon Secours Health Systems Ltd* [2004] IEHC 78.
13.   The watershed year was 1994, the year in which the McRoberts manoeuvre was first advocated in a popular UK publication.

account given by the first defendant of the delivery there was 'a large element of reconstruction of events based upon his professional knowledge and expertise' and that he was 'left with the unshakeable impression that much of that detail resulted from a reconstruction of events, in a genuine effort by the first named defendant to recover what he perceived to be an actual memory of the events'.

[12.52] Whilst both mother and father described the delivery of the plaintiff in different terms, there was substantial convergence between their accounts. They were in exact agreement on the fact that the position of the mother was not changed to the left lateral position and that supra pubic pressure was not applied by anyone. They also agreed that the delivery took place very rapidly, in the space of about three and a half to four minutes at most from the removal of the electrode from the baby's scalp to enable the ventouse to be applied.

[12.53] Interestingly, the judge was also influenced by a note made by the first defendant shortly after the birth of the plaintiff which read: '20th January, 1996, 23.45 vacuum assisted delivery because failure to progress in second stage and CTG dips difficulty delivering right shoulder?. Fracture clavicle'.

[12.54] It was remarkable that the first defendant would have noted in the record merely 'difficulty delivering right shoulder'. This led O'Neill J to the conclusion that he had neither formed the view that there was a shoulder dystocia, nor made a diagnosis of shoulder dystocia at the time of delivery. The judge also considered it remarkable that no mention at all was made in the note of the procedure used to overcome shoulder dystocia.

[12.55] The first defendant gave an incredible explanation, saying that he had been trained to make short notes rather than long notes on the basis that shorter ones are more likely to be read. This did not convince the judge who said: 'the universal desirability of brevity simply fails to explain an omission such as this from this note. A single short additional sentence was all that was required, to say that shoulder dystocia had been encountered and was overcome by the McRoberts manoeuvre'.

[12.56] It was held that, on the balance of probabilities, the plaintiff's injury was caused by the application of excessive traction to her head during delivery. She was delivered in the space of about four minutes or less from removal of the electrode from the scalp, in all likelihood, on the first contraction after delivery of the head in circumstances whereby the defendant had not diagnosed shoulder dystocia and where he applied excessive traction, without resorting to any variant of the McRoberts manoeuvre or the application of supra pubic pressure. The fact that the baby was in excellent condition tended to indicate that the plaintiff was not deprived of oxygen for any significant time, and certainly not for the seven minutes that would have been required to put the mother in the left lateral position and then to adopt the McRoberts manoeuvre with delivery on a subsequent contraction.

[12.57] Not long after that decision, the plaintiff in *Keogh v Dowling and Connolly*[14] alleged failure to detect and properly deal with shoulder dystocia and in failing to do so, applying unnecessary lateral traction which resulted in his Erb's palsy. The plaintiff was born on 29 July 2000, six years after the watershed.

[12.58] Johnson J, in dismissing the claim, held that the onus of establishing that on the balance of probabilities there was a shoulder dystocia which was undetected and untreated had not been discharged. Remarkably, no alternative theory was advanced by the defendant by way of explanation for the injury sustained in this case. Surely it would have been in the interests of justice that the defendant at least be called upon to offer an alternative theory for the causation of injury.

[12.59] The obstetrician whom the plaintiff's mother had been attending throughout her pregnancy was not available on the date she was admitted to hospital and so the second defendant was covering for him. Both of the parties reached a consensus that the plaintiff suffered a brachial plexus injury; that it was mild to moderate in degree; and that it was suffered at or before the time of his birth.

[12.60] During the course of the delivery, the ventouse which had been applied twice slipped off, and so a Neville Barnes forceps was applied. The second defendant recorded that the Neville Barnes forceps produced an easy delivery of a male infant and that he was in good condition. Some 40 minutes later however it was noted that the plaintiff's right arm was not functioning properly.

[12.61] The plaintiff's mother gave evidence that she was given an epidural but yet she felt a very strong pulling traction at the time prior to the emergence of the baby's head. She said that there was no delay between the emergence of the head and the remainder of the delivery. The second defendant gave evidence that, albeit she had no personal recollection of the birth, her notes were very straightforward. She said she was satisfied that if there had in fact been a shoulder dystocia, she would have detected it and recorded it.

---

14. *Keogh v Dowling and Connolly* [2005] IEHC 359.

[12.62] It was agreed between the experts for both parties that shoulder dystocia is an element in the majority of cases involving this type of injury but a dispute arose as to how big that majority was.

[12.63] The plaintiff's expert was of view that in 5.9 per cent of cases shoulder dystocia does not take place. He was of the view that there must have been an undetected problem which was not recognised. He relied on an article[15] which stated that in 5.9 per cent of the cases there was no obvious explanation and 'no identifiable indicator of the application of unusual force in the course of delivery, that is, they were not delivered by assisted or breech delivery and did not have shoulder dystocia or other injuries and were not macrosomic' but went on to say that 'the most important factors associated with the occurrence of brachial plexus syndrome or Erb's palsy had been reported previously were shoulder dystocia, assisted delivery and high birth weight'. On the other hand, the defendant's expert was of the view that in up to 25 per cent of cases shoulder dystocia does not take place. He said that had there been a shoulder dystocia, there would have been a delay between the emergence of the head with the forceps and the delivery of the trunk.

[12.64] Johnson J was very impressed with the defendant's witnesses and found the authorities relied on by the defendant compelling, particularly one[16] which stated that 'these traumatic injuries are not necessarily a result of shoulder dystocia although Erb's palsy is usually considered to be specifically associated with shoulder dystocia no perinatal risk factors could be identified in about one third of Erb's palsy, which most likely have arisen in urethra [sic]'. The judge was of the view that such a figure from an authoritative book on obstetrics would appear to fly completely against the statistics alluded to by the plaintiff's expert.

[12.65] He went on to say that the delivery, though assisted, was perfectly normal and simple and the notes indicated, in his view, that the case fell within that range wherein shoulder dystocia was not a feature in the cause of brachial plexus.

Everard v HSE[17] was an unusual case involving a brachial plexus injury following an operative vaginal delivery during which it was alleged by the

15. Evans-Jones, Kay, Weindling, Cranny, Ward, Bradshaw and Hernon, *Congenital Brachial Plexus Palsy Incidences, Causes and Outcome in the United Kingdom and the Republic of Ireland,* Arch Dis Child Fetal Neonatal Ed 2003; 88:F185-F189.
16. *Turnbull's Obstetrics* (3rd edn) 596.
17. *Everard v HSE* [2015] IEHC 592.

defendant that shoulder dystocia did not occur – but the McRoberts manoeuvre was employed 'prophylactically'. The court surprisingly found that the injured shoulder was posterior at the time of delivery – based solely upon one abdominal palpation in early labour – and that the injury could therefore not have resulted from inappropriate traction.

[12.66] In *Ellis v Royal Surrey County Hospital*[18] there was acceptance of the relatively new theories that the maternal forces of labour could cause brachial plexus damage, and that the application of traction was not the only explanation. The delivery was on 19 February 1995, a year after the watershed.

[12.67] In *Rashid v Essex Rivers Healthcare NHS Trust*[19] experts on both sides were in agreement that considerable force would be required to have caused the claimant's injury. The case highlighted the importance of the position of the fetus just before delivery; if the injured shoulder is posterior, the claimant will struggle to succeed. In this case the judge found that this was a posterior shoulder injury. The defence argument on 'endogenous forces of labour' was accepted after a thorough review of the defence papers was undertaken.

[12.68] This can be contrasted with cases where the endogenous forces of labour argument was rejected, such as in *Sutcliffe v Countess of Chester Hospital NHS Trust*[20] where it was found that the brachial plexus injury was caused by the application of excessive traction in the presence of unrecognised shoulder dystocia.

[12.69] In *Jackson v Bro Taf Health Authority*[21] the claim that a brachial plexus injury and left sided Erb's palsy was caused because at birth a midwife applied excessive traction was dismissed. The court heard expert evidence of the common practice adopted when dealing with shoulder dystocia, and that the midwives had followed that practice during the claimant's birth. There was also evidence before the court that Erb's palsy cases were not being prevented even where detailed notes showed perfectly competent management. There was no reason to believe that the claimant's injury was caused by the midwives' negligence. They were acting in accordance with what was regarded at the time as good practice. Andrew Smith J declined to infer from the injury itself negligence for which the defendants could be held responsible. The delivery was on 25 July 1987, seven years before the watershed.

---

18. *Ellis v Royal Surrey County Hospital* [2003] EWHC 3510 (QB).
19. *Rashid v Essex Rivers Healthcare NHS Trust* [2004] EWHC 1338 (QB).
20. *Sutcliffe v Countess of Chester Hospital NHS Trust* [2002] Lloyd's Rep Med 449.
21. *Jackson v Bro Taf Health Authority* [2002] EWHC 2344 (QB).

[12.70] In *Croft v Heart of England NHS Foundation Trust*[22] Hickinbottom J found that in spite of their undoubted honesty, the parents were mistaken about the midwife straddling the mother on the birthing bed. He considered their recollection of the midwife repeatedly and/or forcefully pulling the baby's head in the period between delivery and the calling of assistance also to be mistaken. The parents could not persuade the court that the midwife pulled the baby's head repeatedly, or at any time with excessive force. Once diagnosed, she stopped all traction; she called for immediate assistance; and, in relation to that assistance, no causative negligence was alleged.

[12.71] In *Sardar v NHS Commissioning Board*[23] Haddon Cave J found that the injury was to the claimant's posterior shoulder, which meant the game was up. The judge made many comments about alternative explanations for anterior shoulder injury, all of which, in the light of his finding of fact, were *obiter*. The claimant failed to establish liability on the part of the defendant for the severe Grade 4 right-sided brachial plexus injury sustained during his birth on 23 October 1989, five years before the watershed. His injury left him with permanent Erb's palsy and a significant loss of function in the right arm, as well as Horner's syndrome, a right-sided palsy affecting the eyelid and pupil. To manage to extract such a grossly macrosomic baby without serious hypoxic injury was quite an achievement and no judge could possibly have found for the claimant in the circumstances.

[12.72] Courts have found in favour of plaintiffs who successfully made allegations that shoulder dystocia should have been predicted and Caesarean section performed in order to avoid the complication.

[12.73] *Holsgrove v South West London Strategic Health Authority*[24] illustrates how the issue of consent can arise in a shoulder dystocia case. The claimant's parents successfully argued that had Caesarean section been discussed it would have been opted for, in circumstances where a previous baby daughter's delivery had been complicated by shoulder dystocia and there was a significantly increased risk of recurrence. The parents had raised concerns prior to delivery

---

22. *Croft v Heart of England NHS Foundation Trust* [2012] EWHC 1470 (QB). This case was taken at a time of new medical research into delivery and brachial plexus injury. The 'Draycott Paper' ('A Template for Reviewing the Strength of Evidence for Obstetric Brachial Plexus Injury in Clinical Negligence Claims' Clinical Risk (May 2008), 14: 96-100) concluded that causes of injuries were multifactorial and more in line with the level of propulsion used during delivery.
23. *Sardar v NHS Commissioning Board* [2014] EWHC 38 (QB).
24. *Holsgrove v South West London Strategic Health Authority* [2004] EWHC 501 (QB).

but nonetheless were not told of their options, which should have included Caesarean section.

[12.74] The claimant suffered cerebral palsy with ataxic left hemiplegia affecting her left arm and leg, Erb's palsy affecting her right arm as well as mental disability. All of the foregoing arose due to the manner of her delivery, which was complicated by shoulder dystocia. The claimant was born on 14 January 1993, a year before the watershed.

[12.75] Hunt J held that the claim could succeed because the claimant's parents should have been told of the option of Caesarean section and the relative risks, but were not. Given the traumatic nature of their older daughter's birth, on the balance of probabilities, the parents would have opted for Caesarean section.

[12.76] A seven-judge Supreme Court in *Montgomery v Lanarkshire Health Board*[25] was invited to depart from the decision of the House of Lords in *Sidaway v Board of Governors of the Bethlem Royal Hospital and the Maudsley Hospital*[26] and to reconsider the duty owed by a doctor to a patient in relation to advice about treatment. The professional standard was rejected in favour of the prudent patient standard. It was unanimously held that a woman has a right to information about any material risk in order to make an autonomous decision about how to give birth.

[12.77] The mother in *Montgomery* was in her first pregnancy and suffered from insulin-dependent diabetes. It was agreed that the risk of shoulder dystocia occurring during such a vaginal delivery was 9 to 10 per cent in the case of diabetic mothers.

[12.78] Nonetheless, she was not told of the risk of shoulder dystocia. In the opinion of her obstetrician, the possibility of this complication causing a serious problem for her baby was very small. Although the mother had repeatedly expressed concerns about giving birth vaginally, the obstetrician gave evidence that she routinely chose not to explain the risk of shoulder dystocia to diabetic women because if she did explain it then everyone would ask for a Caesarean section and further, it was not in the maternal interests for women to have Caesarean sections.

[12.79] During vaginal delivery the umbilical cord was occluded, depriving the baby boy of oxygen. He was born with severe disabilities including brachial plexus injury. It was found that had the mother been advised of the risk of

---

25. *Montgomery v Lanarkshire Health Board* [2015] UKSC 11.
26. *Sidaway v Bethlem Royal Hospital Governors* [1985] AC 871.

shoulder dystocia and the potential consequences discussed with her dispassionately, and the alternative of an elective Caesarean section, she would probably have elected to be delivered of her baby by Caesarean section. It was not in dispute that her baby would then have been born unharmed.

[12.80] The court rejected the 'therapeutic exception' argument, holding it is not intended to enable doctors to prevent their patients from making an informed decision. Rather, it is the doctor's responsibility to explain to her patient why she considers that one of the available treatment options is medically preferable to the others, having taken care to ensure that her patient is aware of the considerations for and against each of them.

[12.81] Whatever the obstetrician may have had in mind, it did not look like a purely medical judgment. As Lady Hale noted, it looked like a judgment that vaginal delivery is in some way morally preferable to a Caesarean section: so much so that it justifies depriving the pregnant woman of the information needed for her to make a free choice in the matter. A patient is entitled to take into account her own values, her own assessment of the comparative merits of giving birth vaginally and of giving birth by Caesarean section, whatever medical opinion may say, alongside the medical evaluation of the risks to herself and her baby.

[12.82] The Supreme Court emphasised eloquently the necessity to impose legal obligations so that 'even those doctors who have less skill or inclination for communication, or who are more hurried, are obliged to pause and engage in the discussion which the law requires. This may not be welcomed by some healthcare providers; but the reasoning of the House of Lords in *Donoghue v Stevenson*[27] was no doubt received in a similar way by the manufacturers of bottled drinks'.

[12.83] *Montgomery* acknowledges that patients are 'widely treated as consumers exercising choices' and shows that the doctor-centred approach in consent cases does not reflect the modern doctor–patient relationship within maternity services, which is a welcome move away from the traditional, paternalistic 'doctor knows best' philosophy.[28]

---

27. *Donoghue v Stevenson* [1932] AC 562.
28. O'Mahony, 'If women are to give medical consent, they must have all the information' (2015) Irish Times, 30 March.

CONCLUSION

[12.84] OBPI is unusual in that in the 1980s and 1990s there was a plethora of evidence, mostly from the US, seeking to show that the majority of brachial plexus injury occurred without shoulder dystocia. This literature led to the hypothesis that a significant proportion of brachial plexus injury was due to 'maternal propulsive forces'. The methodology by which this was obtained was and remains highly suspect.

[12.85] The plaintiff is often at a disadvantage because of the paucity of the defendant's notekeeping. It is not uncommon to find no record whatever of the side of the occiput at any time during the labour, hence at delivery no certainty of which shoulder was anterior. A reliable observer who can tell the court to which side the baby's head turned after delivery is invaluable in this regard, but of course, most birth partners will have other priorities.

[12.86] OBPI is particularly difficult in this jurisdiction also because the defendant is not obliged to produce any lay evidence concerning what will be alleged was done at delivery until after the entirety of the plaintiff's case has been exposed.

Chapter 13

OBSTETRIC ANAL SPHINCTER INJURY

INTRODUCTION

[13.01] The head of the human baby is uncomfortably large for the passage through the maternal birth canal. Whilst the tissues of the vagina are relatively distensible, the last few centimetres are prone to tearing. Damage is usually confined to skin and the superficial muscles of the perineum, but the proximity to the anus renders that structure, and particularly its sphincter, vulnerable to injury.

[13.02] The anal sphincter is a complex structure (figure 13.1) composed of two principal parts. The whole of the bowel has a muscle layer surrounding it, a layer which contracts and propels the contents forwards towards the anus. That muscle layer is continued right until the end and forms the internal sphincter. Like the remainder of the muscle in the bowel wall it is composed of smooth (involuntary) muscle, under the control of the autonomic nervous system. The external sphincter is a separate structure and is composed of striated (voluntary) muscle, supplied by the pudendal nerve. Unlike all other voluntary muscle the resting state of the external sphincter is to be contracted, thus assuring continence at all times. It can of course be voluntarily relaxed during defaecation.

Figure 13.1

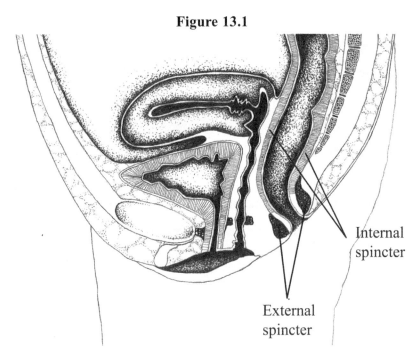

Internal
spincter

External
spincter

[13.03] Injuries to the perineum and anus are classified according to their severity and importance:

First degree   Injury to perineal and/or vaginal skin only;

Second degree   Injury to skin and muscle but not extending to the anal sphincter;

Third degree   Injury to the perineum (usually with injury to skin and superficial muscles) plus:

3a; less than 50 per cent of the external anal sphincter is torn,

3b; more than 50 per cent of the anal sphincter is torn,

3c; both external and internal sphincters are torn,

Fourth degree   Injury to the anal sphincter and to the anorectal mucosa.

First-degree tears often require no treatment unless they are bleeding.

Second-degree tears, involving some muscle, do require repair and should be repaired in layers, vaginal skin first, then muscle, then perineal skin. Such tears heal well and usually have no long-term effects.

[13.04] Episiotomy is a surgical incision deliberately made through skin and muscle so as to limit the extent of spontaneous tearing and in particular to protect the anal sphincter by directing any tear away from that structure. In modern obstetrics episiotomy has become a somewhat political issue. There are those who believe that episiotomy should be avoided, at almost any cost, and that it is just one examination of the 'medicalisation' of childbirth. There are also learned papers which purport to show that a spontaneous second-degree tear heals better and with less long-term side effects than the clean surgical incision of episiotomy. No matter how counter-intuitive such a belief is, it is nevertheless held by many. The difficulty of course is to compare like with like and since most second-degree tears are of much less depth and severity than episiotomy, they do, unsurprisingly, heal rapidly and well.

[13.05] The chief purpose of episiotomy is to protect the anal sphincter, directing any tear well away from that structure so as to preserve continence. There is now good evidence that a properly placed episiotomy does so protect the anal sphincter in the majority of cases.[1] The protective effect of episiotomy is strongly related to the angle at which it is cut. The recommendation is that a 'medio-lateral' episiotomy should be cut at an angle of 45° from the fourchette (figure 13.2). There is a 50 per cent relative reduction in the risk of sustaining a third-degree tear observed for every 6° away from the perineal midline that an episiotomy is cut.[2] There was in some hospitals, particularly in the United States, a practice of midline episiotomy, recommended on the basis that the tissues in the midline are less vascular and therefore heal better. In the 21st century there is now no justification for a midline episiotomy with its greatly increased risk of extension into the anal sphincter.

---

1. De Leeuw, Stuijk, Vierhout and Wallenburg, 'Risk Factors for Third Degree Perineal Ruptures During Delivery' (2001) 108 British Journal of Obstetrics and Gynaecology 383–387.
2. Daly, O'Connell, O'Herlihy, 'Does the Angle of Episiotomy Affect the Incidence of Anal Sphincter Injury?' (2006) BJOG: An International Journal of Obstetrics and Gynaecology.

Figure 13.2

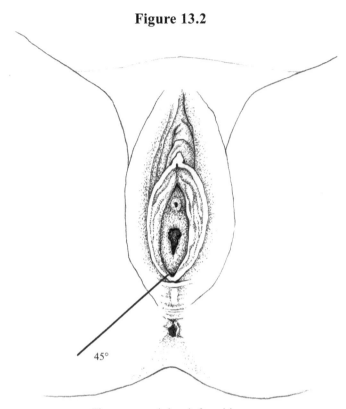

45°

The recommended angle for episiotomy

[13.06] The social consequences for the patient who suffers an anal sphincter injury are potentially immense. Whilst good immediate repair restores continence in the majority (see below) it does not do so in every case and, if there is failure of recognition and/or delay in repair, the results are often poor. Secondary repair is less likely to restore continence. Life-long anorectal incontinence is an injury of truly horrendous consequence for the sufferer, destroying professional, social, reproductive and sexual life.

ALLEGATION OF FAILURE TO PREVENT THIRD- AND FOURTH-DEGREE TEARS

[13.07] The highest risk factor for anal sphincter injury is a forceps delivery. Because the forceps occupy space around the baby's head they are much more likely to inflict anal sphincter injury than is the ventouse. Other significant but less powerful risk factors are shoulder dystocia, a prolonged second stage of labour and a first vaginal delivery. Save only in forceps delivery (where episiotomy is an essential requirement) the performance of episiotomy becomes a matter of judgment. Sometimes that judgment is impaired by unreasoning prejudice on the part of the accoucheur against incision of the perineum.

[13.08] If episiotomy is to be performed it should be medio-lateral (45°) and if it is not, the potential plaintiff has reasonable grounds for complaint. In all circumstances involving anal sphincter injury where an episiotomy has been performed, it is essential that the expert should have the opportunity of examining the plaintiff so as to identify the position of the scar before any secondary attempt at repair is carried out.

[13.09] Episiotomy, like any other intervention, requires consent on the part of the mother and she is of course fully entitled to decline. It is however essential that the real risks and benefits of episiotomy are fully explained to her before she makes such a decision.

ALLEGATION OF FAILURE TO DETECT INJURY

[13.10] The RCOG guideline on the management of third and fourth degree perineal tears[3] recommends that:

> All women having a vaginal delivery with evidence of genital tract trauma should be examined systematically to assess the severity of damage prior to suturing. All women having an operative vaginal delivery or who have experienced perineal injury should be examined by an experienced practitioner trained in the recognition and management of perineal tears.

[13.11] So much is common sense. If the injury is not looked for it will probably not be found. Most hospitals require doctors and midwives repairing perineal injury to indicate both before and after doing so that the anal sphincter has been examined and is intact. There is a significant literature that suggests the presence of 'occult' injury following vaginal delivery. The term occult means hidden from sight, concealed from view, difficult to detect. The occult injury is simply not there to be seen. Such injuries may be anal sphincter injuries occurring alone without any other evidence of perineal trauma. Equally, in the presence of an episiotomy or a second-degree tear, an anal sphincter injury towards the back of the sphincter and well away from the vaginal tear would be properly described as occult. If the sphincter injury is at the front, between 10 o'clock and 2 o'clock on the imaginary clock face, then the presence of an

---

3. *Greentop Guideline No 29*. RCOG, *The Management of Third- and Fourth-Degree Perineal Tears* (March, 2007) (currently under review and with publication anticipated sometime in 2015).

episiotomy or a vaginal tear will reveal that injury to any competent practitioner looking for it. Occult injury is not a plausible explanation for missing an anterior quadrant sphincter injury in the presence of an episiotomy.

ALLEGATION OF INADEQUATE REPAIR

[13.12] The RCOG guideline lays down the strict criteria for adequate anal sphincter repair. The chief components are:

- the surgeon;

- the operating circumstances;

- the suture materials;

- surgical technique; and

- post-operative care.

The surgeon

[13.13] The guideline recommends that an obstetric anal sphincter repair should be performed by appropriately trained practitioners and 'formal training in anal sphincter repair techniques is recommended as an essential component of obstetric training'. It is not appropriate for these repairs to be undertaken by doctors with no previous experience and, at least on the first few occasions of such a repair, every obstetric registrar should be supervised by a consultant.

The circumstances

[13.14] The guideline recommends 'repair of third- and fourth-degree tears should be conducted in an operating theatre, under regional or general anaesthesia'. The reason for the operating theatre is self-evident. The question of anaesthesia perhaps is not. The clue is in the function of the sphincter. As explained above, the voluntary (external) element of the sphincter is made up of striated (voluntary) muscle but its resting state is to be permanently contracted. It follows therefore that when the sphincter is divided the ends vigorously retract away and cannot easily be re-apposed. They can certainly never be re-apposed unless there is profound anaesthesia affecting the nerve supply of all components of the sphincter. Hence there must be general anaesthesia or a regional block; skin infiltration and pudendal nerve block are not sufficient adequately to relax the sphincter. The ends of the sphincter otherwise tend to retract into the sphincter pit and have to be elevated before they can be repaired.

Suture material

[13.15] The guideline recommends fine sutures of polydiaxanone (PDS) or polyglactin (vicryl). Older materials such as catgut and softgut should not be employed.

Post-operative care

[13.16] The immediate post-operative care should include a broad-spectrum antibiotic and stool softening laxatives, to reduce the incidence of dehiscence. All women should be offered physiotherapy and pelvic floor exercises from about six weeks after repair. All women who have had such a repair should be reviewed at about 6 to 12 weeks by a consultant and, if continence problems continue should be referred early to a colorectal surgeon.

PUDENDAL NEUROPATHY

Prof Michael Keighley

Clinical testing

[13.17] Neuropathy is a clinical diagnosis based on exclusion and specific features. The give-away is a patch of anaesthesia on the perineum, often around the anus and or at the back of the posterior vulva. Sometimes the impaired sensation can be more extensive with vaginal sensory loss, impaired sensation of bladder filling and reduced rectal sensation but these are extremes, almost certainly represent a neuropathy involving more than the afferent fibres from the pudendal nerve and are probably due to sacral nerve root trauma. The pudendal nerve provides motor innervation to the external anal sphincter and other muscles of the pelvic floor. It also shares the motor innervation of the voluntary element of the urethral sphincter. Thus the classic finding is a failure of contractility of the anal sphincter and muscles supporting the rectum on command. This type of testing depends upon the complete cooperation of the patient. There are other reasons why a non-neuropathic muscle may fail to contract.

Neuropathy with or without an anatomical defect in the sphincters

[13.18] Neuropathy may occur with or without an anal sphincter injury. Professor Keighley[4] finds that in his experience of 81 severe obstetric injuries over the last five years, only two women had a neuropathy alone with a completely intact anal sphincter and pelvic floor whilst 33 had a neuropathy and some anatomical defect in the anal sphincter.

---

4. Personal communication.

Tests of function

[13.19] Is there a test you may ask? Answer: no. Historically there were two tests. The electromyographic (EMG) method has been abandoned. The alternative is to measure pudendal nerve terminal motor latency with a special finger stall. This test has also been abandoned but, curiously, there is one institution in this jurisdiction which continues to use EMG testing and claims that it provides useful data. Professor Keighley is of the opinion that clinical testing as outlined above is more useful in clinical practice.

Transient or permanent

[13.20] As in all neurological injury there may be recovery in some, partial recovery in others and no change in the rest. Recovery if it occurs is usually complete in two years but substantial recovery may be seen in a year. In this author's experience about half of the neuropathies following childbirth recover, thus perineal anaesthesia may disappear and contractility of the striated sphincters may recover in 12 to 18 months.

Clinical effects

[13.21] Permanent loss of vaginal sensation may compromise orgasm, and psychosexual issues are common.

[13.22] The non-contractile sphincter and pelvic floor results in incontinence of flatus, urgency and urge incontinence, there is often some impairment of rectal evacuation but most distressing of all is passive incontinence due to lack of sensation and the inability to close the sphincter in an emergency. Thus mothers affected by this can soil themselves without their being aware of it.

[13.23] Women with a permanent neuropathy almost always are doubly incontinent. There is leakage of urine sometimes without knowing about it and the ability to stop the flow is also compromised.

[13.24] Pudendal neuropathy after two years is permanent and incurable.

Causes

[13.25] The literature on causation is generally dated and unhelpful. The classical teaching is that the risk is related to the duration of second stage.[5] The second stage is variously defined. By some it implies duration of pushing

---

5.   Allen et al, 'Pelvic floor damage and childbirth: a neurophysiological study', BJOG 770–779; and Sultan et al, 'Anal-sphincter destruction during vaginal delivery', (1993) 329 N Engl J Med 1905–11.

(modern view) by others it is the duration of full dilatation of the cervix. Not all mothers are asked to push at full dilatation. Defining full dilatation depends on how often a vaginal examination takes place during labour.

[13.26] The risk of pudendal neuropathy is not linear with time. The risky bit is the final descent and birth of the head pressing on the pudendal nerves as they leave the pelvis. Thus a big baby and a small pelvis increase that risk. An obstructed pelvic outlet and perineum also increase the risk especially in the latter case if an episiotomy is not used.

[13.27] Then we come to excessive force. If there is an urgent need to deliver or if there is a mal-rotation involving deflexion, there is less available room for the baby to come out. Under such situations excessive force may be used to deliver the baby which may result in a neuropathy. Most obstetricians condemn this practice of using excessive pulling but inexperienced practitioners if they panic may simply pull on the forceps too hard. Forceps are being designed at the moment so as to be able to record the force that is applied in order to prevent this cause of neuropathy.

[13.28] Caesarean section may not protect from neuropathy if operative delivery takes place at an advanced stage in labour when the presenting part is on the pelvic floor.[6]

PROGNOSIS

[13.29] Immediate repair gives good results with 60 to 80 per cent asymptomatic in 12 months. Residual symptoms usually affect either incontinence of flatus or the persistence of urgency of defaecation.

[13.30] Under no circumstances should any woman who has suffered an anal sphincter injury give birth vaginally again. The sad fact is of course that those women who suffer long-term incontinence of faeces seldom achieve pregnancy, in any event, for their ability to enjoy sexual intercourse is severely impaired. Sometimes a permanent colostomy is preferable to the complete loss of anal sphincter control and persistent soiling.

---

6.   Fynes at al, 'Cesarean Delivery and Anal Sphincter Injury', (1998) 92 Obstet Gynaecol 496–500.

RECTO-VAGINAL FISTULA

[13.31] If the vaginal skin and underlying muscle are torn the mucosa (the thin membrane lining the rectum and anal canal) is exposed and may be torn, creating a communication between the anus/rectum and the vagina. If this communication is not closed, or the closure breaks down, a persistent communication will form between the rectum and the vagina (a recto-vaginal fistula) allowing the persistent discharge of faecal fluid. Occasionally such a fistula may develop between the rectum and perineum.

[13.32] It is not necessary to tear the anal sphincter in order to produce such a fistula; occasionally a 'button-hole' tear in the mid vagina with a surgical instrument will produce the same result. The most common accident of this kind occurs when a small edge of vaginal skin is caught in the rim of a ventouse cup; as the operator draws the fetus down the vagina the trapped skin is torn off to reveal a defect in the posterior vaginal wall. Such accidents cannot occur if the operation is conducted with proper care.

[13.33] Such injuries must be recognised and repaired in layers by an experienced surgeon if a permanent fistula is to be prevented. Secondary repair is always much more difficult and may involve a temporary colostomy.

THE IMPORTANCE OF SWAB COUNTS AND THE 'RETAINED SWAB' CASES

[13.34] Whilst the counting of swabs, before and after surgery in any body cavity is now a ritual deeply ingrained in the consciences of all theatre staff and surgeons, it would appear not to be so in the case of perineal repair. Whilst most hospitals have procedures requiring the counting of swabs before and after perineal repair, it is surprising how often that process fails and swabs are left within the vagina, to the detriment of the repair and to the patient's recovery. Such retained articles are often discovered only days later (usually by the public health nurse) and all, not least the patient, are astonished when the offensive article is removed from the vagina and the persistent odour, of which the woman has complained for several days, finally disappears. There is no excuse for it and the retention of such a swab must necessarily be indicative of a lack of care. The consequences are often more than trivial and may contribute both to breakdown of the wound and to ascending infection, jeopardising subsequent fertility.

THE LAW

[13.35] Perineal damage is an area of increasing medico-legal interest. The pelvic floor is also where obstetric and colorectal disciplines, if not minds, meet.[7] Litigation relating to obstetric anal sphincter injury usually concerns one of three allegations:

- the injury could have been prevented by proper care;
- the injury was inflicted during childbirth but was missed by the attendants and therefore not repaired;
- the repair was improperly conducted and, as a consequence, failed to restore continence.

[13.36] When anal sphincter injuries are missed it is because women are not properly examined in the third stage of labour. An injury can remain unrecognised and only be subsequently repaired when the patient, weeks or months following the injury, complains of anal incontinence. Secondary repair often yields disappointing results. In order for a plaintiff to succeed in her claim, she must prove that primary repair would, on the balance of probabilities, have restored her continence.

[13.37] In *Warnock v National Maternity Hospital*[8] the plaintiff successfully claimed damages for anal sphincter injury sustained by her during the course of the operative birth of her first child in 2004. It was found that had her injury been detected at the time of the birth rather than when it was ultimately discovered some 20 months later, the probability was that it would have been amenable to effective repair and treatment.

[13.38] Following failed ventouse and a right medio-lateral episiotomy, the plaintiff's treating doctor, a specialist registrar in obstetrics, achieved delivery of a healthy baby by means of Neville Barnes forceps. Unfortunately, the plaintiff sustained a significant third-degree tear of both her internal and external anal sphincter which went undetected and she was left with significant ongoing problems of faecal incontinence attributable to her injury.

[13.39] The plaintiff's problems which had initially been mild increased markedly during the course of her second pregnancy and it was necessary to deliver her second baby by Caesarean section.

---

7.   Eddy, 'Litigating and quantifying maternal damage following childbirth' (1999) 5(5) Clinical Risk 178–180.

8.   *Warnock v National Maternity Hospital* [2010] IEHC 25.

[13.40] The plaintiff made her case on liability on seven grounds. On the first five of those grounds, the court held against the plaintiff. Those grounds were:

(a) that the practices and philosophy of the defendant hospital were at the relevant time not in conformity with good obstetric practice and exposed the plaintiff unnecessarily to the risk of an injury such as that which she sustained;

(b) a double instrumental operational delivery should not have been attempted in the instant case;

(c) there should have been a trial of instrumental delivery in the operating theatre;

(d) the baby should have been delivered by Caesarean section either before or following the failed ventouse application;

(e) alternatively, if a forceps delivery was to be attempted following a failed ventouse procedure, it should only have been carried out by a consultant or under the supervision of a consultant. On this occasion the doctor concerned was not a consultant.

[13.41] Essentially the court had to decide whether the doctor should have elected for a trial delivery in the operating theatre and/or a Caesarean section once she noted that this baby was presenting in the occiput posterior position. Surprisingly, the evidence of the defendant's experts was favoured, that trial of instrumental delivery in an operating theatre was not particularly well evaluated and was not common practice in Irish maternity hospitals. The plaintiff failed to establish a breach of duty of care on that ground. As for the question of Caesarean section, given that there would have been equal or even higher risks associated with it at that stage of the labour, the doctor was acting within the reasonable parameters of professional discretion in opting to proceed with an operative vaginal delivery. Accordingly, the court held against the plaintiff on issues (a) to (e).

[13.42] The remaining two grounds upon which the plaintiff succeeded were:

(f) excessive traction was applied during the course of the forceps delivery and such excessive force caused the plaintiff's injury;

(g) the plaintiff's injury was detectable and capable of prompt repair by the exercise of reasonable care but the doctor failed to exercise such reasonable care.

[13.43] As regards causation of the tear, the plaintiff's treating doctor said that she used no excessive force or traction when applying the forceps. Following the delivery, she said she examined the plaintiff's anal sphincter on two occasions by means of a bidigital examination using all due care and diligence and found no defect. She contended that, notwithstanding careful examination, a significant number of such anal sphincter injuries pass undetected and are 'occult' in nature, and that the plaintiff's injury was not one which was reasonably discoverable.

[13.44] Kearns P was satisfied that excessive traction was not applied during the forceps delivery, and that delivery was quite rapidly achieved after two contractions. Howsoever, he said he was finding as a fact that the tear to the plaintiff's internal and external anal sphincter was nonetheless caused during the course of the forceps delivery, noting that even spontaneous vaginal deliveries can result in perineal tears as the literature demonstrates.

[13.45] On the issue of the discoverability of the anal sphincter tear, however, Kearns P preferred the evidence led on behalf of the plaintiff.

[13.46] The plaintiff's colorectal expert gave evidence of the dimensions of the defect in question and as to the position of the injury towards the front of the anus, a circumstance which rendered the injury more readily detectable. Two opportunities were provided to carry out an effective examination, he said: a visual examination and a bidigital examination of rectum and vagina.

[13.47] The court was not satisfied that a visual inspection would necessarily have revealed the nature of the damage. However, as the plaintiff's expert pointed out, the episiotomy has a crucial significance in another way. It provided a major diagnostic opportunity when it came to the bidigital examination.

[13.48] The doctor had no precise recollection of the plaintiff's case but described her usual practice, which she would have followed on this occasion. She told the court that she must have found the external anal sphincter to be intact. The notes in this regard recorded only that she ticked a box on a *pro forma* sheet. She did this once only and provided no further note to say she had conducted a second check. But it would have been a very simple matter to tick the box twice or to insert a 'x2' note beside the box on the sheet to denote that two such examinations had in fact taken place.

[13.49] The court concluded that she did not, in fact, conduct such a test, or, if she did, it was not carried out as it ought to have been. The fact that following closure of the episiotomy she carried out a further bidigital examination (although this was not anywhere recorded), also supported the conclusion that she did not conduct such a check or did not do so on this occasion in her usual thorough manner.

[13.50] Kearns P found that this was not an 'occult' injury, stating 'it is a false logic to argue that, because [the doctor] did not find the tear that it must therefore follow that it was occult in the sense of being undiscoverable'.[5]

[13.51] It was held that the injury was in a frontal position where it was more readily discoverable. A careful bidigital examination of the external sphincter injury would or should have revealed the third-degree tear. The discovery of the damage to the external sphincter would also have flagged the existence of the internal sphincter damage. There was failure to diagnose and promptly treat both injuries sustained by the plaintiff.

[13.52] The plaintiff in *Kelly v Lenihan*[9] was awarded €255,500 in damages by Abbott J for injuries arising from negligence on the part of the defendant, a nominee on behalf of the National Maternity Hospital, in assisting the delivery of her third baby in 1994. At the end of the plaintiff's labour, she had suffered a significant tear injury.

[13.53] In the delivery of her first two children, it had been necessary to perform an episiotomy. Her third child was in a persistent occipito-posterior position. Evidence was given which was not contradicted by the defendant, that a student midwife had told the plaintiff to push before the second stage of labour.

[13.54] Although it was repaired, the plaintiff's tear injury caused serious faecal incontinence which had to be treated with a colostomy which, it was accepted, was likely to be permanent. The plaintiff was largely confined to the home and was hampered functionally, socially and in her family relationships. Albeit the colostomy bag improved the plaintiff's life, she suffered irritation where it was attached to the stoma and consequent social embarrassment by reason of odours and threats of odours. She got into the habit of carrying a coat or an article of clothing in front of her where the appliance was attached.

[13.55] But for her injury, it was accepted that the plaintiff would have returned to work by July 2001. She still intended to return to work and would probably do so about two years after the hearing of the case, but her earning ability would be reduced as a result of her condition.

[13.56] It was the practice in Dublin maternity hospitals to restrict the use of episiotomy and to rely on a high level of care by midwives in ensuring measured breathing and pushing of the mother and stretching of the perineum. There were differing schools of thought as to when or whether an episiotomy should be carried out.

---

9.   *Kelly v Lenihan* [2004] IEHC 427.

[13.57] The application of the more restrictive school of episiotomy in the Dublin maternity hospitals was not one which could be rejected in favour of a more liberal use of planned episiotomy.

[13.58] The midwifery regime was critical to the effectiveness of the practice as carried out in the Dublin hospitals. The tear caused to the plaintiff arose by reason of the non-establishment of a management regime or a breakdown in the management regime.

[13.59] In the alternative, the defendants were liable because they had, by their choice of a school of opinion, relied on a high duty of care represented by a management regime, the breach of which exposed the plaintiff to an added risk of a tear. Applying the rule in *McGhee v National Coal Board*,[10] the defendant had, by adopting this policy, foreseen the possibility of damage and, it was held, should bear its consequences.

[13.60] In *M v HSE*[11] the plaintiff, who was awarded €87,400, gave birth to a baby boy in 2001 at Our Lady of Lourdes in Drogheda during a forceps delivery which caused a third-degree tear of her anal sphincter. In a detailed judgment, Charleton J examined both the issue of the management of the plaintiff's labour and the response to the tear of her anal sphincter.

[13.61] The plaintiff claimed that the intervention by forceps would have been unnecessary and the tear injury avoided had the labour been allowed to proceed to a non-instrumental birth. She argued that oxytocin was not discontinued at the appropriate time and claimed that the tear was caused by the episiotomy cut being made at the wrong angle, one that was too close to the midline, and that the diagnosis and repair was inadequate.

[13.62] Since experts for both sides accepted that the initial administration of oxytocin was appropriate, all that stood between them was the time at which it should have been stopped. Charleton J was for the most part not convinced that the earlier stopping of oxytocin would have made a substantial difference.

[13.63] The court found that there was no want of appropriate care in managing the labour. There was insufficient evidence to establish a probability that there was any failure of ordinary care by a midwife, or by the doctor in the management of the labour. It was probable that at a later stage in the labour, instrumental intervention into the birth would have been necessary in any event.

10. *McGhee v National Coal Board* [1973] 1 WLR 1.
11. *M v Health Service Executive* [2011] IEHC 339.

[13.64] There was no doubt that during the course of delivery, the plaintiff's anal sphincter was ruptured; however the extent of that rupture was disputed. Whether the rupture arose by reason of a want of care in cutting the episiotomy with a view to ensuring a swift delivery also remained in issue. Even if it did not so arise, the identification and proper management of the tear was essential. The plaintiff claimed that the repair was inadequate however the rupture was caused, whereas the defendant claimed that the response of the hospital to the tear was in accordance with normal standards of care at the time. While the present condition of the plaintiff was not disputed, the future prognosis for her condition was the subject of controversy. The defendant claimed that the plaintiff's condition was due to pudendal neuropathy and was not due to the anal sphincter tear.

[13.65] The court was satisfied that the doctor did what the hospital required her to do at that time. The issue was whether that procedure was incorrect. It was established that the injury to the anus was a 3B injury. The injury did not involve, as the doctors' notes seemed to indicate, a few superficial fibres. Instead, the court was satisfied that the anal ultrasonography established that a more extensive injury existed after childbirth along the track of the external anal sphincter. The real difficulty for an attending doctor, in this context, is identifying the torn ends, which retract, and bringing them together for repair. The degree of retraction can vary depending on the classification of the injury as 3A or 3B in accordance with the guidelines. The court was satisfied that the guidelines apply to both, as they apply to a complete tear of the external anal sphincter.

[13.66] The attending doctor described the injury that she thought she saw in accordance with the current hospital procedures. If the plaintiff had been treated under correct hospital procedures, in place through appropriate measures from 2002, the description would have been more reliable and the repair under general or regional anaesthetic much more suitable. The plaintiff argued in relation to the repair that it wasn't conducted in an acceptable manner according to the standard of practice that pervaded at the time and it failed to ensure an adequate examination. One of her experts stated:

> I can only imagine that 'a few fibres gone' implies a less than adequate examination and I know that the Plaintiff didn't have an anaesthetic to allow a fuller examination … I deal with sphincter injuries at the time that they occur and I am more interested in their depth, rather than the quadrant affected and my assumption, which may or may not be wrong, is that this was more than simply a superficial tearing of a few fibres … but I have not gauged that according to how many degrees there were or how

many – if you've got a ring and the ring is broken, the ring is broken, is how I see it as an obstetrician.

[13.67] If the hospital had appropriate procedures and guidelines in place or disseminated appropriate information, the plaintiff would have been immediately brought to theatre and an assistant would have been sought. Proper lighting would then have been available. In addition, general or regional anaesthesia was necessary. The purpose of regional or general anaesthesia is to relax the muscle so that the torn ends of the anal sphincter may be identified, brought together, and repaired. Regrettably, this was not done. The result was that the anal sphincter of the plaintiff was compromised. The responsibility, in that regard, attached to the defendant hospital in the management and organisation of a busy maternity unit. Ordinary care demanded that such a unit be kept reasonably up to date in important thinking in medical science. Since these guidelines were extremely important, involving a commonly occurring injury, and making practical and difficult to dispute suggestions, they should have been implemented. Instead, the hospital did not expect to deal with anal sphincter injuries in this way and had no procedures in place to which the doctor could reasonably have been expected to turn. That was a fault in hospital management. In 2002, however, the guidelines were implemented. Had the guidelines been implemented in 2001, the year prior to that, it was clear on the evidence that a better outcome, with a probability of no compromise to the anus, would have been established.

[13.68] In relation to pudendal neuropathy, on the evidence, the opinion of the colo-rectal expert for the plaintiff emerged as more probable. He described what was looked for in any diagnosis of pudendal nerve injury, saying there are three components looked for:

> One is anaesthesia, she has none. One is perineal descent, she has none. The other is failure of contraction of the sphincters in the pelvic floor, it is reduced, but she has some. So, in my clinical judgment, there is no evidence of pudendal neuropathy, and in any event it doesn't fit with the obstetric history.

[13.69] The court found on the balance of probability that the plaintiff's injury was caused not by pudendal neuropathy, but by the sphincter tear.

[13.70] As to the prognosis for the plaintiff, the court did not think that she would reach the stage where it would be necessary to consider vagal nerve stimulation. Good results had been achieved in consequence of reawakening awareness of the pelvic floor through physiotherapy. It was clear that this would be a burden on the plaintiff's life, but she had ample intelligence and determination in following through in the amelioration of her injury and she would achieve good results in psychotherapy with expert assistance. On the other side, however, it was taken into account that the plaintiff was 33, the future would be long and managing the problem would require serious effort.

[13.71] The appellant in *Priestley v Harrogate Health Care NHS*[12] gave birth for the first time in 1992. She brought an action against the defendant for the admitted negligent manner in which certain birth procedures were carried out and the consequences of those procedures as treated thereafter.

[13.72] The claimant was a nurse employed at Harrogate District Hospital, and what could have been more natural, therefore, than for her to choose to have her first born in that hospital. When her time came, an obstetrician negligently performed an episiotomy which resulted in a third-degree tear.

[13.73] Unfortunately, initial attempts to repair the damage were also unsatisfactory, with the unfortunate consequence that the claimant was left suffering from incontinence and periodic bouts of anal pain, due to a condition known as proctalgia fugax, which, while it lasted, rendered her incapacitated.

[13.74] Two issues remained for resolution on appeal: causation and quantum of damages. The trial judge found in favour of the claimant on the issue of causation and also held that she was entitled to damages on the basis that she was and would remain unemployable.

[13.75] The defendant unsuccessfully appealed against the damages finding on the ground that the trial had been rendered unfair by the judge's partiality, as could be inferred from his expressed view in relation to the defendant's expert medical report and the interventions that the judge had made during the course of the trial which had been designed to assist the claimant.

[13.76] The claimant found herself medically retired in 1997 on the basis that she was unfit for continued employment and thereafter was in receipt of a pension. Her claim to be entitled to be retired did not rely entirely on her evidence, but also upon the opinions of an occupational health physician, a surgeon in the employment of the defendants and her general practitioner.

[13.77] The trial judge accepted the plaintiff's evidence to the effect that she found it impossible by virtue of her condition to follow any kind of appropriate employment. She spoke of the suddenness with which these episodes of incontinence and pain came upon her. Against that there was evidence from two occupational health physicians, one being an employee of the defendant and the other of a different health authority. Their view was that, given a sympathetic

---

12.   *Priestley v Harrogate Health Care NHS* [2002] EWCA Civ 183.

employer, it was possible for the claimant to follow some kind of employment within the hospital service.

[13.78] Having come to a clear view that the claimant's evidence was credible, accurate and reliable, the trial judge came to the conclusion that her claim to be entitled to loss of earnings for the balance of her working life had been made good. Mantell LJ thought that the conclusion reached was properly arrived at and not vulnerable to attack on appeal.

[13.79] Consideration then had to be given to the ground of complaint that the trial judge showed partiality from an early stage, demonstrated by an expression of a preliminary view and followed up by interventions in the proceedings which were designed to assist the claimant and disadvantage the defendant. There was nothing worthy of forming a ground of appeal, and certainly nothing upon which an appeal might be allowed.

[13.80] On the second occasion, however, it appeared that the trial judge's intervention was possibly designed to prevent counsel for the claimant making what some might consider to have been a tactical mistake. The court accepted that some criticism of the trial judge was justified but nonetheless, it was not an intervention which could have had any possible bearing on the outcome of this hearing.

[13.81] The third ground arose out of circumstances whereby the trial judge took the opportunity when one of the two witnesses to whom he had referred earlier, had, on the face of it, concluded his evidence, in the sense that he had been examined in chief and cross-examined, to ask a number of questions himself. This is standard procedure.

[13.82] The trial judge was clearly concerned about one matter, that it seemed that neither of those two experts had considered the impact upon the issue of the claimant's employability or the fact that her bouts or attacks came on without any kind of warning. It was to that end that the trial judge asked a number of questions – and it was suggested far too many questions – aimed at getting the witness to grapple with that particular problem. However, the court noted that a judge is not required to stay out of the arena completely and that he is entitled, in his attempt to reach a just solution to the matters which are being litigated in front of him, to intervene if he thinks it necessary.

[13.83] It did not appear that the trial judge exceeded the boundary or the limits within which he was required to perform his judicial function. What occurred was not such as could possibly support an appeal.

CONCLUSION

[13.84] Whatever the precise factual matrix of an anal sphincter injury claim, for the plaintiff it is an affliction of truly horrendous consequences.

[13.85] In most of these cases a moment's forethought and a simple strategy, such as episiotomy, would have avoided the injury entirely.

[13.86] The case law illustrates that failure to detect, discover or diagnose anal sphincter injury is a wrong which will be difficult to defend. A plaintiff may be able to prove that had her injury been spotted in time, it would have been amenable to prompt repair, sparing her some or all of the horrendous sequelae which flow from this most awful injury.

[13.87] There are also those cases where the anal sphincter injury was recognised but the 'repair' was inadequate.

[13.88] A claim will require both obstetric and colorectal expert reporting. Where there is a significant loss of earnings aspect, this too will have to be supported by appropriate expert evidence.

Chapter 14

FAILED STERILISATION

INTRODUCTION

[14.01] Numerous methods have been described to achieve sterility for women whose reproductive ambitions have been fulfilled. No perfect method has yet been invented and every operation so far attempted has a failure rate. There are even a handful of reports in the world literature of women who have conceived following hysterectomy.

[14.02] Most of the methods so far attempted have involved interference with the Fallopian tube. In the first half of the last century a number of surgical procedures were described, aiming to divide the Fallopian tube so as to prevent the meeting of sperm and ova. The most successful of these was the operation invented by Pomeroy,[1] an operation that still has much to recommend it when sterilisation is undertaken at the same time as Caesarean section. The principle of the operation is illustrated in figures 14.1–14.4. At laparotomy a loop of Fallopian tube is elevated and an absorbable tie is placed around the base of the loop. The tube is then excised above the tie. Because the material employed is rapidly absorbed and serves only to prevent bleeding, the two cut ends drift apart and it is the gap which sterilises the woman. Other methods which involved permanent sutures carried much higher failure rates simply because they allowed the two cut ends to stay together, increasing the risk of 'recanalisation' (see below).

Figure 14.1.1

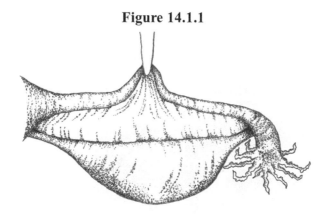

---

1.   Bishop and Nelms, 'A simple method of tubal Sterilization' (1930) 30(4) New York State Journal of Medicine (15 February) 214–216.

Figure 14.1.2

Figure 14.1.3

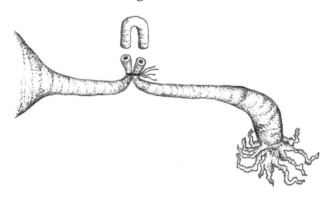

Figure 14.1.4

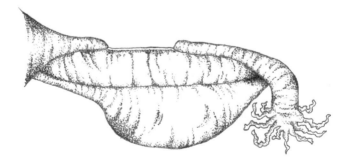

[14.03] In the second half of the 20th century these 'surgical' methods were replaced by laparoscopic procedures, involving diathermy destruction of a portion of tube, the placement of metal clips (Hulka-Clemens and Filshie) or silastic rings (Falope). A third type of procedure was introduced at the turn of the century and involved the hysteroscopic placement of material into the proximal end of the Fallopian tube so as to block it. The most popular of these (Essure) gained some popularity in the first few years of the century but has since been found not only to have a significant failure rate but also to produce unpleasant side effects. At present the two principal methods of sterilisation employed are tubal ligation (at the time of Caesarean section) or the application of Filshie clips (as a standalone procedure).

[14.04] Sterilisation has become less popular in recent years because of the greatly increased efficiency of temporary methods of birth control, principally the Mirena intrauterine system. The failure rates from the Mirena are similar to those for most methods of sterilisation and have the merit of being reversible and of reducing menstrual blood flow.

TUBAL LIGATION

[14.05] Repeat Caesarean section may provide an opportunity for tubal ligation, if the patient wishes it. The abdomen being already open and the anaesthetic applied, the additional procedure of sterilisation hardly adds anything to the risk of the operation. For this purpose the Pomeroy is still the method of choice and it is essential that the suture material employed is rapidly absorbed. Provided the gap between the cut ends of the tube is of sufficient length, natural repair of the tube is most unlikely to occur. When however the two cut ends stay together there is a possibility that some kind of 'recanalisation' will occur. The muscle of the Fallopian tube cannot of course be replaced but the epithelium (endosalpinx) has remarkable powers of regeneration and will grow across a narrow bridge of scar tissue to reconnect the two sections of cut tube.

LAPAROSCOPIC STERILISATION – FILSHIE CLIPS

[14.06] The Filshie clip can be applied through a laparoscope, a procedure that takes no more than 10 minutes. The clips are designed to cover the narrow part of the Fallopian tube, the isthmus (figure 14.2). The clip is not designed so as to cover the ampulla of the Fallopian tube, and if applied there will almost certainly fail to occlude the lumen. Sterilisation is not achieved by the presence of the Filshie clip which will often, having destroyed the tube within it, fall away, sometimes remaining attached to the broad ligament, sometimes falling free into the peritoneal cavity. As with the Pomeroy technique, it is the gap that sterilises the woman, not the presence of the clip.

Figure 14.2

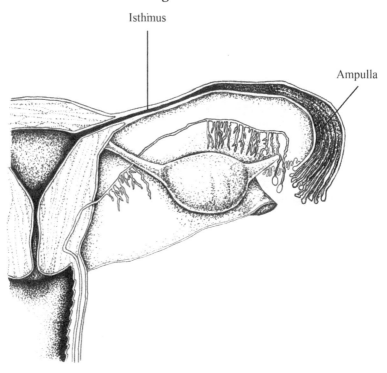

CAUSES OF FAILURE

[14.07] Sterilisation may fail for a variety of reasons:

1.   the patient may already have been pregnant at the time of the operation. It is therefore essential that the operation is only ever performed in the first half of a menstrual cycle, within two weeks of the last menstrual period. To operate late in the cycle is to risk missing a pregnancy that is already present;

2.   the operation was performed on the wrong structure. This error is more common at laparoscopy than at laparotomy but it may occur in any circumstance. The round ligament, a near-by structure, may be mistaken for the Fallopian tube as, on occasion, may the ovarian ligament. There can be no defence to operating on the wrong structure;

3.   a Filshie clip is applied to the wrong part of the Fallopian tube, to the ampulla, instead of the isthmus, thus failing completely to occlude the lumen;

4. the operation succeeded in dividing the Fallopian tube but natural healing (recanalisation) has occurred.

RECANALISATION

[14.08] Because this phenomenon can occur following a competent performance of sterilisation, it is essential that the patient is warned when giving consent to the procedure, that it cannot be guaranteed. Even with the best surgical techniques failures will occasionally occur. The defendant will usually suggest where sterilisation has failed that it is indeed recanalisation that is to blame. The onus is of course on the plaintiff to prove otherwise. Recanalisation is not always a good excuse even if it can be shown to have occurred. If, using the Pomeroy technique, the surgeon uses a permanent material to ligate the tubes, such as silk or nylon, the result is to keep the two cut ends of the tube close together and to make recanalisation more likely. The use of such material would constitute a breach of duty.

[14.09] In most other circumstances proof of recanalisation would provide the perfect defence. In order to succeed the plaintiff would need to show that recanalisation had not happened and that the tube had never been properly divided. The appearances of the Fallopian tube after recanalisation are characteristic and immediately identifiable by histopathology. The peritoneal surface and the endosalpinx are both epithelial linings that can regenerate and will be replaced. However, the muscle of the Fallopian tube cannot regenerate and can be replaced only by scar tissue. Where recanalisation has occurred therefore there will be a narrow portion of Fallopian tube which, when examined will be shown to have no muscle in its wall, just two epithelial tubes separated by scar tissue. If no such narrow portion of the tube can be demonstrated and if the entire Fallopian tube has its muscle wall intact then it is certain that that Fallopian tube has never been divided.

THE LAW

Introduction

[14.10] A failed sterilisation claim will ordinarily be brought because an unplanned pregnancy has occurred. The claim made is that a pregnancy has been endured and a baby born who would not have been born but for the negligence on the part of those who incompetently performed the sterilisation procedure.

[14.11] The usual type of claim made is that the sterilisation operation was negligently performed. Many modern cases involve the application of clips to the Fallopian tubes, so this will mean arguing that the clips were either wrongly applied or applied to the wrong structure. Where a woman becomes pregnant within a few months of her sterilisation, it is likely that a clip was not properly applied to the tube. Sometimes in response to this a defendant will try to argue that recanalisation occurred soon after the procedure. The plaintiff who seeks to persuade a court that her failed sterilisation is not due to recanalisation, a natural healing process, must arrange for her Fallopian tubes to be examined by a histopathologist with clear instructions to identify or exclude 'recanalisation'.

Investigation of the cause of failure

[14.12] Since there is potentially an innocent cause for failure the onus is on the plaintiff to prove that in her particular case the surgeon was at fault and the healing was not due to 'natural' causes. For that it is necessary for the plaintiff to submit to a second surgical procedure at which the Fallopian tubes are removed in their entirety and sent to a reliable histopathologist with the question to be answered: 'Have both of these Fallopian tubes been subject to a competent procedure for sterilization?'

[14.13] The histopathologist can answer that question because, if the entirety of the Fallopian tube on each side has an intact muscle coat then no competent sterilisation procedure has occurred.

[14.14] Neither will there be a defence to a case where the clip is found on the tube but it is not properly occluding the lumen. Care should be taken to ensure that the clip properly occludes the lumen of the tube. If in doubt, the patient should be advised to undergo a test of tubal patency.[2]

Pre-operative counselling

[14.15] Counselling in consent for sterilisation is unusually tricky and causation will remain a problem in cases of failure to warn about the risk of innocent failure.[3] There are many other ways in which a woman may control her fertility and it is essential, in making the choice for sterilisation, that she understands its advantages and drawbacks. The doctor must make sure that she understands two conflicting principles:

1. all sterilisation operations have a failure rate, even when competently performed;

---

2. *McLennan v Newcastle Health Authority* [1992] 3 Med LR 215.
3. Jones, 'Failed sterilization and omission to warn: the causation problem' (1998) 4 Clinical Risk, 12–16

2. sterilisation is intended to be permanent and it may not be possible at a later date to reverse it.

Compensation

[14.16] A new child is generally seen as a cause of celebration, not litigation.[4] The law on failed sterilisation has unique features, especially when the result of negligence involves the birth of a child and when the issues are closely linked with public policy.[5] Can the loss incurred by having to feed a newborn baby really be offset by the ensuing smile and gurgle – when the cost of the former is calculable and the value of the latter is not?[6]

[14.17] Our courts have considered and decided on failed sterilisation actions, and followed the reasoning of the House of Lords in *McFarlane v Tayside Health Board*.[7] According to the 'burden v benefit' rule in that case, the benefits of having a healthy child outweigh any financial burdens incurred in rearing that baby.[8]

[14.18] Where a sterilisation has been performed ineffectively or negligently and it fails, an action can be maintained. General damages will be allowed for the pain, suffering and inconvenience of pregnancy and childbirth and any psychological injury suffered as a result. Special damages will be allowed to cover costs arising directly out of the pregnancy. These specials might include the losses incurred by way of time taken off work, purchase of maternity clothing and of course, medical costs.

[14.19] Although the costs of rearing a healthy child are not recoverable, the question of whether the costs of rearing a disabled child born in these circumstances would be allowed remains as yet unanswered.[9] In this regard, the

4. Donnelly M, 'The Injury of Parenthood: The Tort of Wrongful Conception' (1997) 48(1) Northern Ireland Legal Quarterly 10.
5. Donnelly, 'Legal actions for negligence relating to sterilisation' (1996) 2(1) MLJI 21–24.
6. Weir, 'The unwanted child', case comment (2000) Cambridge Law Journal 238.
7. *McFarlane v Tayside Health Board* [2000] 2 AC 59. This overturned, but did not formally overrule, the Court of Appeal judgment in *Emeh v Kensington, Chelsea and Westminster Area Health Authority* [1985] QB 1012 which had been the settled law for 15 years.
8. Based on the concept of distributive justice and public policy the child was deemed to be 'a blessing'. Moreover, such damages for the child's maintenance would be pure economic loss and so not recoverable.
9. Damages for the extra costs of rearing a disabled child were dealt with in England in *Parkinson v St James and Seacroft University Hospital NHS Trust* (contd .../)

McFarlane decision has proved to be unpopular with the English Court of Appeal, which has latched on to the principle of distributive justice as a device for allowing recovery where the child[10] or parent[11] is disabled.[12]

[14.20] The claim is, of course, brought by the parent, usually the mother – the child has no claim. In this regard, a careful eye needs to be kept on the clock as the statute of limitations is only two years from the date on which the pregnancy was identified. It may be open to a plaintiff to argue that she did not know of the negligence which caused her pregnancy until she was in receipt of expert medical opinion on the matter. However, it is safer to assume that the two-year statutory period begins to run from the moment the plaintiff discovers she is pregnant.

[14.21] This is a particularly onerous burden since the plaintiff will have no opportunity to investigate the cause of failure until after the completion of the wrongful pregnancy.

[14.22] The plaintiff in *Byrne v Ryan*[13] sought damages for negligence arising out of a failed sterilisation. She had undergone a tubal ligation at the Coombe Hospital following which she went on to bear two children.[14]

[14.23] The first part of the plaintiff's claim was for the physical consequences of the failed sterilisation. The second part was for the costs involved in rearing

---

9.   (contd) [2001] EWCA Civ 530, [2001] 3 All ER 97. A mother who had undergone a negligently performed sterilisation was held to be entitled to recover damages for the costs of providing for the special needs and extra expenses of her son who was conceived after the operation and who was born with significant disabilities but could not recover any sum in respect of the basic costs of his maintenance. A claim is therefore possible for the unplanned birth of a disabled child, but the ordinary costs of raising the child (ie had the child not been disabled) have to be discounted.

10. *Parkinson v St James and Seacroft University Hospital NHS Trust* [2001] EWCA Civ 530, [2001] 3 All ER 97.

11. *Rees v Darlington Memorial Hospital NHS Trust* [2002] EWCA Civ 88. On appeal, however, the House of Lords overruled the decision to allow recovery and awarded a conventional sum in recognition of harm done to the claimant's autonomy [2003] UKHL 52.

12. Maclean, 'Distributing the Burden of a Blessing' (2004) Journal of Obligations and Remedies 1, 23–45

13. *Byrne v Ryan* [2009] 4 IR 542.

14. In the related High Court case of *Byrne v Ryan* [2007] IEHC 206 the estranged husband of the plaintiff in the above case sought damages to recover the costs of rearing the two children. His claim was dismissed.

the two children she gave birth to, until such time as they would cease to be dependant on their parents. An Irish court had to examine for the very first time the entitlement to recover damages for the cost of rearing a healthy child born subsequent to a failed sterilisation.

[14.24] The plaintiff first had to prove that the operation in question was a failure and that its failure was as a result of the negligence of the consultant who carried it out.

[14.25] There was no dispute but that the surgeon had failed to apply the clip to the plaintiff's left Fallopian tube. He was a consultant of very considerable experience when he carried out the operation. Kelly J came to the conclusion that that his failure was one which no medical practitioner of equal specialist status and skill would have been guilty of if acting with ordinary care. To quote one of the experts: 'If you put the clip on the wrong place and there are no extenuating circumstances, the operator has got to face the music for that'.

[14.26] It transpired that a clip had been attached, not to the Fallopian tube as intended, but to nearby tissue. The presence of adhesions did not constitute an extenuating circumstance such as would excuse what occurred. There was a breach of the duty of care owed to the plaintiff.

[14.27] All three experts who gave evidence accepted that tubal ligation is not always successful and that it does have a recognised failure rate. The consent form executed by the plaintiff recognised that the operation may not be successful, stating: 'I understand that there is a possibility that I may not become or remain sterile'.

[14.28] The defendant contended that by executing this consent form the plaintiff 'consented to that risk of failure', thus relieving the consultant of any liability. Kelly J could not accept such a proposition, and said:

> It is not a consent to the carrying out of a failure; still less is it a consent to the carrying out of the operation in a negligent fashion. It merely records the plaintiff's understanding that there is a possibility of failure. It might be possible to draft a form of consent which would exclude liability on the part of a doctor for negligent treatment but there is no attempt to do so here.

[14.29] Some months after her tubal ligation the plaintiff discovered that she was pregnant. When she was seen in the antenatal clinic, there was some confusion as to whether she had become pregnant before or after the tubal ligation. The plaintiff formed the impression that she was already pregnant at the time of the sterilisation. None of the doctors who saw her during the course of her pregnancy informed her that her sterilisation procedure had failed.

[14.30] After the birth of her daughter, the plaintiff was discharged without being told that her tubal ligation had failed. No contraceptive was prescribed and the plaintiff subsequently became pregnant again. Her GP, at that point certain that the tubal ligation had failed, advised her on contraceptive measures after the birth of her son. The plaintiff later had to undergo a second tubal ligation.

[14.31] It was held that the defendant was liable for the failed sterilisation. The claim for the costs associated with rearing the two children however, was disallowed.[15] As a matter of policy, it would not be fair or reasonable to visit a doctor who negligently performed a sterilisation operation with the cost of rearing a healthy child. This view might be justified by the opinion that the benefits of a healthy child outweighed any loss incurred in rearing the child. This decision blended more harmoniously with the value placed by the Constitution upon the family and the dignity and protection afforded to human life. Accordingly, the plaintiff was not entitled to damages in respect of rearing her daughter and son.

[14.32] An award of €90,000 damages was made in respect of the second tubal ligation and the pregnancy and birth of the two children. It should, however, be noted that the liability for pain, suffering and inconveniences related to the pregnancies and second sterilisation was conceded by the defendants. Some of Kelly J's remarks suggest that he would not have ruled that way had the matter been disputed. Damages had, rather unusually, been agreed in the sum of €381,678 for the upbringing of the two children, but this portion of the claim was dismissed.

[14.33] *Hurley Ahern and Ahern v Moore and Southern Health Board*[16] involved a couple who claimed negligence on the part of the defendants for a failed laparoscopic sterilisation involving the application of clips. The mother's claim was allowed but the father's claim was disallowed.

[14.34] The plaintiff mother gave birth by way of emergency Caesarean section to a baby boy who had severe physical defects and died at six months of age. She had a painful and difficult pregnancy and post-natal recovery. Very shortly after

---

15. In *Fletcher v Commissioners of Public Works* [2003] 1 IR 465, the Supreme Court held that it was proper to exclude an award of damages in certain circumstances on the grounds of policy.
16. *Hurley Ahern and Ahern v Moore and Southern Health Board* [2013] 1 IR 205.

his birth, the baby was transferred to Our Lady's Hospital in Crumlin where he was kept for the remainder of his short life. His parents were understandably distraught and the whole experience left indelible scars on their psyches.

[14.35] The plaintiff had a blood condition making pregnancy more complicated and a cause of anxiety; she was in hospital for two weeks after the birth; thereafter she had a traumatic period of six months until the baby's death. Moreover, there were actual special damages incurred solely because of baby's condition.

[14.36] The first defendant's operation note and her evidence did not absolve her from liability by confirming correct application of the clips. Ryan J was of the view that there was no reasonable probable explanation for the pregnancy if the sterilisation had been carried out properly.

[14.37] With regard to the claim of the father which was tacked on to the mother's claim, the submissions cited the *obiter* comment of Baroness Hale in *Parkinson v St James and Seacroft University Hospital NHS Trust*[17] where she stated:

> I must say something about fathers ... this is not a debate in which the differences between the sexes can be ignored. The primary invasion of bodily integrity and autonomy is suffered by the mother. If the object of the operation was to prevent that particular mother becoming pregnant, the proximity between her and the defendant is as close as it can be. Even if the object of the operation (and later advice) was to render the father infertile, the proximity between his partner and the defendant is quite close. In both cases the nature of the harm to her is entirely clear and predictable, although it may vary in degree. Of the two types of harm, one can only be suffered by her. The other in my view is properly conceptualised as the obligation to care for and bring up the child. That too is, in the great majority of cases, primarily borne by her. However, there are cases where it is shared, more or less equally, or where the primary carer is the father. My tentative view is, however, that, if there is a sufficient relationship of proximity between the tortfeasor and the father who not only has but meets his parental responsibility to care for the child, then the father too should have a claim.

[14.38] However, it was unnecessary for Ryan J to express a concluded view in the instant case since the child died at six months. The defendants submitted that the father had no claim because he sustained no injury; neither was there a question of nervous shock. Travel expenses and earnings losses during the

---

17. *Parkinson v St James and Seacroft University Hospital NHS Trust* [2002] QB 266.

baby's illness were said to be pure economic loss and therefore were not compensable. The law simply did not permit recovery in this father's case.

[14.39] The mother's claim in respect of the physical effects of pregnancy and birth was of a kind that was expressly conceded but not decided in the *Byrne* case: there is no entitlement because pregnancy, with all its features of discomfort and pain, including that of the birth process, is a natural condition and not an injury. This echoed counsel's submissions which were accepted by the House of Lords in *McFarlane*. The emotional toll of this pregnancy and its aftermath did not amount to nervous shock or psychiatric illness.

[14.40] Ryan J acknowledged that the questions of principle, logic and policy that arise in assessing damages in cases of failed sterilisations have been debated in courts around the world. He noted that in the one decided Irish case, *Byrne v Ryan*, the issue was expressly conceded, so it was unnecessary for Kelly J to adjudicate on the question in that case. He went on to state that:

> the approach of the House of Lords in *McFarlane* is to be preferred and I adopt the conclusions of their lordships in that case. It is of course correct to say that the speeches do not follow the same lines of reasoning but that does not detract from the status of the case as an authority representing mainstream thought on this topic in the common law world. In this jurisdiction, there is also, as Kelly J points out, a constitutional dimension that supports the central conclusion.

[14.41] Ryan J considered that damages should not be confined to the moment of birth but should extend for the six months of the infant's life, saying:

> I think it would be difficult to justify a rule that cut off recovery in respect of tragic and affecting circumstances that framed and exacerbated the recoverable pain, suffering and inconvenience. The experiences that followed and resulted from the negligence in this case were a continuum.

On a test of remoteness as advanced by Lord Hope in *McFarlane*, the post-natal six-month period was to be included.

[14.42] The plaintiff mother was awarded €100,000 in general damages for the failed sterilisation, the pregnancy, delivery and the extra operation arising from the defendants' negligence. The period during which the infant survived (six months) was also included. Although the father had undoubtedly suffered some of the distresses which she had, the law did not permit recovery of compensation in his case. Ryan J went on to observe that, while the plaintiffs had been 'of course entitled to decide that [the plaintiff] would be sterilised for purely family planning reasons', the case was 'arguably stronger' because her sterilisation had been medically warranted.

[14.43] It is submitted that the Irish judiciary would have difficulty in moving past the conferred rights of the unborn child within the Constitution and further to this, they may not even be able to provide a distinction between a healthy child and an unhealthy child for the purposes of establishing case law and ultimately legislation regarding these important legal issues.[18]

[14.44] *Buckley v O'Herlihy and National Maternity Hospital*[19] involved a different type of claim, one which arose from the plaintiff's laparoscopic tubal ligation which was carried out by the first defendant at the second defendant's hospital.

[14.45] The plaintiff argued that the warning given to her by the first defendant was inadequate and that she should have been warned of the risk of an inadvertent injury to a blood vessel and that the complications which arose from her surgery were not competently dealt with. While the plaintiff had signed a consent form, no mention had been made of any risk associated with the procedure of laparoscopy. The issue arose as to the legality of the warning provided and the manner in which the hospital had dealt with the complications. Extensive evidence was provided as to the risks involved and the complications.

[14.46] O'Keeffe J found that a warning should indeed have been given to the plaintiff. If the plaintiff had received the warning, she would not in any event have opted to forego the procedure.

[14.47] The court accepted the plaintiff's account of the bleeding she suffered and the evidence of the nurse informing the first defendant as to the ooze of blood from the laparoscopy site. O'Keeffe J considered that further investigation would likely have revealed that the bleeding from the laparoscopy site could have been greater than 'oozing' and that the nurse ought to have investigated this bleeding further. Details of such investigations should have been disclosed in the hospital notes and could also have been relayed to the first defendant directly prior to his examination. If the first defendant had been informed by the nurse of the report of the plaintiff's bleeding episode, then the first defendant would have carried out a more extensive investigation than he did and this failure amounted to a breach of duty. There was a further failure on the part of the second defendant to advise the plaintiff to return to hospital at a stage when the blood loss may not have been as great as it went on to become.

---

18. McInerney, 'To Be or not to Be Born? – Ireland's Position on Wrongful Birth and Wrongful Life Actions' (Paper to the Law Society, 2011).

19. *Buckley v O'Herlihy and National Maternity Hospital* [2010] IEHC 51.

[14.48] The plaintiff was left with a scar at the umbilical incision and pain and discomfort albeit she would have been left with some permanent scarring in any event, had the matter been dealt with promptly. In such circumstances she would not have endured the difficulties which she did over the course of two days, the subsequent bleeding, laparotomy and the stay in the Intensive Care Unit of St Vincent's Hospital.

[14.49] The plaintiff succeeded as against the second defendant and was awarded €70,000 plus agreed special damages.

CONCLUSION

[14.50] Sterilisation operations, like any other surgical procedures, are prone to complications, some of which will be the result of negligence. Our courts have adopted with approval the reasoning in *McFarlane*, meaning that claims for failed sterilisation are now relatively small. If a healthy child is born following a failed sterilisation general damages will be modest, but may be enhanced by way of any psychological injury suffered by the mother (for example following miscarriage or death of the child). Special damages will cover all of the additional expenses associated with the pregnancy and birth. Care costs until adulthood are not recoverable. The case of a disabled child born following a failed sterilisation is a scenario on which our courts have not yet adjudicated.

PART V
QUANTUM OF DAMAGES

Chapter 15

QUANTUM

INTRODUCTION

[15.01] The word quantum simply means amount. The task of plaintiff lawyers in preparing the evidence on quantum so as to maximise damages involves identifying all headings of loss under which damages may be recovered and procuring reports from the best experts to address each of the headings of loss under which claim will be made as appropriate. This chapter will deal with those aspects of quantum which are particularly relevant in birth injury cases.

[15.02] The assessment of damages for personal injuries and death is one of the most challenging and demanding of judicial functions. Judges endeavour to achieve a just satisfaction for the injured person and to elaborate principles which will achieve this result in the context of changing social and economic conditions which colour the reasonable expectations of injured persons and society as to what constitutes such a just satisfaction.[1] At the end of the 1980s, jury trials were abolished in personal injury actions.[2] The objective was to achieve greater certainty and predictability in the assessment of damages.

COMPENSATORY DAMAGES

[15.03] *Restitutio in integrum* is the objective of compensation for injury – reparation, in so far as this is possible in the circumstances. The intention of compensatory damages is to restore the plaintiff, so far as is possible by an award of money, to the *status quo ante* in respect of past and prospective losses pecuniary and non-pecuniary caused by the wrong,[3] subject to the qualification that the damages should not be too remote. Barton J in *Bennett v Cullen*[4] observed that, compensation of itself cannot restore the plaintiff to their pre-accident position. Whilst financial loss can be made good via a money award, he

---

1. White, *Irish Law of Damages for Personal Injuries and Death* (Butterworths, 1989) preface.
2. Courts Act 1988, s 1.
3. See the *dicta* of Lord Blackburn in *Livingstone v Rawyards Coal Co* (1880) 5 App Cas 25.
4. *Bennett v Cullen* [2014] IEHC 574.

quoted with approval Lord Morris of Borth-y-Gest's observation in *H West & Son Ltd v Shephard*[5] that '… money cannot renew a physical frame that has been battered and shattered. All that judges and courts can do is to award sums which must be regarded as giving reasonable compensation'.

[15.04] Money, of course, is an imperfect means of compensating for a wrong done. In birth injury cases, it is par for the course that the negligence will have had 'a transforming effect on the plaintiff's life'.[6] In this regard, at trial in a cerebral palsy claim, 'day in the life' footage can be of assistance in giving the court a glimpse of the reality of daily life for the plaintiff.

[15.05] Who can envy a judge faced with the task of assessing 'how much'? However, judges constantly do have to grapple with that difficult question. Evaluating quantum of damages is a very important task for which judges rely on both precedent and experience in order to come up with suitable figures. If a just solution is to be provided to a person injured contrary to law, it must be on the principle that the wrong suffered is put right or corrected as best compensation and the law can. The issue ought to be how best this is to be done, not simply protecting the profits of insurers.[7]

MECHANISM OF COMPENSATION

[15.06] The principles and approach traditionally adopted by the Irish courts to assessing damages have been very much conditioned by the fact that the plaintiff is only going to receive one lump sum payment to cover all categories of loss in a single, once and for all award. Consequently future losses must be reduced to present value by taking a complex variety of factors into consideration. The award has to account for all losses, both past and future, and the tremendously difficult assessment will have to be made at trial. This undoubtedly imperfect model was retained due to the certainty and finality it brings to claims – and to the defendant's financial liability. Notwithstanding those benefits there has long been recognition that the disadvantages of the

---

5.   *H West & Son Ltd v Shephard* [1964] AC 326.

6.   Per O'Neill J in *Nelson v McQuillan and Ors* [2013] IEHC 152. The plaintiff was awarded €591,297 in circumstances where the defendant was found to have failed to diagnose the plaintiff's symphysis-pubis dysfunction and failed to manage her pregnancy so as to avoid progression to symphysiotomy.

7.   Pierse, 'Guessing Damages in Personal Injuries Cases – A Practitioner's View' (2005) 23 ILT, 43–48.

current system outweigh the advantages.[8] Legislation allowing judges an alternative means of awarding damages, by way of periodic payment orders (PPOs), has been dreadfully delayed.[9]

[15.07] With lump sum payments significant uncertainty exists; unlike Oliver Twist, the plaintiff cannot come back and ask for more. Cross J in *Russell v HSE*[10] queried the effectiveness of our current method of assessing damages for future loss stating that it 'can be seriously undermined by uncertainties affecting assumptions made as to the plaintiff's future personal circumstances and future investment returns and inflation rates'. Irvine J in the Court of Appeal[11] in *Russell* emphasised once again the 'frailty and injustice' of the lump sum system of compensation, stating that '[i]t is surely time to catch up with those jurisdictions who have addressed this fundamentally flawed and unjust system by the introduction of legislation to permit awards be made by way of periodic payment order'.

[15.08] While PPO legislation was awaited, the *ad hoc* practice built up of catastrophic injury cases being settled on an interim basis. That involved the payment of compensation in full and final settlement of certain parts of the plaintiff's claim and the adjournment of the case for a stated period of time with the balance of the claim to be dealt with on the adjourned trial date. One advantage of the interim settlement is that it allows the plaintiff to set up a high quality care system which can be relied on when the case comes back to court in terms of claiming that what the plaintiff had in terms of care, therapy, etc, before the matter came back to court on the adjourned trial date should be maintained or improved as the case may be.

---

8. The Law Reform Commission reported on the subject in its 1996 *Report on Personal Injuries: Periodic Payments and Structured Settlements* (LRC 54-1996). The President of the High Court established a Working Group which was to consider the possibility of introducing compensation by way of periodic payment order (PPO). In 2010 the Working Group recommended the introduction by way of legislation of a mechanism of PPO compensation for cases involving compensation for catastrophic injuries. O'Mahony, 'Another day, another dollar – periodic payment orders for catastrophic injury claims in Ireland' (2013) 2 MLJI, 107–110.

9. Such delay was bemoaned, and mention must be made of the always welcomed (by plaintiffs) statements on the issue made from the seat of the High Court Personal Injuries List Judge, and in particular made by Irvine J during her time in that position.

10. *Russell v HSE* [2014] IEHC 590.

11. (5 November 2015) Court of Appeal.

[15.09] Cases have come before the court for assessment of damages only where disagreement has arisen between parties as to mechanism of compensation. In the *Russell* case Cross J refused the defendant's submission that the matter should proceed on the basis of a periodic payment order and held that:

> The plaintiff through his next friend is entitled to proceed to have his case assessed in its finality in accordance with the law as it stands. Even in the absence of an express agreement and settlement that the plaintiff is so entitled to proceed, I believe that exceptional and almost unimaginable factors would have to ensue to prevent a plaintiff, who is well advised by solicitor and counsel, to have his case determined in accordance with the law.

That such a jurisdiction exists to intervene in exceptional circumstances was also recognised by the judge who held that 'exceptional' and what he described as 'almost unimaginable factors' would have to ensue to prevent a plaintiff, who is well advised by lawyers, to have his case determined in accordance with the law.

[15.10] Similarly in *O'Neill v National Maternity Hospital*[12] Barton J held that 'in the absence of a statutory framework to provide for structured settlements and/or the making of periodic payment orders; there being no agreement between the parties as to how best to proceed, and absent any exceptional circumstances or factors which would warrant the court in the exercise of its inherent jurisdiction intervening in the best interests of the plaintiff otherwise than in accordance with the expressed wishes of the plaintiff's mother and next friend', the defendant's application would be refused, noting that the rules of court were not to become 'a vehicle to carry into effect periodic payment orders as a means of assessing damages in the absence of and as a substitute for a statutory framework established for that purpose'.

[15.11] These cases illustrate, if illustration is necessary, the urgent necessity of bringing forward long-promised legislation to amend the law in this area.

[15.12] Eventually, in May 2015 the Minister for Justice published the heads and general scheme of the Civil Liability (Amendment) Bill which is to introduce PPO compensation in catastrophic injuries cases.

[15.13] A periodic payment is a payment made to a plaintiff on a periodic basis for a particular heading of expense/loss. Payments are index-linked to cater for changes in the cost of goods and services over time. Certain risks posed by uncertainties to which the plaintiff is subjected in the case of lump sum

---

12. *O'Neill v National Maternity Hospital* [2015] IEHC 160.

compensation are avoided in the case of PPO compensation, for example the risk that the plaintiff lives for longer than the life expectancy assumed when calculating lump sum compensation, the risk that lump sum compensation invested does not earn the income expected when lump sum compensation was calculated, the risk that inflation rises at a higher rate than was catered for when lump sum compensation was calculated, and the risk that a party with whom money is invested fails to honour its contractual obligations.

[15.14] Having waited for so long for PPO legislation in Ireland the hope was that the legislation would be satisfactory. The Irish legislators had the opportunity to observe the learning experience with PPO compensation in other jurisdictions. The Irish could have taken the best features from the PPO systems in other countries and avoided the mistakes made in other countries. It will for example be a serious shortcoming of the PPO legislation in Ireland if it does not contain a suitable provision for the making of variation orders – such a provision is not included in the revised draft general scheme published in May 2015.[13] Their surprising absence could hurt either side in a case.

[15.15] The draft PPO legislation has stated that PPO compensation will only be available in cases involving catastrophic injury where the plaintiff will require lifelong care and assistance. The court is to have power to impose PPO compensation in a case in which the parties do not consent to such, but only having first heard what the parties have to say in relation to method of compensation and decided that compensation by way of PPO is in the best interests of the plaintiff.

[15.16] It states that the headings of loss in respect of which a PPO can be made are future cost of care, cost of future medical treatment, and cost of future occupational therapy and assistive technology requirements. It provides that future loss of earnings can be compensated for by way of a PPO only where the parties consent to this. It provides that the court may make provision in a PPO that the amount to be paid under a certain heading is to increase or decrease by a certain amount on a certain date or dates in accordance with the plaintiff's changing circumstances. This caters for a heading of expense in which there are what are referred to as 'stepped multiplicands', for example the care

---

13. If a PPO includes a facility for re-entering a matter in certain circumstances (in order to apply for the making of a variation order) then a type of case in which under-compensation can be avoided is the case in which the plaintiff's condition deteriorates resulting in the requirement for a higher level of care or other/additional services/goods not catered for when lump sum compensation was calculated.

requirements of a person with spastic quadriplegia who is confined to a wheelchair will change as that person progresses from young childhood to teenage years to adulthood. It provides that if a case is to settle and the settlement is to involve compensation by way of PPO the settlement must be ruled by the court (the purpose of this provision is that it is intended that the court will play a superintendent role to guard against a PPO compensation arrangement being entered with a defendant who may not be in a position to meet its future liabilities). It provides that the court is to make a PPO only once satisfied that continuity of payment on foot of the order is reasonably secure. Continuity of payment on foot of a PPO is deemed to be reasonably secure when the defendant is a State authority, when the compensation is eligible for cover from the Insurance Compensation Fund in case of default by the defendant, or when the defendant can provide evidence to satisfy the court that continuity of payment is reasonably secure.

[15.17] The draft PPO legislation provides that annual payments will be index-linked to the Irish Harmonised Index of Consumer Prices (HICP) as published by the Central Statistics Office (CSO). The draft legislation provides that the indexation rate applicable is to be reviewed every five years, and the rate can be changed by regulations when this is deemed appropriate. In England indexes relating to specific fields of work are used, eg the ASHE 6115 index which relates specifically to wages paid to care assistants and home carers. It will be interesting to see how the power to change the indexation rate by regulations is used. Some have criticised the linking to the HICP, saying that we should be capable of having a more sophisticated device in place.

[15.18] For the purpose of safeguarding the interests of the plaintiff, the draft PPO legislation provides that payments on foot of a PPO cannot be assigned, charged, or commuted without prior approval of the court.

GENERAL DAMAGES

[15.19] General damages are designed to compensate a plaintiff for all past and future pain, suffering, distress and loss of amenity of life. They are presumed in law to flow from the wrong and do not have to be specifically pleaded. Three elements, fairness to the plaintiff, fairness to the defendant, and proportionality to the general scheme of damages awarded by a court, fall to be determined.[14]

---

14. See the *dicta* of Denham J in *Nolan v Murphy* [2005] 4 IR 461, [2005] IESC 17.

[15.20] In assessing general damages in catastrophic injury claims, the courts have been careful to take into account a number of factors including:

(a) the fact that the catastrophic nature of the injuries may be such that no award of damages will be adequate to compensate the injured plaintiff;

(b) that in awarding general damages the court should attempt to take a detached and objective approach and consider the full award on a 'global' basis, taking into account any additional awards of damages to the plaintiff including sums to compensate for past and future care, past and future loss of earnings and other special damages; and

(c) that there should be no punitive element in the award of general damages.[15]

[15.21] In England and Wales and in Northern Ireland there are judicial guidelines for the assessment of general damages which are updated every so often. In Ireland, guidance as to the appropriate levels of compensation was introduced by virtue of the provisions of s 22 of the Civil Liability and Courts Act 2004 whereby courts must have regard to the Book of Quantum prepared and published by the Personal Injuries Assessment Board under the Personal Injuries Assessment Board Act 2003.

[15.22] The 'constellation of factors' which is relevant to the heading of general damages means that any assessment is 'inevitably impressionistic'.[16] Indeed, whilst courts do the best they can, 'psychiatric and psychological injuries are probably always under-regarded'.[17]

CAP ON GENERAL DAMAGES

[15.23] When deciding on a suitable figure for general damages for catastrophic injuries the courts have long recognised that a limit must exist as to how much can be awarded under that heading. In 1984, our Supreme Court placed a cap or ceiling of £150,000 on the amount of general damages recoverable for pain and suffering alone.[18] In 2009, while the recession was in full force, that cap was re-

---

15. See the *dicta* of Quirke J in *Myles v McQuillan and North Eastern Health Board* [2007] IEHC 333.

16. *Totham (protected party) v King's College Hospital NHS Foundation Trust* [2015] EWHC 97 (QB).

17. *Lalor v National Maternity Hospital* [2015] IEHC 423.

18. *Sinnott v Quinnsworth Ltd* [1984] ILRM 523.

examined by Quirke J in *Yun v MIBI and Anor*[19] who concluded that the equivalent value of the cap at that time was €500,000. He then indicated that as a result of the reduction in wealth and living standards that the cap should be reduced and it was accordingly set at €450,000 and has remained so until now: Quirke J stated:

> the limit or cap on general damages might more usefully be described as a guide. It is simply the present threshold beyond which further monetary compensation for a catastrophically injured person has probably become relatively meaningless. It is not a yardstick against which other awards of general damages should, necessarily, be measured.

In a similar vein, in *Fagan v Griffin*[20] Cross J observed:

> It is of course important to note that what was decided [in *Sinnott v Quinnsworth*] was that there was a cap on general damages – not that general damages in cases that fail to reach the standards of being the most extreme should suffer pro rata diminution.

[15.24] In the course of his judgment in *O'Riordan v Dempsey and Anor*[21] Cross J stated that, with the recent improvement in Ireland's economy, the 'cap' on recoverable general damages should be increased, stating 'it is quite possible that the sum should now be €500,000'. In setting the cap in *Yun* Quirke J assumed an annual return of 3 per cent in accordance with the figure of 3 per cent for real rate of return assumed in *Boyne v Dublin Bus and Anor.*[22] However since then the High Court has decided on a lower real rate of return (see below).[23] This strengthens the argument in favour of raising the cap on general damages.

[15.25] In *Kearney v McQuillan*[24] the Supreme Court dismissed an appeal on liability of a decision to award a symphysiotomy victim compensation, but did reduce damages. It was considered that whilst liability must be assessed by the standards of the time; the damages issue may be analysed with the benefit of hindsight. The court illustrated the difference between this and other types of cases by stating:

> In doing justice in the assessment of damages, a court must have regard to the wide range of cases which may come before it. Such cases may

---

19. *Yun v MIBI and Anor* [2009] IEHC 318.
20. *Fagan v Griffin* [2012] IEHC 377.
21. *O'Riordan v Dempsey and Anor* [2014] IEHC 523.
22. *Boyne v Dublin Bus and Anor* [2003] 4 IR 47.
23. *Russell v HSE* [2014] IEHC 590.
24. *Kearney v McQuillan and North Eastern Health Board* [2012] ILRM 377, [2012] IESC 43.

involve plaintiffs who have sustained catastrophic physical injuries such as tetraplegia or other extensive neurological damage with devastating psychological consequences. Such cases may involve persons with most serious brain damage who cannot move any part of their body, but who nonetheless have insight into their condition. In such instances there have indeed been awards of general damages for past and future pain and suffering totalling €450,000. But it must be borne in mind such awards, in general damages, have been made in circumstances where such persons have sustained injuries that are, truly, catastrophic. In other such cases, the physical injuries involved may have been grossly deforming, or the outcome of negligence may have been cerebral palsy. Associated physical and psychological consequences may involve a total inability to live independently, to work, or to engage in any form of meaningful social life.

Accordingly, the Supreme Court substituted a total award of €325,000 general damages for both past and future general damages in place of the award in the High Court of €450,000.[25]

[15.26] Geoghegan J in the Supreme Court in *Gough v Neary and Anor*[26] said he had always understood that the principle of the 'cap' applied only to very substantial damages cases where there was a high element of special damages particularly loss of earnings, stating:

> In my view, there is no compulsory 'cap' if there is no 'omnibus sum' or in other words if the special damages are low. On the other hand that does not mean that the 'cap' figure cannot be taken into account in a general way in assessing the appropriate general damages in a non-cap case.

The plaintiff had suffered the loss of her womb and was utterly traumatised. Johnson J in the High Court[27] had appreciated the depths of despair to which the plaintiff had been put and that the effect on her had been catastrophic. A figure for general damages of €150,000 to date plus €100,000 in the future, totalling €250,000 was awarded. The Supreme Court, in allowing that part of the appeal in relation to quantum of general damages, held that the test to be applied by an appellate court in deciding whether to alter an award of damages is whether there was any reasonable proportion between the actual award of damages and what the court, sitting on appeal, would be inclined to give. The court did not interfere with the amount of €150,000 damages for pain and suffering to date but considered that having regard to the psychiatrist's evidence in particular, a figure of €50,000 was appropriate for pain and suffering into the future. It

---

25. *Kearney v McQuillan and North Eastern Health Board* [2012] IEHC 127.
26. *Gough v Neary and Anor* [2003] 3 IR 92, [2003] IESC 39.
27. *Gough v Neary and Anor* (15 November 2002) HC.

allowed the appeal on quantum to the extent of reducing the award for general damages of €250,000 to €200,000.

[15.27] The Medical Protection Society at the beginning of 2015 proposed a reduction in the entitlement of a catastrophically injured patient in Ireland to the amount specified by law in Queensland, Australia: *circa* €275,000! Why we should not have a maximum tariff similar to Northern Ireland, which is £575,000, is anybody's guess.[28]

SPECIAL DAMAGES: PAST

[15.28] Special damages result from the particular circumstances of the case; they include all out-of-pocket expenses and loss of earnings incurred by a plaintiff due to injury. Individual heads of special damage must be specifically pleaded.

[15.29] It goes without saying that record keeping is very important to support a claim for items of special damages arising in the period prior to trial particularly for mundane items such as travelling expenses.

[15.30] In a catastrophic injury case such as that involving an infant suffering cerebral palsy who faces a life-long dependency, the sum awarded in special damages predominates, and the cost of care will usually be the biggest heading of claim. For the first few years of life however the cost of care will not be as significant as in later years, because a baby or very young child will require a certain amount of care even if she does not have any disability. At the very outset care will usually be provided by family members. The claim made for the cost of such will be a claim in respect of 'gratuitous care'. Sadly the courts have at times made some very harsh rulings on this heading of claim.[29] If a deduction is to be made it should have a rational basis – in particular it should be made with reference to the rates/amounts payable on income tax, USC, and social insurance contributions, and a factor which should then be taken into account which will increase the amount of compensation is that of interest.

[15.31] In terms of gratuitous care the following sensible general application statement of principle, which has been followed in some subsequent cases, was

---

28. http://www.jsbni.com/Publications/personal-injury-guide/Pages/Injuries-involving-paralysis.aspx.
29. *Yun v MIBI and Anor* [2009] IEHC 318; *O'Brien v Derwin and Anor* [2009] IEHC 2; *Conley v Strain* [1988] 1 IR 628.

made by Walsh J in a dissenting judgment in *Doherty v Bowaters Irish Wallboard Mills Ltd*:[30]

> It is certain that the plaintiff will require attention. If he continues to live with his parents, the fact that his parents, even if able to provide the attention by their own efforts, might be willing to do so is entirely a chance, though it may well be a happy chance for the plaintiff; but, even if such a contingency is in the realms of probability for the limited period of the lifetimes of the parents, it does not follow that the plaintiff ought not to, or might not, reimburse them or remunerate them to the same extent as he would in the case of other attendants.

[15.32] A claim for past gratuitous care should be particularised with as much detail as possible. When quantifying the claim it should be borne in mind that where appropriate a higher rate of pay should be applied for evening, weekend, and bank holiday care. The plaintiff should be prepared to counter a proposal for a deduction in the amount to be awarded under this heading.

[15.33] A factor which should be taken into consideration is that of interest. The plaintiff should also seek to have appropriate adjustments made to awards in respect of past expenses/losses to reflect the fact that there is a delay in compensation being given for same. Section 22(1) of the Courts Act 1981 provides as follows:

> Where in any proceedings a court orders the payment by any person of a sum of money (which expression includes in this section damages), the judge concerned may, if he thinks fit, also order the payment by the person of interest at the rate per annum standing specified for the time being in section 26 of the Debtors (Ireland) Act, 1840, on the whole or any part of the sum in respect of the whole or any part of the period between the date when the cause of action accrued and the date of the judgment.

[15.34] In *Yardley v Brophy*[31] O'Neill J was tasked with deciding what method to adopt in adjusting figures for past expenses incurred to reflect the fact that compensation was being awarded several years after the expenses in question were incurred. The major element of the claim in terms of past expenses was the cost of care between 1992 and the date of judgment in the case in 2008. The plaintiff's actuary submitted figures applying the Courts Act rate of interest of 8

---

30. *Doherty v Bowaters Irish Wallboard Mills Ltd* [1968] IR 277.
31. *Yardley v Brophy* [2008] IEHC 14.

per cent. In deciding what method to adopt in adjusting the figures in question O'Neill J stated:

> I am satisfied that using the Courts Act interest rate is not an appropriate and fair method bringing historical cost up to present day values because the 8% rate of interest greatly exceeds the prevailing rates of inflation over the intervening years. Clearly, the best way of doing this is to increase the historic figure annually in accordance with inflation as reflected in the Consumer Price Index, or depending on the particular cost involved, some other more relevant measure of inflation ... I propose to adopt the addition of average rate of inflation of 3.1% or the uplifting of values by 24% as the best and fairest method of bringing historical values to their present day equivalent. I am of the view that this approach is best suited to rendering justice between these parties.

SPECIAL DAMAGES: FUTURE

[15.35] In catastrophic injury claims in which the case is brought to conclusion within a few years of the injuries being first suffered the bulk of the award of damages will be in respect of future special damages, unless the plaintiff has a very short life expectancy.

[15.36] For traditional lump sum compensation a multiplier-multiplicand approach is taken to the calculation of appropriate compensation for headings of expenses/losses arising in the future. The appropriate compensation is the product of the multiplicand and the multiplier (ie the relevant multiplicand multiplied by the appropriate multiplier).

[15.37] The multiplicand is the recurring periodic (annual/monthly/weekly) expense/loss under a particular heading. For headings of future expenses/losses quantum reports will be procured from experts in the relevant fields of expertise.

[15.38] For the purpose of determining the appropriate multiplier to apply to a given multiplicand the most significant factor is the duration over which the expense/loss will arise. If the expense/loss will arise for the remainder of the plaintiff's life then of course the key issue is her life expectancy. The amount of an expense or a loss under a particular heading may vary over time and in such case a number of calculations can be made using what are commonly referred to as 'stepped multiplicands' and 'split multipliers'. An assumption will have to be made on the likely real rate of return so that the appropriate discount rate can be applied to the multiplier, and this will involve consideration of interest rates and inflation rates (technically this adjustment could be a positive factor, but because it has historically been a negative factor (reduction) the term 'discount rate' has been used). Assumptions will also have to be made in relation to taxation if income on compensation is taxable and in relation to other contingencies.

LIFE EXPECTANCY

[15.39] It is generally only in the most serious cases associated with severe physical disability that life expectancy is adversely affected such as the serious neurological disability encountered in those with cerebral palsy as a result of birth-related injury. Quantum in a cerebral palsy case is influenced by three principal factors: level of insight, physical limitations and life expectancy. The higher each of these is, the higher the damages will be. The estimate of life expectancy by courts was traditionally one of the most troublesome but also one of the most important factors in determining quantum. From a clinical perspective, the question of how long a disabled child will live was often asked of paediatricians and paediatric neurologists.

[15.40] There are some major general risk factors which are recognised as leading to an earlier death and which help in the prediction of life expectancy: immobility, problems with nutrition and swallowing, ie whether the child has to be tube-fed, epilepsy, visual impairment, continence and renal failure, cognitive and psychological problems. The presence or absence of these risk factors has to be taken into account. The more risk factors present, the greater the risk to life.

[15.41] The CSO publishes data on life expectancy. The Irish Life Tables No 16 deal with life expectancy by age in the period 2010–2012. The figures published are period life expectancies. Period expectation of life at a given age for 2010–2012 is the average number of years a person would live if she/he experienced age-specific mortality rates for that time period throughout her/his life. The Irish Life Tables No 16 are representative of the mortality experience in Ireland in 2011 by using the 2010, 2011, and 2012 estimates and census of population and deaths registered in those three years. The life table should reflect the normal mortality conditions at about the time of the census. A census has traditionally been held every five years.

[15.42] Over the years many epidemiological studies on the subject of life expectancy for children with cerebral palsy have been published. The two centres which have produced the studies/publications that have been most prominent from the point of view of lawyers are California (Strauss and Shavelle) and Liverpool (Hutton, Pharaoh, and Cooke). These studies correlate life expectancy with types of functional impairment. It will be appreciated that in the case of children functional abilities may change over time. It goes without saying that assessments of the plaintiff should be carried out close to trial and on foot of same expert opinion on life expectancy given so that the evidence in this regard is up to date at trial stage.

[15.43] Strauss and Shavelle have argued that it is not clinicians who should give the evidence on life expectancy, but rather statisticians or actuaries: that the clinician's role should be to assess the plaintiff, and thereafter the opinion on life expectancy should be given by a statistician or an actuary. Their argument has not held sway in this part of the world.[32]

[15.44] The evidence on life expectancy should be given by a clinician (paediatrician or paediatric neurologist) who uses the published empirical data as a basis on which to provide an opinion on the plaintiff's life expectancy. The clinician will assess the plaintiff's level of functioning for the purpose of deciding what group identified in the published data is the best fit for her. The applicable figure for life expectancy will then be fine-tuned to the specifics of the plaintiff's case by making adjustments in the form of adding to or subtracting from the base figure for life expectancy to reflect identified 'positives' or 'negatives' in the plaintiff's case.

[15.45] Life expectancy for the severely disabled is improving all the time. Modern rehabilitation helps to minimise risk from unnecessary complications and improves life expectancy, and increased survival will continue to be the pattern.[33] In future years, possible changes in lifestyle, medical advances, and new discoveries in genetics will have a bearing on life expectancies.

[15.46] In the case of *Robshaw v United Lincolnshire Hospitals NHS Trust*[34] in terms of adjustments to be made to the life expectancy prediction it was held that it was legitimate to increase the life expectancy prediction considering the quality of future care that the plaintiff would receive following the award of damages in his case.

[15.47] In cases being dealt with on a once-and-for-all lump sum basis, lawyers should deal in the optimal manner with the issue of life expectancy so as to achieve the best result possible for the plaintiff, being familiar with the concept of longevity risk and where appropriate utilising that concept to best effect, eg to

---

32. *B v The Royal Victoria Infirmary & Associated Hospitals NHS Trust* [2002] EWCA Civ 348; *Arden v Malcolm* [2007] EWHC 404 (QB).

33. Barnes, 'Life Expectancy' and Rosenbloom, 'Neurological Disability in Childhood' in *Medical Aspects of Personal Injury Litigation* (Blackwell Science, 1997).

34. *Robshaw v United Lincolnshire Hospitals NHS Trust* [2015] EWHC 923 (QB).

weigh in favour of the case being put on behalf of the plaintiff on the issue when there is a dispute as to whether a particular adjustment should be made to the figure for life expectancy. Longevity risk refers to uncertainty in future trends in mortality rates and the impact of same on the long-term probability of survival of an individual, and is usually taken to refer to the risk of subjects living for longer than was expected when a forecast of their life expectancy was made.

REAL RATE OF RETURN

[15.48] Present value is a term used to describe the present value of a series of future payments, assuming a particular rate of return. The adjustment to a multiplier that has come to be known as the discount rate is based on the real rate of return – the excess of the nominal rate of return over the relevant inflation rate. In simple terms this adjustment reflects the expected excess of investment income (which adds to the value of an award of damages) over inflation (which reduces the value of an award of damages). The lower the discount rate the higher the multiplier and the higher the award of damages.

[15.49] Following the decision in *Boyne v Dublin Bus and Anor*[35] a real rate of return of 3 per cent was assumed when applying a discount rate when calculating multipliers. The issue was re-visited in 2014, prior to which for a number of years plaintiffs had been threatening to challenge the then prevailing assumed real rate of return, and to that end had been lining up investment managers and economists to give evidence if the threatened challenge was to be proceeded with.

[15.50] It was in the case of *Russell v HSE*[36] that the assumption on real rate of return which up to then had been made was challenged. The plaintiff submitted that assuming a real rate of return of 3 per cent was unfair and necessitated an investment in equities which was excessively risky, that a real rate of return of 0 per cent or close to 0 per cent should be assumed, with the lump sum compensation being invested in a portfolio of Index-Linked Government Securities. Expert evidence was heard from investment managers and economists. A number of statements were made by Cross J which are relevant to the question of the scope of the decision. Referring to the Minister for Justice's power to prescribe the discount rate by way of Regulations he said 'I do not see that a "one size fits all" rate could easily or fairly be fixed by the Minister, given the different needs and different levels of risk appropriate to different funds, as well as the different lengths funds are required to last.' Emphasising the fact that he was dealing with a case involving a plaintiff who was very severely disabled

---

35. *Boyne v Dublin Bus and Anor* [2003] 4 IR 47.
36. *Russell v HSE* [2014] IEHC 590.

Cross J said 'Whereas the House of Lord in *Wells v Wells*, applied its "no risk" reasoning to all plaintiffs, not just plaintiffs such as Gill who are totally dependent on their fund surviving throughout the time to provide for their care, and where there is considerable logic to that approach, I am not dealing with all plaintiffs. I am dealing with Gill Russell, who is totally dependent upon his fund lasting him for his agreed life span'. In relation to the question of whether a different discount rate should be applied in cases involving plaintiffs less severely disabled than the plaintiff in the case before him Cross J said '[w]ere I to be deciding on an appropriate multiplier for a plaintiff, such as in the *Boyne* case, who required investment of a sum for loss of earnings, and I am not so deciding, then it is very likely that a 3 per cent real rate of return or the equivalent would be appropriate'. On the same point Cross J, in dealing with the case before him, said 'I find that a prudent investor on behalf of the plaintiff given the absolute necessity to ensure that his fund will not be dissipated would invest in a safest possible portfolio, whether of ILGS or in a mixed fund with substantially less equities to give greater security than an ordinary plaintiff who suffered a diminution in his earning capacity'.

The defendant accepted from the outset the principle of 'full compensation', but argued in its submissions that the court should have regard to the 'position of the defendant'. Cross J said the duty to be 'fair to all' cannot result in the plaintiff being under-compensated: 'The fact that the defendant in this case and in many such cases is, in effect, the State and the taxpayer, is no more a reason to diminish the award from some misguided sense of "public policy" than it would be to increase the award just because the State represents a "deep pocket". (Irvine J in the Court of Appeal similarly held that 'It is not part of the court's function ... to consider the effect any such award may have on matters such as the finances of the HSE, on insurance premiums or on the State's resources ... Policy matters are for the Oireachtas'.)

The plaintiff argued that a different rate should apply to earnings-related losses. In deciding on this point Cross J stated that to apply different rates for different headings of loss is to add uncertainty to litigation, and did not consider this good practice. He stated that a preferable approach is to take into account any differential in wage inflation when calculating the final figure for the multiplier. Noting that a substantial proportion of the plaintiff's damages would be for future cost of care Cross J decided to reduce the assumed real rate of return by ½ per cent to allow for wage inflation. The point arose as to whether there should be a further reduction to cater for medical inflation but it was decided that such further reduction should not be made.

[15.51] In deciding on the real rate of return to be expected Cross J based his calculation on the yields to be expected from Index-Linked Government

Securities. The yield applying for investment at the then present time was taken to be ½ per cent. It was assumed that the rate of yield on such investment would increase over the course of the plaintiff's lifetime, and 1 per cent was added to the overall real rate of return to cater for this. This gave a rate of return of 1½ per cent. It was held that to cater for expected wage inflation a reduction of ½ per cent should be made to the rate of return, giving a rate of 1 per cent for a heading to which wage inflation applied. Cross J's decision in *Russell* was upheld by the Court of Appeal.[37] The following clarification was provided by Irvine J in the Court of Appeal (at para 156 of the judgment):

> The court notes that the trial judge, having concluded that a real rate of return based upon investment in a portfolio of ILGS should be set at 1.5%, reduced that rate to 1% to take account of future wage inflation, a factor only relevant to the computation of the cost of future care. However, from his judgment and order it appears that he then proceeded to use the 1% rate for the purpose of calculating certain categories of pecuniary loss of a non care nature. No submissions were addressed to this issue. Given that a rate of 1% was considered appropriate solely by reason of the potential impact of wage inflation, the use of 1% rather than 1.5% to calculate any category of pecuniary loss other than future care would appear inappropriate.

TAXATION

[15.52] The general rule is that income on a lump sum award is subject to tax. However, there is an important exception – s 5 of the Finance Act 1990 covers compensation paid to a person 'who is permanently and totally incapacitated by reason of mental or physical infirmity from maintaining himself' and provides that income earned on investment of such compensation is not taxable income if it is the sole or main income of the person. That exception to the general rule was introduced following controversy in relation to the issue of taxation of income on the compensation received by the plaintiff in *Dunne v National Maternity Hospital and Anor.*[38] In cases where income on lump sum compensation is taxable, a net interest rate is calculated following calculation of the entire lump sum and the net income from investment of the lump sum – this net interest rate gives a multiplier adjusted to cater for tax on investment income.

---

37. (5 November 2015) Court of Appeal (judgment per Irvine J in the Court of Appeal).
38. *Dunne v National Maternity Hospital and Jackson* [1989] IR 91.

COST OF CARE

[15.53] A brain-damaged infant will require a comprehensive regime of nursing care. Reports dealing with both past and future care will have to be commissioned. In most cerebral palsy cases the largest heading of claim is the cost of future care. The practicalities of the plaintiff's day-to-day living have to be dealt with in detail, as do night-time arrangements. The number of carers required has to be decided; the issue of transfers is important in this regard. The number of hours of care or cover (night-time sleep-in cover) to be provided by each carer also has to be decided. There have been relevant developments in the rates of pay for persons providing home-care in recent years, including by the Financial Emergency Measures in the Public Interest Acts and the Consolidated Salary Scales for Public Health Sector Employees (in particular the hourly rate for a multi-task carer/home-help/care assistant). Care providers or agencies such as Enable Ireland, the Irish Wheelchair Association, and the Centre of Independent Living have their own stances on the given hourly rates. Considering the flux that there has been in this area in recent years and the ongoing changes, this chapter will not go into further detail on this heading of claim.

PHYSIOTHERAPY

[15.54] In cerebral palsy cases it is routine to commission from a suitable physiotherapist expert a report dealing with extent of disability, prognosis, required therapy at present and into the future, and the costing of such therapy. The physiotherapist expert will often include in his report recommendations in respect of types of accessory physical therapies which are different to what would be considered traditional physiotherapy, such as hydrotherapy and hippotherapy.

ACCOMMODATION

[15.55] In *Barry v National Maternity Hospital and Anor*[39] O'Neill J decided how compensation for accommodation should be calculated in a catastrophic injuries case in which a specially-adapted home is required. The plaintiff claimed the full cost of acquiring a suitable property and carrying out appropriate works to adapt the property for the plaintiff's needs. The position taken by the defendant, referring to the approach adopted by the English Court of Appeal in *Roberts v Johnstone*,[40] was that the plaintiff should only be entitled

---

39. *Barry v National Maternity Hospital and Anor* [2011] 3 IR 80.
40. *Roberts v Johnstone* [1989] QB 878.

to recover the additional expense of accommodation over-and-above what would have been her expenditure on accommodation if she had not suffered the injuries the subject of her case, and the defendant asserted that the measure of such over-and-above expense is either the loss on the investment of capital used to meet the additional expense or alternatively the cost of acquiring capital to meet that expense, using a real rate of return to calculate same. Furthermore the defendant asserted that the value of the plaintiff's parents' house (from which the family would move) should be deducted, as should the enhanced value resulting from the adaptations to be carried out to the property to be acquired.

[15.56] Setting about making his decision O'Neill J stated as follows:

> The starting point in the necessary analysis of the relevant factors which should lead to the appropriate resolution, are the ordinary principles which govern the ascertainment of compensatory damages. The compensation to be paid by the defendants must, insofar as money can do it, put the plaintiff in the same position as she would be in, if the wrongdoing had not occurred. That involves a consideration of the actual effects of the wrongdoing on the plaintiff, and also a consideration of where the plaintiff would be, and how her life would progress, if she had not suffered the injury in question ... If the plaintiff had not suffered these injuries, the probability is that her life would take the normal course, in the sense that she would have attended school, probably progressed into employment, and in due course, acquired her own accommodation, either with or without the aid of a husband or partner. Thus, factors to be taken into account are that the plaintiff would have acquired accommodation in the future by expending her own income for that purpose. Therefore, what she has to be compensated for is the additional cost of accommodation beyond that which she would, in the ordinary course, herself have incurred in the course of her life, had her capacity to provide for her own accommodation not been destroyed by the injuries suffered. In my view, that is the core decisive principle which must govern the ascertainment of the amount of compensation to be paid to the plaintiff in respect of her future accommodation needs.

[15.57] O'Neill J quoted a passage from the judgment of Walsh J in the Supreme Court in *Doherty v Bowaters Irish Wallboard Mills Ltd*[41] which, he said:

> makes it clear that where a house is to be purchased for the purposes of providing for the accommodation needs of a disabled plaintiff, the value of the capital asset which will accrue to the plaintiff must be discounted, and only the additional cost of providing the necessary accommodation,

---

41.   *Doherty v Bowaters Irish Wallboard Mills Ltd* [1968] IR 277.

but which does not result in an enduring or appreciating asset, can be the subject matter of compensation to be paid by the tortfeasor. Thus, the principle seems to be that the defendant is only obliged to compensate for that part of the additional cost of providing accommodation, which is a 'wasting expenditure' or, in other words, an expenditure on assets which will be consumed over the expected lifetime of the plaintiff.

[15.58] O'Neill J held that the defendant was entitled to credit commensurate with the value of the benefit to the plaintiff of having accommodation provided for her by her parents during her childhood or minority. At the time of the trial the plaintiff was one of a family of four – but he stated that 'she may find herself sharing this accommodation with more children before too long; indeed, that is a probability'. In terms of the factors taken into account in deciding on the extent of the benefit to the plaintiff of having accommodation provided for her during her childhood or minority O'Neill J stated:

> Having regard to the nature of the occupation of a family home by any individual child and having regard to the number of adult and child occupants of this house during the plaintiff's minority, I would be of the view that the plaintiff's benefit in this regard could not be considered to exceed one-sixth of the value of the house.

Credit was to be given to the defendant for this one-sixth share of the plaintiff in her family home. He dealt with the issue of setting off the value of the then present family home against the value of the property to be purchased for the plaintiff as follows:

> the plaintiff's parents' obligation to provide accommodation to the plaintiff would end, in all probability, with the expiration of the plaintiff's minority or soon thereafter. This corresponds approximately to about one-half of the plaintiff's life expectancy. Thus, in my opinion, it necessarily follows that insofar as the first named defendant seeks to have the entire value of the current family home taken into account as representing the value of, or a part of the value of the plaintiff's future accommodation for the duration of her life expectancy, there must be an apportionment of that value to reflect the fact that, upon reaching adult status, the plaintiff would, but for her injuries, no longer have that accommodation available to her as of right, nor, indeed, as a matter of probability, would she continue to avail of it, having assumed normal adult status, and from then on availing of the normal opportunities of life, including obtaining her own accommodation. Thus, in my view, to reflect the fact that the family home would, but for her injuries, only be available to the plaintiff for approximately half of her current expected lifespan, the benefit to the plaintiff of her share in that accommodation must be reduced by a half to reflect this. Thus, I have to come to the conclusion that her benefit in this regard is equivalent to one-twelfth of the value of the house.

[15.59] O'Neill J dealt with of the issue of the enhancement of the value of the property to be acquired by virtue of the adaptations to it as follows:

> Like the Law Commission in the United Kingdom, I prefer the approach adopted in the case of *Willett v. North Bedfordshire Health Authority* [1993] PIQR, Q 166, to the approach taken in the *Roberts v. Johnson* case to the treatment of the cost of alterations. In my view, this approach is much more consistent with the core reasoning applicable to the acquisition of assets with an enduring capital value, as set out in the *Doherty v. Bowaters* case and in *Roberts v. Johnson*. Using this approach, one identifies that portion of the cost of the alterations which does not produce any enhancement of value and that is treated then as a wasted or wasting asset, which, of course, is what it is. The balance of the cost of alterations which, in fact, produces an enduring capital value, is then treated in exactly the same way as the purchase cost of a new house for the purposes of calculating compensation to be paid by a tortfeasor. In order not to put in the hands of a plaintiff the full enduring capital cost, the compensation is calculated actuarially based on the assumption of a 3% return on capital multiplied by the appropriate multiplier.

LOSS OF EARNINGS

[15.60] In a claim for loss of earnings on behalf of a child who has suffered injuries at birth the following headings should, as appropriate, be covered:

(a) loss of earnings during the late teens and early twenties if it is the case that the plaintiff would likely but for her injury engage in temporary/part-time work while undergoing education and/or training during these years;

(b) loss of earnings up to retirement age or expected time of death if sooner than normal retirement age (this period can be divided into parts if appropriate because of increases in pay as a career advances);

(c) loss of earnings during the 'lost years' if the plaintiff is expected to die before normal retirement age; and

(d) loss of related benefits such as pension benefits.

[15.61] Calculating loss of earnings which will likely be suffered by a child who has suffered injury at birth is a rough science. Sometimes it will be necessary to make the relevant assessment when the child has not started formal education or when the child has only been in formal education for a short time. In such cases a vocational consultant will interview family members and will consider the family educational history and working history for the purpose of forecasting how the plaintiff would have fared in terms of her working life if she had not suffered the injuries in respect of which claim is made in her case. Before the vocational consultant furnishes a report he should be furnished with copies of reports of other experts in the case which relate to physical and mental impairments suffered by the plaintiff. In terms of impact on the plaintiff's ability for education, reports should, if appropriate, be procured from a neuropsychologist (who will report on cognitive functioning), a speech and language therapist, and an educational psychologist. Where available school/ educational reports and exam results should be available. At trial, evidence should, as appropriate, be called from one or more of the plaintiff's teachers or other competent persons from her school or educational institution.

[15.62] A 'lost years' earnings claim refers to a claim for loss of expected earnings during those years of working and earning that the plaintiff has lost out on due to reduced life expectancy resulting from the defendant's negligence. The authority relied on in support of lost years earnings claims is the following statement made by Walsh J in the Supreme Court in *Doherty v Bowaters Irish Wallboard Mills Ltd*:[42]

> The evidence of the actuary called on behalf of the plaintiff was that the capitalised value at the date of the trial of the plaintiff's loss of earnings for the future would be £9,335. That was on the assumption of an actual life expectancy of 28½ years. This figure was taken and acted upon on the assumption that the plaintiff was not entitled to recover, as part of his damages, any sum in respect of the loss of wages for the number of years by which his expectation of life had been reduced, which in this case was approximately ten years. On this matter the learned trial judge expressed the view that that was the correct legal position. In my opinion the period or the length of time by which the expectation of life has been reduced must also be taken into account, though of course for that particular period the sum to be considered would not be the gross loss of wages for the period but the surplus, if any, after providing for what it would have cost him to live during those years if he had not had the accident.

[15.63] Since *Reddy v Bates*[43] it has been the practice in appropriate cases to apply a percentage deduction to the figure awarded for future loss of earnings to reflect certain risks applying to the plaintiff's future working life. Five such risks were identified in *Reddy*.[44] In the Supreme Court Griffin J stated the following

---

42.   *Doherty v Bowaters Irish Wallboard Mills Ltd* [1968] IR 277.
43.   *Reddy v Bates* [1983] IR 141.
44.   The five risks identified were: unemployment, redundancy, illness, accident and marriage prospects.

in relation to the figure claimed for future loss of earnings as put forward by way of evidence from an actuary (note: Reddy was female):

> this figure does not take into account the marriage prospects of the plaintiff; nor does it take into account any risk of unemployment, redundancy, illness, accident or the like. It assumes that the plaintiff, if uninjured, would have continued to work, week in and week out, until retirement. In effect, it is based on the assumption that there would have been guaranteed employment, at a constantly increasing annual rate of wages, until retirement or prior death ... Whilst the mathematical calculations made by an actuary may be constant and correct, they should be applied in the particular circumstances of every case with due regard to reality and common sense ... There is now a high rate of unemployment not only in this country but in Great Britain and in most of the member States of the European Economic Community. The great increase in recent years in the number of employees becoming redundant and in the number of firms being closed – firms which would have been regarded hitherto as of unshakeable financial soundness – must inevitably lead to the conclusion that there is no longer any safe, much less guaranteed, employment. In my view, this is a factor which juries should be required to take into account in assessing future loss of earnings in any given case, but the matter should be canvassed in evidence and in argument.

[15.64] In *Laffan v Quirke and Anor*[45] Hogan J, in making a 20 per cent deduction for contingencies to the figure to be awarded in respect of future loss of earnings, made the following remarks:

> Perhaps I suffer from hopeless optimism, but it is nonetheless realistic to expect that the economy will recover – and perhaps significantly recover – over the coming decade. Human nature being what is, just as we often mistake of assuming that booms will never end, we must nevertheless not make the converse mistake of assuming that these very difficult times will not end at some stage, even if this present recession is one of unparalleled severity.

[15.65] The *Reddy* deduction for contingencies is notoriously unpredictable.[46]

---

45. *Laffan v Quirke and Anor* [2012] IEHC 250.
46. In England, since 1994 there has been guidance for calculating a deduction for labour market hazards in the form of a set of figures published as part of the Ogden Tables – these proposed deductions for labour market risks were stated based on a study of activity, unemployment, and sickness rates observed in large scale cross-sections of the labour force carried out by Haberman and Bloomfield. The proposed deductions for labour market hazards set out in the Ogden Tables are smaller than the deductions that had been made by the courts prior to the first publication of the relevant figures in the Ogden Tables.

OTHER HEADINGS OF FUTURE EXPENSES

[15.66] In addition to those discussed above, there are several headings of future expenses which regularly arise but will not be discussed here. Lawyers should know how best to deal with the details which arise under each heading, and of course it is important to instruct the best possible expert to deal with each heading. Such further headings include occupational therapy aids/appliances, assistive technology aids/appliances, speech and language therapy, medical expenses, cost of medication, orthotic devices, visual aids, hearing aids, other treatments/therapies, case management, additional home insurance expenses, travelling expenses, additional vehicle-related expenses including insurance for carers driving vehicle, additional holiday expenses, investment management, and costs relating to wardship.

A WORD ON AGGRAVATED AND EXEMPLARY DAMAGES

[15.67] In certain claims, further amounts may be claimed for aggravated or exemplary damages. In *Conway v INTO*[47] Finlay CJ in the Supreme Court identified aggravated damages as compensatory damages which were 'in part a recognition of the added hurt or insult to a plaintiff who has been wronged, and in part also a recognition of the cavalier or outrageous conduct of the defendant'. In *Swaine v The Commissioners for Public Works in Ireland*[48] the Supreme Court again considered the circumstances in which a court can award aggravated damages. O'Neill J in the High Court had awarded the plaintiff aggravated damages in the sum of £15,000 for his chronic reactive anxiety neurosis caused by the negligence of the defendants in exposing the plaintiff to the risk of contracting mesothelioma in circumstances whereby he had been exposed to large quantities of asbestos dust during the course of his employment with them. The defendants contested the aggravated damages aspect of the award and their appeal was allowed. It was generally accepted that a court could award aggravated damages where compensatory damages were increased by reason of:

(a) the manner in which the wrong was committed;

(b) the conduct of the wrongdoer after the commission of the wrong; and

(c) the conduct of the wrongdoer in the defence of the claim.

---

47. *Conway v INTO* [1991] 2 IR 305, [1991] ILRM 497.
48. *Swaine v The Commissioners for Public Works in Ireland* [2003] 1 IR 521, [2003] IESC 30.

While the defendants were unquestionably guilty of 'the grossest negligence', that factor, of itself, was not sufficient to entitle the plaintiff to aggravated damages. The Supreme Court held that the circumstances in which an award of aggravated damages could be made did not typically arise in cases of negligence and, if they did, were not a ground for increasing the amount of compensatory damages. The cases in which one would expect to find awards of aggravated damages were those in which the damages were traditionally described as being 'at large' and in which it could be said that the intention of the defendant to commit the wrong was frequently a pre-condition to liability.

[15.68] In *Philp v Ryan*[49] the Supreme Court made an award of €55,000 in aggravated damages due to the behaviour of the defendants in the preparation and presentation of their case, in circumstances where the defendant had appealed quantum and the plaintiff cross-appealed. The case involved a doctor who had negligently failed to diagnose the plaintiff's prostate cancer and later deliberately and knowingly altered a clinical record to suggest that he had recommended further tests. The delay in diagnosis and treatment had shortened the plaintiff's life-expectancy. While blame attached to the defendant for having altered the clinical notes in the first place, equal if not greater blame attached to his legal advisors who, having been informed of this fact, did not inform the plaintiff's solicitors of the true facts. Not disclosing the alteration was misconduct on their part. The loss suffered was greatly increased due to the grossly improper behaviour of both the defendant and his legal advisors, which Fennelly J described as 'reprehensible in the highest degree'. In *Daly v Mulhern*[50] the plaintiff in a road traffic accident claim was awarded an additional €10,000 in aggravated damages due to the conduct of the defendant in the defence of the claim up to and including the trial of the action whereby after receiving a letter from the plaintiff's solicitor, he denied that the accident ever occurred and maintained that stance throughout the action.

[15.69] Exemplary damages are designed to punish the defendant for particularly offensive behaviour and as such are a form of punitive damages. There should be no punitive element in an award of general damages, but punitive or exemplary damages may be sought separately in the limited number of special cases.[51] Without intentional misconduct or conscious recklessness of a serious level however, a successful argument in favour of such an award in a

49. *Philp v Ryan* [2004] 4 IR 241.
50. *Daly v Mulhern* [2008] 2 IR 1.
51. *Myles v McQuillan and North Eastern Health Board* [2007] IEHC 333.

medical negligence case will be extremely rare.[52] Irish courts have consistently maintained that exemplary damages may be awarded only in the most exceptional of cases and O'Flaherty J in *McIntyre v Lewis*[53] remarked that such awards should be kept on a tight rein.

[15.70] Aggravated and exemplary damages are more easily argued for in claims for assault, battery, trespass to the person, breach of constitutional rights of the plaintiff and the intentional infliction of emotional suffering and distress.

FATAL INJURIES

[15.71] Sadly litigation sometimes arises from death of mother or baby.

[15.72] Neonatal death (death in the new born period) arises chiefly because of infection or oxygen lack. The factors giving rise to cerebral palsy will, if not arrested, lead to fetal demise. The approach to investigation is in every way similar to that discussed with survivors.

[15.73] Maternal death is fortunately extremely rare.[54] The commonest causes are pulmonary embolus, infection, haemorrhage and neurological complications (such as intracranial haemorrhage) from hypertensive disease. An inquest is an invaluable aid to the exploration of the facts. In the 21st century no mother should die in hospital from infection or haemorrhage.

[15.74] Part IV of the Civil Liability Act 1961 provides that where there has been a wrongful death such as would have entitled the injured deceased person, but for her death, to maintain an action and recover damages, the wrongdoer shall be liable to an action for damages for the benefit of her dependants. Only one action for damages may be brought against the same defendant in respect of a death.[55] One collective action is brought by the statutory dependants as a single group. A 'dependant' is any one of those parties listed in s 47(1)[56] who has suffered injury or mental distress as a result of the death.

---

52. A decision of the Privy Council on appeal from the courts of New Zealand in *A v Bottrill* [2003] 1 AC 449 held that intentional misconduct or conscious reckless however was not an essential prerequisite of the court's discretionary jurisdiction to make such an award.
53. *McIntyre v Lewis* [1991] 1 IR 121, [1990] IESC 5.
54. Probably fewer than 10 in 100,000 maternities.
55. Civil Liability Act 1961, s 48.
56. A spouse, parent, grandparent, step-parent, child, grandchild, step-child, brother, (contd .../)

[15.75] It must be remembered that a fatal injury action involving a claim for mental distress is separate and distinct from an action for nervous shock. The defendant whose negligence caused the death may also owe a duty of care to a close relative of the deceased in their own right.[57] Stillbirth (death before delivery) may also give rise to a claim in nervous shock.

[15.76] The damages recoverable in a fatal injury case are damages for mental distress as a solatium for injured feelings, loss of dependency and expenses like funeral expenses. There is a statutory cap on the total amount recoverable for mental distress for all of the dependants. The current cap is €35,000.[58]

PREPARING FOR TRIAL

[15.77] Prognosis of injury will set the timetable for settlement or trial. If prognosis is unclear then settlement or trial may be a long way off. As regards the necessity of an interim payment, lawyers should ask:

1. does the plaintiff need money now?

2. if so, for what?

3. does the lead medical expert confirm the need?

4. is other expertise required and if so, on what issue?[59]

PAYMENT OUT OF FUNDS

[15.78] Where funds have been lodged to the separate credit of a minor until they reach 18, it is possible to apply to the Master of the High Court on the minor's behalf for payment out before the minor reaches 18. If the order by which the funds were lodged has not expressly directed that future applications regarding the minors funds can be made to the Master, application must be made

56. (contd) sister, half-brother, half-sister, a divorcee of the deceased or a person who had been co-habiting with the deceased as husband or wife for a continuous period of at least three years prior to date of death.

57. In *Courtney v Our Lady's Hospital Ltd* [2011] 2 IR 786, [2011] 2 ILRM 328, [2011] IEHC 226 a mother was awarded €150,000 in respect of nervous shock resulting from witnessing the death of her child, and €10,500 in respect of legal representation at the child's inquest.

58. Civil Liability Act 1961 (Section 49) Order 2014 (SI 6/2014).

59. Adapted from Goldrein and de Haas, 'Preparing for Trial' in *Personal Injury Major Claims Handling: Cost Effective Case Management* (Butterworths, 2000).

to the High Court.[60] Any award of costs made will only be for the purpose of covering the necessary outlay incurred in court fees.

[15.79] It is wise to have the plaintiff made a ward of court if as a result of her injury she is unable to manage her property.

APPEALING QUANTUM

[15.80] If either side is unhappy with an award they may take an appeal against it on the basis that it was too high or too low. It became the general rule that awards for general damages should only be interfered with if the disparity between the views of the Supreme Court and each item of the award is not less than 25 per cent.[61] If quantum is appealed and if the appeal court is of the view that the damages awarded to a plaintiff are unsustainable, it may order a retrial or, more commonly, set aside the trial court's judgment and enter such judgment as it thinks proper.

---

60. RSC, Ord 63, r 12(1).
61. *Reddy v Bates* [1983] IR 141, [1984] ILRM 197.

EPILOGUE

'Lord, thou are art hard on mothers …' Those were the words of Patrick Pearse in 1916. Almost one hundred years later and a lot has changed for mothers and their babies, yet much remains to be done. It is not so much where the needle of the compass is currently pointing, but in which direction we now want it to move.

My hope is that procedural reforms will be introduced in medical negligence litigation to provide efficiency and economy in the fair determination of claims. Even before litigation arises, that there will be a cultural change whereby the so-called 'duty of candour' becomes ingrained in everyday clinical practice and where medical professionals are open and honest with their patients when things go wrong. And before ever getting to the stage where things go wrong, that proper risk management strategies will be implemented throughout maternity services in Ireland so that mistakes are recorded and remembered and as a result, less likely to be repeated.

The stand-alone maternity unit is an anachronism. Every one of our maternity units should be in the same building complex as a multi-disciplinary teaching hospital.

The development of risk management protocols in Irish hospitals is clearly at an early stage. Where is the Adverse Incident Report, or the Root Cause Analysis? Time after time we have seen that what patients who bring a claim want most of all is to be given an explanation for what happened and where appropriate an apology, along with an assurance that lessons have been learned and changes made so that what happened to them will not happen to somebody else. In those cases where compensation is not required to cover, for example, long term care costs for a disabled child, it could feasibly be said to be the only reason for suing. Litigation can certainly be a force for good – provided there is a proper risk management feedback loop.

To compel more openness and communication at the earliest opportunity would in many cases obviate the need for protracted litigation. Medical mistakes will often be accepted if freely admitted and frankly explained but such opportunities, unfortunately, are rarely availed of. The Health Service Executive and State Claims Agency launched a national policy on open disclosure two years ago but the practice of keeping quiet when things go wrong is so prevalent in our medical culture that, sadly, it is hard to believe the creation of new policy will change all that. Trying to create a common culture of openness and honesty on the present foundation of denial and defensiveness is like building on sand. To bring about real change, surely we need a legal duty of candour.

If a way could be found to bring the desirable level of openness and communication into legal proceedings, and in particular into the denial and admission part of pleadings, a great number of issues otherwise litigated, surely would become non-issues, with very considerable savings in both time and costs. Positive pleadings should be mandatory on both sides. Lay evidence, in the form of sworn witness statements, should be in court at the beginning of a trial. The privilege which at present remains in expert reports after they are disclosed and exchanged seriously disadvantages the plaintiff. Since the privilege is only lifted when the author of a report enters the witness box, the plaintiff's experts are never in a position to criticise the defence experts whilst the defence experts can when they come to give their evidence, discuss and criticise the plaintiff's experts. The Medical Negligence Working Group acknowledged the need for reform of our current rules by way of pre-action protocols and case management but despite promise after promise, successive Ministers have failed to act on their sound proposals.

A trial is not fair if the procedural dice are loaded in favour of one side or the other. There are at present a great many difficulties facing plaintiffs which are not faced by defendants. There is the excessive cost of funding the investigation of a claim, the lack of any adequate civil legal aid, the complexity of issues involved and the delays encountered, along with the restrictive two-year limitation period. Worst of all is the hostile approach so often adopted by defendants who have all the facts of the case at their fingertips but who fail to admit liability at an appropriate stage so that the injured patient spends years trying to prove there was negligence, running up costs all the time with an admission, if one is forthcoming, only being made at the eleventh hour. It is indeed highly regrettable that defendants often continue this pattern of delay for years before accepting responsibility and resolving claims, even in the most clear-cut cases. The Fabius Maximus tactics serve nobody.

What we should hope for and work for, is a quicker, more cost-effective and fairer litigation procedure, and one which encourages learning from mistakes. The aim of procedural reform should be twofold: providing a fair trial for both sides and doing so in a cost-effective and time-efficient manner. Justice is not achieved by a war of attrition in which victory is a prize to be awarded to the party with the greatest resources and the most money.

With the introduction of fair procedural rules, a great number of cases will surely not reach trial stage; they will be compromised at an appropriate time. The twin objectives of achieving a just and proper result in medical negligence actions and doing so as speedily and economically as possible will have been achieved and this will be in the interests of everybody involved.

I hope that we can muster the strength and determination to steer our system in the right direction. With conscience as our compass, I believe we will get there.

Appendix

SUPPORT SERVICES

I. BEREAVEMENT SERVICES

Anam Cara

Support for grieving parents and families. Aimed at networking families.

Tel: 01 4045378

www.anamcara.ie

Féileacáin (Stillbirth and Neonatal Death Association of Ireland)

Group meetings, low cost counselling, memory boxes, cold cots, family workshops, information and remembrance services.

Tel: 085 2496464

www.feileacain.ie

A Little Lifetime Foundation

Formerly known as Irish Stillbirth and Neonatal Death Association (ISANDS).

Group meeting, handprint and footprints booklets, information, follow up support.

Tel: 01 8829030

www.isands.ie

II. MATERNAL MENTAL HEALTH SUPPORT SERVICES

Nurture

Counselling and supports surrounding pregnancy and childbirth/maternal mental health illnesses for women, partners and their families.

Tel: 01 8430930

www.nurturecharity.org

III. BIRTH INJURY SUPPORT SERVICES

Cerebral Palsy Ireland

087 2990318

www.healing.ie

Special Education Support Service (SESS)

Tel: 021 4254231

www.sess.ie

Enable Ireland

Tel: 01 872 7155

www.enableireland.ie

Erbs Palsy Friends and Family

Tel: 086 6666200

www.erbspalsy.ie

IV. ADVOCACY SERVICES

Patient Focus

Tel: 01 8851611

www.patientfocus.ie

AIMS Ireland

www.aimsireland.com

Irish Patients Association

Tel: 01 2722555

www.irishpatients.ie

INDEX

[all references are to paragraph number]

A

Abortion
    failure of pregnancy, and, 11.02

Abuse of oxytocin
    breach of duty, and, 8.04
    clinical risk management, and, 1.13
    contraction frequency, 6.41–6.42
    fetal distress, and, 6.43–6.47
    fetal scalp sampling, 6.32
    generally, 6.34–6.40
    rupture of uterus, and, 6.83
    twin delivery, 6.134

Acute near total asphyxia
    bradycardia, 9.08–9.10
    damage occurring after onset of
      insult, 9.11–9.16
    elements, 9.07
    introduction, 9.01–9.07
    other evidence, 9.06
    review of evidence that damage
      ensue well after bradycardia
      lasting longer than 10 minutes,
      9.69–9.103
    review of working backward
      method, 9.24–9.49
    review of working forward
      method, 9.17–9.23
    summary, 9.64–9.68
    10–25 minute principle, 9.17–9.23
    therapeutic cooling, 9.58–9.63
    units of time of less than 5 minutes,
      9.50–9.57
    use of methods, 9.05
    working backward method, 9.04
    working forward method, 9.03

Administration of medical treatment
    causes of action, and, 2.06

Aggravated damages
    compensation, and, 15.67–15.68

Anal sphincter injury
    anatomy, 13.02
    classification, 13.03
    clinical risk management, and, 1.13
    consequences, 13.06
    episiotomy, 13.04–13.05
    failure to detect, 13.10–13.11
    failure to prevent third- and
      fourth-degree tears, 13.07–13.09
    inadequate repair
      circumstances, 13.14
      introduction, 13.12
      post-operative care, 13.16
      surgeon's identity, 13.13
      suture material, 13.15
    introduction, 13.01–13.06
    pudendal neuropathy, and
      case law, 13.35–13.83
      causation, 13.25–13.28
      clinical effects, 13.21–13.24
      clinical testing, 13.17
      conclusion, 13.84–13.88
      legal claims, 13.35–13.83
      neuropathy with or without
        anatomical defect in
        sphincters, 13.18
      permanent, 13.20
      prognosis, 13.29–13.30
      recto-vaginal fistula,
        13.31–13.33
      swab counts, 13.34
      tests of function, 13.19
      transient, 13.20

Anal sphincter injury (contd)
RCOG guideline
failure to detect, 13.10
inadequate repair, 13.12
social consequences, 13.06

Anembryonic pregnancy
failure of pregnancy, and, 11.01

Antenatal care
cerebral palsy, and, 8.03
clinical risk management, and, 1.12

Apgar scoring system
cerebral palsy, and, 5.18

Appeals
damages, and, 15.80

Asphyxia
see also **Cerebral palsy**
acute near total asphyxia
bradycardia, 9.08–9.10
damage occurring after onset of
insult, 9.11–9.16
elements, 9.07
introduction, 9.01–9.07
other evidence, 9.06
review of evidence that damage
ensue well after bradycardia
lasting longer than 10 minutes,
9.69–9.103
review of working backward
method, 9.24–9.49
review of working forward
method, 9.17–9.23
summary, 9.64–9.68
10–25 minute principle,
9.17–9.23
therapeutic cooling, 9.58–9.63
units of time of less than 5
minutes, 9.50–9.57
use of methods, 9.05
working backward method, 9.04
working forward method, 9.03

chronic partial asphyxia
introduction, 10.04–10.15
overview, 10.01–10.03
timing of damage, 10.16–10.29
clinical risk management, and, 1.13
introduction, 10.01–10.03
timing of onset of fetal brain
damage
acute near total asphyxia,
9.01–9.103
chronic partial asphyxia,
10.04–10.29

Assault and battery
causes of action, and, 2.06

Autonomy
consent, and, 4.04

B

Battery
consent, and, 4.08

Birth asphyxia
see also **Cerebral palsy**
generally, 5.12
timing of damage, 9.01–9.103

'Bolam' test
consent, and, 4.16

'Born-alive' rule
causes of action, and, 2.08

Brachial plexus injury (OBPI)
anatomy
case law, 12.41–12.83
conclusion, 12.84–12.86
defences
introduction, 12.22
maternal propulsion,
12.32–12.39
mechanism of labour, and,
12.23–12.25
posterior shoulder injury,
12.26–12.31

Brachial plexus injury (OBPI) (contd)
definition, 12.03–12.04
diabetic mothers, 12.09
Erb-Duchenne paralysis, 12.03
Erb's palsy, 12.04
generally, 12.03–12.04
good practice, 12.10–12.21
HELPERR, 12.17
introduction, 12.01–12.02
legal claims, 12.41–12.83
macrosomia, 12.07–12.08
maternal propulsion, 12.32–12.39
McRoberts manoeuvre,
12.15–12.16
mechanism of labour, 12.23–12.25
posterior shoulder injury,
12.26–12.31
RCOG guideline
generally, 12.17
introduction, 12.02
risk factor, 12.07
shoulder dystocia, 12.01–12.02
'turtle' effect, 12.07

Bradycardia
see also **Cerebral palsy**
generally, 9.08–9.10

Brain disorders
cerebral palsy, and, 5.06–5.11

Breach of contract
causes of action, and, 2.05

Breach of duty
cerebral palsy, and, 8.02–8.05

Breach of statutory duty
causes of action, and, 2.07

C

Capacity of patient
consent, and, 4.11–4.13

Cardiotocograph (CTG) trace
see also **Cerebral palsy**

baseline artefact, 6.22–6.23
classification, 6.24
decelerations of the fetal heart,
6.11–6.21
generally, 6.02–6.10
legal claims, and, 8.33–8.41

Causation
cerebral palsy, and, 8.06–8.20
civil procedure, and, 2.16–2.22
consent, and, 4.25–4.29
pudendal neuropathy, and,
13.25–13.28

Causes of action
civil procedure, and, 2.05–2.10

Cerclage
failure of pregnancy, and, 11.07

Cerebral palsy
abuse of oxytocin
contraction frequency, 6.41–6.42
fetal distress, and, 6.43–6.47
generally, 6.34–6.40
acute near total asphyxia
bradycardia, 9.08–9.10
damage occurring after onset of
insult, 9.11–9.16
elements, 9.07
introduction, 9.01–9.07
other evidence, 9.06
review of evidence that damage
ensue well after bradycardia
lasting longer than 10 minutes,
9.69–9.103
review of working backward
method, 9.24–9.49
review of working forward
method, 9.17–9.23
summary, 9.64–9.68
10–25 minute principle,
9.17–9.23
therapeutic cooling, 9.58–9.63

Cerebral palsy (contd)
  units of time of less than 5
    minutes, 9.50–9.57
  use of methods, 9.05
  working backward method, 9.04
  working forward method, 9.03
  antenatal errors, 8.03
  Apgar scoring system, 5.18
  assessment, 5.05
  birth asphyxia
    generally, 5.12
    timing of damage, 9.01–9.103
  bradycardia, 9.08–9.10
  brain disorders, 5.06–5.11
  breach of duty, 8.02–8.05
  cardiotocograph (CTG) trace
    baseline artefact, 6.22–6.23
    classification, 6.24
    decelerations of the fetal heart,
      6.11–6.21
    generally, 6.02–6.10
    legal claims, and, 8.33–8.41
  causation, 8.06–8.20
  causes
    abuse of oxytocin, 6.34–6.47
    birth asphyxia, 5.12
    brain disorders, 5.06–5.11
    cord problems, 6.48–6.67
    generally, 5.14
    intrauterine fetal surveillance,
      6.01–6.33
    kernicterus, 5.13
    medico-legal aspects, 5.15–5.18
    placental malfunction, 6.68–6.78
    rupture of uterus, 6.79–6.136
  chronic partial asphyxia
    introduction, 10.04–10.15
    overview, 10.01–10.03
    timing of damage, 10.16–10.29
  classification
    birth asphyxia, 5.12
    generally, 5.03–5.05

    kernicterus, 5.13
    underlying brain disorders,
      5.06–5.11
  cord problems
    abnormalities, 6.55–6.56
    introduction, 6.48
    obstruction, 6.49–6.54
    prolapse, 6.57–6.67
  diplegia, 5.03
  'fetal distress', 6.01
  fetal scalp blood sampling,
    6.27–6.31
  functional impact, 5.05
  Gross Motor Function
    Classification System (GMFCS),
    5.05
  hemiplegia, 5.03
  intrapartum trace, 6.25–6.26
  intrauterine fetal surveillance
    cardiotocograph trace, 6.02–6.24
    fetal scalp blood sampling,
      6.27–6.31
    intrapartum trace, 6.25–6.26
    introduction, 6.01
    meconium in the liquor, 6.33
    overview, 5.14
  introduction, 5.01–5.02
  kernicterus
    generally, 5.13
    overview, 5.14
  labour errors, 8.04
  legal claims
    antenatal errors, 8.03
    breach of duty, 8.02–8.05
    cardiotocograph (CTG),
      8.33–8.41
    causation, 8.06–8.20
    introduction, 8.01
    labour errors, 8.04
    operative vaginal delivery,
      8.66–8.86
    placental failure, 8.42–8.65

Cerebral palsy (contd)
  legal claims (contd)
    postnatal errors, 8.05
    quantum, 8.87–8.89
    resuscitation failure, 8.21–8.32
  Manual Ability Classification, 5.05
  meaning, 5.01–5.02
  medico-legal aspects, 5.15–5.18
  motor function impairment
    assessment, 5.05
    generally, 5.04
    introduction, 5.02
  MRI, 5.06
  muscle tone, 5.04
  operative vaginal delivery
    breech delivery, 6.124–6.131
    caput, 6.106
    descent, 6.102
    engagement, 6.104
    forceps delivery, 6.109–6.111
    generally, 6.99–6.108
    head level, 6.103
    introduction, 6.84
    legal claims, and, 8.66–8.86
    mal-rotated head, 6.114–6.122
    moulding, 6.106
    obstetric forceps, 6.110–6.111
    outlet forceps, 6.109
    position, 6.101
    station, 6.105–6.107
    trial of operative delivery, 6.123
    twin delivery, 6.132–6.136
    ventouse, 6.112–6.113
  other cases, 5.13
  oxytocin abuse
    contraction frequency, 6.41–6.42
    fetal distress, and, 6.43–6.47
    generally, 6.34–6.40
    rupture of uterus, and, 6.83
  placental failure, 8.42–8.65

placental malfunction
  acute, 6.77–6.78
  chronic, 6.70–6.76
  generally, 6.68–6.69
postnatal errors, 8.05
quadriplegia, 5.03
quantum, 8.87–8.89
resuscitation
  airway, 7.18–7.24
  assessment of newborn,
    7.10–7.15
  breathing, 7.25–7.28
  circulation, 7.29–7.30
  common errors, 7.38–7.39
  difficult delivery, 7.01
  drugs, 7.31–7.32
  guidelines, 7.17
  intrauterine growth restriction,
    7.01
  introduction, 7.01–7.04
  macrosomia, 7.01
  meconium staining, 7.01
  method, 7.16–7.32
  physiology, 7.05–7.09
  post-resuscitation care,
    7.33–7.36
  prematurity, 7.01
  risk factors, 7.01
  special considerations, 7.37
  thick meconium staining, 7.01
  underlying physiology,
    7.05–7.09
resuscitation failure, 8.21–8.32
rupture of uterus
  'clamping down', 6.80
  direct injury, 6.84
  generally, 6.79–6.81
  obstructed labour, 6.82
  operative vaginal delivery,
    6.99–6.136
  oxytocin abuse, 6.83
  scarred uterus, 6.85–6.98

Cerebral palsy (contd)

scarred uterus

augmentation of labour,
6.97–6.98

decision to allow VBAC,
6.91–6.96

generally, 6.85–6.89

incidence of rupture, 6.90

induction of labour, 6.97–6.98

spasticity, 5.04

tetraplegia, 5.03

timing of onset of fetal brain
damage

acute near total asphyxia,
9.01–9.103

chronic partial asphyxia,
10.04–10.29

introduction, 10.01–10.03

umbilical cord problems

abnormalities, 6.55–6.56

introduction, 6.48

obstruction, 6.49–6.54

prolapse, 6.57–6.67

underlying brain disorders,
5.06–5.11

vaginal birth after Caesarean
section (VBAC), 6.91–6.96

Children under 16 years

consent, and, 4.41–4.45

Chronic partial asphyxia

see also **Cerebral palsy**

introduction, 10.04–10.15

overview, 10.01–10.03

timing of damage, 10.16–10.29

Civil procedure

basis of claim, 2.04

causation, 2.16–2.22

causes of action, 2.05–2.10

costs, 2.103–2.107

date of knowledge, 2.05

death of claimant, and, 2.97–2.98

disclosure rules, 2.82–2.96

discovery, 2.78–2.81

experts

choice, 3.11–3.18

disclosure of reports, 2.82–2.85

duty, 3.06–3.07

duty to the court, 3.08–3.11

instructions, 3.19

relevant persons, 3.01–3.05

identity of parties, 2.32–2.35

introduction, 2.01–2.04

letter of claim, 2.36–2.39

limitation period

date of knowledge, 2.45–2.49

delay, 2.53–2.66

equitable fraud, and, 2.50–2.51

generally, 2.40–2.52

minors, and, 2.52

negligence, 2.05

nursing negligence, and, 2.42

persons under a disability, and,
2.52

plea of statute bar, 2.43–2.44

trespass to the person, 2.06

medical records, 2.24–2.31

nursing negligence, and, 2.42

pleadings, 2.67–2.75

requests for particulars, 2.76–2.77

standard of care, 2.11–2.15

statement of truth, 3.07

striking out, 2.53–2.66

succession to claims, and,
2.97–2.98

tort actions, 2.01

trials, 2.99–2.102

Claims management system (NIMS)

generally, 1.04

Clinical indemnity scheme (CIS)

generally, 1.04

Clinical risk management
  cascade of events, 1.11–1.13
  definition, 1.02
  delay, 1.11–1.12
  elements
    analysing risk, 1.08
    controlling risk, 1.09–1.10
    identifying risk, 1.07
    introduction, 1.05–1.06
  failure of communication,
    1.11–1.12
  history, 1.03–1.04
  indemnity, 1.04
  introduction, 1.01
  'no blame culture', 1.10
  obstetrics, in, 1.11–1.13
  purpose, 1.01

Compensatory damages
  compensation, and, 15.03–15.05

Consent
  autonomy, 4.04
  battery, 4.08
  'Bolam' test, 4.16
  capacity of patient, 4.11–4.13
  causation, and, 4.25–4.29
  children under 16 years, 4.41–4.45
  clinical risk management, and, 1.13
  departure from professional
    standard, 4.21–4.24
  'Dunne' principles, 4.16–4.20
  emergency Caesarean sections,
    4.37
  female genital mutilation, 4.09
  form, 4.33–4.36
  illegal operation, 4.09
  'informed consent', 4.07
  introduction, 4.01–4.04
  Jehovah's Witnesses, and,
    4.39–4.40
  lack of capacity, 4.13
  method, 4.33–4.36

  paternalism, 4.05–4.06
  physical force or coercion, 4.14
  professional standard, 4.16–4.24
  'prudent patient' standard, 4.14
  refusal of treatment
    generally, 4.37–4.40
    introduction, 4.03
  self-determination, 4.04
  sufficiency of information, 4.15
  timing, 4.30–4.32
  treatment, to, 4.07–4.09
  trespass to the person, 4.08
  use of force, 4.14
  validity, 4.10–4.15
  writing, in, 4.33–4.36

Consortium
  causes of action, and, 2.09

Cord problems
  see also **Cerebral palsy**
  abnormalities, 6.55–6.56
  introduction, 6.48
  obstruction, 6.49–6.54
  prolapse, 6.57–6.67

Costs
  civil procedure, and, 2.103–2.107

D

Damages
  accommodation, 15.55–15.59
  aggravated damages, 15.67–15.68
  appeals, 15.80
  assessment, 15.02
  compensatory damages,
    15.03–15.05
  cost of nursing care, 15.53
  exemplary damages, 15.69–15.70
  fatal injuries
    dependency claims, 15.74
    funeral expenses, 15.76
    introduction, 15.71
    maternal death, 15.73

Damages (contd)
   fatal injuries (contd)
      mental distress, 15.75–15.96
      neonatal death, 15.72
      solatium, 15.76
   future expenses
      accommodation, 15.55–15.59
      loss of earnings, 15.60–15.65
      nursing care, 15.53
      other heads, 15.66
      physiotherapy, 15.54
   general damages
      generally, 15.19–15.22
      limits, 15.23–15.27
   interim payments, 15.78–15.79
   interim settlement, 15.08
   introduction, 15.01–15.02
   life expectancy, 15.39–15.47
   loss of earnings, 15.60–15.65
   lump sum payments, 15.06–15.07
   meaning, 15.01
   mechanism, 15.06–15.18
   nursing care, 15.53
   periodic payment orders,
      15.12–15.18
   physiotherapy, 15.54
   preparation for trial, 15.77
   real rate of return, 15.48–15.51
   restitutio in integrum, 15.03
   special damages
      future, 15.35–15.38
      past, 15.28–15.34
   taxation, 15.52

Date of knowledge
   limitation period, and, 2.05

Death of claimant
   civil procedure, and, 2.97–2.98

Defences
   obstetric brachial plexus injury,
   and

   introduction, 12.22
   maternal propulsion,
      12.32–12.39
   mechanism of labour, and,
      12.23–12.25
   posterior shoulder injury,
      12.26–12.31

Diabetic mothers
   obstetric brachial plexus injury,
      and, 12.09

Diplegia
   cerebral palsy, and, 5.03

Disclosure
   civil procedure, and, 2.82–2.96

Discovery
   civil procedure, and, 2.78–2.81

'Dunne' principles
   consent, and, 4.16–4.20

Dystocia
   clinical risk management, and, 1.13

E

Ectopic pregnancy
   diagnosis, 11.15
   effect, 11.14
   generally, 11.13–11.18
   introduction, 11.01
   meaning, 11.13
   treatment, 11.16–11.18

Emergency Caesarean sections
   consent, and, 4.37

Episiotomy
   obstetric anal sphincter injury,
      and, 13.04–13.05

Erb-Duchenne paralysis
   see also **Obstetric brachial plexus**
      injury
   generally, 12.03

Erb's palsy

see also **Obstetric brachial plexus injury**

generally, 12.04

Exemplary damages

compensation, and, 15.69–15.70

Experts

choice, 3.11–3.18

disclosure of reports, 2.82–2.85

duty, 3.06–3.07

duty to the court, 3.08–3.11

instructions, 3.19

relevant persons, 3.01–3.05

F

Failed pregnancy

abortion, 11.02

anembryonic pregnancy, 11.01

cerclage, 11.07

conclusion, 11.50

diagnosis, 11.08–11.12

ectopic pregnancy

diagnosis, 11.15

effect, 11.14

generally, 11.13–11.18

introduction, 11.01

meaning, 11.13

treatment, 11.16–11.18

incompetent cervix

generally, 11.06

introduction, 11.01

treatment, 11.07

introduction, 11.01–11.07

legal claims, 11.19–11.49

miscarriage

cause, 11.05–11.06

diagnosis, 11.08–11.12

introduction, 11.01–11.03

legal claims, 11.19–11.49

refining adjectives, 11.04

treatment, 11.07

nomenclature, 11.02

reasons, 11.01

stillbirth, 11.03

terminology, 11.02

Failed sterilisation

causes

generally, 14.07

investigation, 14.12–14.14

conclusion, 14.50

counselling, 14.15

filshie clips, 14.06

introduction, 14.01

investigation of cause, 14.12–14.14

laparosopic sterilisation, 14.06

legal claims

compensation, 14.16–14.49

counselling, 14.15

introduction, 14.10–14.11

investigation of cause of failure, 14.12–14.14

pre-operative counselling, 14.15

recanalisation

generally, 14.08–14.09

introduction, 14.07

overview, 14.02

tubal ligation, and, 14.05

sterilisation methods

background, 14.02–14.03

current approaches, 14.04

filshie clips, 14.06

introduction, 14.02

tubal ligation, 14.05

tubal ligation, 14.05

Failure to detect

obstetric anal sphincter injury, and, 13.10–13.11

Failure to prevent tears

obstetric anal sphincter injury, and, 13.07–13.09

Fatal injuries
damages, and
dependency claims, 15.74
funeral expenses, 15.76
introduction, 15.71
maternal death, 15.73
mental distress, 15.75–15.96
neonatal death, 15.72
solatium, 15.76

Female genital mutilation (FGM)
consent, and, 4.09

'Fetal distress'
cerebral palsy, and, 6.01

Fetal scalp blood sampling
cerebral palsy, and, 6.27–6.31

Filshie clips
failed sterilisation, and, 14.06

G

General damages
generally, 15.19–15.22
limits, 15.23–15.27

Gross Motor Function Classification System (GMFCS)
cerebral palsy, and, 5.05

H

Haemorrhage
clinical risk management, and, 1.13

HELPERR
obstetric brachial plexus injury, and, 12.17

Hemiplegia
cerebral palsy, and, 5.03

Hypoxic ischaemia
cerebral palsy, and, 5.14

I

Illegal operations
consent, and, 4.09

Inadequate repair
obstetric anal sphincter injury, and
circumstances, 13.14
introduction, 13.12
post-operative care, 13.16
surgeon's identity, 13.13
suture material, 13.15

Incompetent cervix
generally, 11.06
introduction, 11.01
treatment, 11.07

Infarction
cerebral palsy, and, 5.14

Inflammatory response sundrome
cerebral palsy, and, 5.14

Informed consent
see also **Consent**
generally, 4.07

Interim payments
damages, and, 15.78–15.79

Interim settlement
damages, and, 15.08

Intracranial haemorrhage
cerebral palsy, and, 5.14

Intrapartum trace
cerebral palsy, and, 6.25–6.26

Intrauterine fetal surveillance
see also **Cerebral palsy**
cardiotocograph trace, 6.02–6.24
fetal scalp blood sampling, 6.27–6.31
intrapartum trace, 6.25–6.26
introduction, 6.01
meconium in the liquor, 6.33
overview, 5.14 15

Intrauterine growth restriction
neonatal resuscitation, and, 7.01

Intrauterine infection
cerebral palsy, and, 5.14

J

Jehovah's Witnesses
consent, and, 4.39–4.40

K

Kernicterus
see also **Cerebral palsy**
generally, 5.13
overview, 5.14

L

Labour errors
cerebral palsy, and, 8.04

Lack of capacity
consent, and, 4.13

Letter of claim
civil procedure, and, 2.36–2.39

Life expectancy
damages, and, 15.39–15.47

Limitation period
date of knowledge, 2.45–2.49
delay, 2.53–2.66
equitable fraud, and, 2.50–2.51
generally, 2.40–2.52
minors, and, 2.52
negligence, 2.05
nursing negligence, and, 2.42
persons under a disability, and,
2.52
plea of statute bar, 2.43–2.44
trespass to the person, 2.06

Loss of earnings
damages, and, 15.60–15.65

Lump sum payments
damages, and, 15.06–15.07

M

Macrosomia
neonatal resuscitation, and, 7.01

obstetric brachial plexus injury,
and, 12.07–12.08

Major obstetric haemorrhage
clinical risk management, and, 1.13

Malformation of brain
cerebral palsy, and, 5.14

Manual Ability Classification
cerebral palsy, and, 5.05

Maternal propulsion
obstetric brachial plexus injury,
and, 12.32–12.39

McRoberts manoeuvre
obstetric brachial plexus injury,
and, 12.15–12.16

Meconium
neonatal resuscitation, and, 7.01

Medical records
civil procedure, and, 2.24–2.31

Medical treatment
causes of action, and, 2.06

Meninigitis
cerebral palsy, and, 5.14

Miscarriage
cause, 11.05–11.06
diagnosis, 11.08–11.12
introduction, 11.01–11.03
legal claims, 11.19–11.49
refining adjectives, 11.04
treatment, 11.07

MRI
cerebral palsy, and, 5.06

N

Negligence
causation, 2.16–2.22
Dunne principles, 2.14
introduction, 2.05
standard of care, 2.11–2.15

Neonatal resuscitation
   airway, 7.18–7.24
   assessment of newborn, 7.10–7.15
   breathing, 7.25–7.28
   circulation, 7.29–7.30
   common errors, 7.38–7.39
   difficult delivery, 7.01
   drugs, 7.31–7.32
   guidelines, 7.17
   intrauterine growth restriction, 7.01
   introduction, 7.01–7.04
   macrosomia, 7.01
   meconium staining, 7.01
   method, 7.16–7.32
   physiology, 7.05–7.09
   post-resuscitation care, 7.33–7.36
   prematurity, 7.01
   risk factors, 7.01
   special considerations, 7.37
   thick meconium staining, 7.01
   underlying physiology, 7.05–7.09

Nervous shock
   causes of action, and, 2.10

NIMS
   generally, 1.04

Nursing care
   damages, and, 15.53

O

Obstetric anal sphincter injury
   anatomy, 13.02
   classification, 13.03
   clinical risk management, and, 1.13
   consequences, 13.06
   episiotomy, 13.04–13.05
   failure to detect, 13.10–13.11
   failure to prevent third- and
      fourth-degree tears, 13.07–13.09
   inadequate repair
      circumstances, 13.14
      introduction, 13.12

      post-operative care, 13.16
      surgeon's identity, 13.13
      suture material, 13.15
   introduction, 13.01–13.06
   pudendal neuropathy, and
      case law, 13.35–13.83
      causation, 13.25–13.28
      clinical effects, 13.21–13.24
      clinical testing, 13.17
      conclusion, 13.84–13.88
      legal claims, 13.35–13.83
      neuropathy with or without
         anatomical defect in
         sphincters, 13.18
      permanent, 13.20
      prognosis, 13.29–13.30
      recto-vaginal fistula,
         13.31–13.33
      swab counts, 13.34
      tests of function, 13.19
      transient, 13.20
   RCOG guideline
      failure to detect, 13.10
      inadequate repair, 13.12
   social consequences, 13.06

Obstetric brachial plexus injury (OBPI)
   anatomy
   case law, 12.41–12.83
   conclusion, 12.84–12.86
   defences
      introduction, 12.22
      maternal propulsion,
         12.32–12.39
      mechanism of labour, and,
         12.23–12.25
      posterior shoulder injury,
         12.26–12.31
   definition, 12.03–12.04
   diabetic mothers, 12.09
   Erb-Duchenne paralysis, 12.03
   Erb's palsy, 12.04

Obstetric brachial plexus injury (OBPI) (contd)
generally, 12.03–12.04
good practice, 12.10–12.21
HELPERR, 12.17
introduction, 12.01–12.02
legal claims, 12.41–12.83
macrosomia, 12.07–12.08
maternal propulsion, 12.32–12.39
McRoberts manoeuvre, 12.15–12.16
mechanism of labour, 12.23–12.25
posterior shoulder injury, 12.26–12.31
RCOG guideline
generally, 12.17
introduction, 12.02
risk factor, 12.07
shoulder dystocia, 12.01–12.02
'turtle' effect, 12.07

Obstetric haemorrhage
clinical risk management, and, 1.13

Operative vaginal delivery
breech delivery, 6.124–6.131
caput, 6.106
descent, 6.102
engagement, 6.104
forceps delivery, 6.109–6.111
generally, 6.99–6.108
head level, 6.103
introduction, 6.84
legal claims, and, 8.66–8.86
mal-rotated head, 6.114–6.122
moulding, 6.106
obstetric forceps, 6.110–6.111
outlet forceps, 6.109
position, 6.101
station, 6.105–6.107
trial of operative delivery, 6.123
twin delivery, 6.132–6.136
ventouse, 6.112–6.113

Oxytocin abuse
breach of duty, and, 8.04
clinical risk management, and, 1.13
contraction frequency, 6.41–6.42
fetal distress, and, 6.43–6.47
fetal scalp sampling, 6.32
generally, 6.34–6.40
rupture of uterus, and, 6.83
twin delivery, 6.134

P

Paternalism
consent, and, 4.05–4.06

Perinatal asphyxia
clinical risk management, and, 1.13

Periodic payment orders
damages, and, 15.12–15.18

Physical force or coercion
consent, and, 4.14

Physiotherapy
damages, and, 15.54

Placental failure
cerebral palsy, and, 8.42–8.65

Placental malfunction
acute, 6.77–6.78
chronic, 6.70–6.76
generally, 6.68–6.69

Pleadings
civil procedure, and, 2.67–2.75

Posterior shoulder injury
obstetric brachial plexus injury, and, 12.26–12.31

Pregnancy failures
abortion, 11.02
anembryonic pregnancy, 11.01
cerclage, 11.07
conclusion, 11.50
diagnosis, 11.08–11.12

Pregnancy failures (contd)
  ectopic pregnancy
    diagnosis, 11.15
    effect, 11.14
    generally, 11.13–11.18
    introduction, 11.01
    meaning, 11.13
    treatment, 11.16–11.18
  incompetent cervix
    generally, 11.06
    introduction, 11.01
    treatment, 11.07
  introduction, 11.01–11.07
  legal claims, 11.19–11.49
  miscarriage
    cause, 11.05–11.06
    diagnosis, 11.08–11.12
    introduction, 11.01–11.03
    legal claims, 11.19–11.49
    refining adjectives, 11.04
    treatment, 11.07
  nomenclature, 11.02
  reasons, 11.01
  stillbirth, 11.03
  terminology, 11.02

Prematurity
  neonatal resuscitation, and, 7.01

Pre-operative counselling
  failed sterilisation, and, 14.15

'Prudent patient' standard
  consent, and, 4.14

Psychiatric injury
  causes of action, and, 2.10

Pudendal neuropathy
  case law, 13.35–13.83
  causation, 13.25–13.28
  clinical effects, 13.21–13.24
  clinical testing, 13.17
  conclusion, 13.84–13.88
  legal claims, 13.35–13.83
    neuropathy with or without
      anatomical defect in sphincters,
      13.18
  permanent, 13.20
  prognosis, 13.29–13.30
  recto-vaginal fistula, 13.31–13.33
  swab counts, 13.34
  tests of function, 13.19
  transient, 13.20

Q

Quadriplegia
  cerebral palsy, and, 5.03

Quantum of damages
  accommodation, 15.55–15.59
  aggravated damages, 15.67–15.68
  appeals, 15.80
  assessment, 15.02
  cerebral palsy, and, 8.87–8.89
  compensatory damages,
    15.03–15.05
  cost of nursing care, 15.53
  exemplary damages, 15.69–15.70
  fatal injuries
    dependency claims, 15.74
    funeral expenses, 15.76
    introduction, 15.71
    maternal death, 15.73
    mental distress, 15.75–15.96
    neonatal death, 15.72
    solatium, 15.76
  future expenses
    accommodation, 15.55–15.59
    loss of earnings, 15.60–15.65
    nursing care, 15.53
    other heads, 15.66
    physiotherapy, 15.54
  general damages
    generally, 15.19–15.22
    limits, 15.23–15.27
  interim payments, 15.78–15.79
  interim settlement, 15.08

Quantum of damages (contd)
    introduction, 15.01–15.02
    life expectancy, 15.39–15.47
    loss of earnings, 15.60–15.65
    lump sum payments, 15.06–15.07
    meaning, 15.01
    mechanism, 15.06–15.18
    nursing care, 15.53
    periodic payment orders,
      15.12–15.18
    physiotherapy, 15.54
    preparation for trial, 15.77
    real rate of return, 15.48–15.51
    restitutio in integrum, 15.03
    special damages
      future, 15.35–15.38
      past, 15.28–15.34
    taxation, 15.52

R

RCOG guideline
    obstetric anal sphincter injury, and
      failure to detect, 13.10
      inadequate repair, 13.12
    obstetric brachial plexus injury,
      and
      generally, 12.17
      introduction, 12.02

Real rate of return
    damages, and, 15.48–15.51

Recanalisation
    see also **Failed sterilisation**
    generally, 14.08–14.09
    introduction, 14.07
    overview, 14.02
    tubal ligation, and, 14.05

Recto-vaginal fistula
    pudendal neuropathy, and,
      13.31–13.33

Refusal of treatment
    generally, 4.37–4.40

    introduction, 4.03

Requests for particulars
    civil procedure, and, 2.76–2.77

Restitutio in integrum
    damages, and, 15.03

Resuscitation
    airway, 7.18–7.24
    assessment of newborn, 7.10–7.15
    breathing, 7.25–7.28
    cerebral palsy, and, 8.21–8.32
    circulation, 7.29–7.30
    common errors, 7.38–7.39
    difficult delivery, 7.01
    drugs, 7.31–7.32
    guidelines, 7.17
    intrauterine growth restriction, 7.01
    introduction, 7.01–7.04
    macrosomia, 7.01
    meconium staining, 7.01
    method, 7.16–7.32
    physiology, 7.05–7.09
    post-resuscitation care, 7.33–7.36
    prematurity, 7.01
    risk factors, 7.01
    special considerations, 7.37
    thick meconium staining, 7.01
    underlying physiology, 7.05–7.09

Risk management
    cascade of events, 1.11–1.13
    definition, 1.02
    delay, 1.11–1.12
    elements
      analysing risk, 1.08
      controlling risk, 1.09–1.10
      identifying risk, 1.07
      introduction, 1.05–1.06
    failure of communication,
      1.11–1.12
    history, 1.03–1.04
    indemnity, 1.04

Risk management (contd)
  introduction, 1.01
  'no blame culture', 1.10
  obstetrics, in, 1.11–1.13
  purpose, 1.01

Rupture of uterus
  see also **Cerebral palsy**
  'clamping down', 6.80
  direct injury, 6.84
  generally, 6.79–6.81
  obstructed labour, 6.82
  operative vaginal delivery,
    6.99–6.136
  oxytocin abuse, 6.83
  scarred uterus, 6.85–6.98

S

Scarred uterus
  see also **Cerebral palsy**
  augmentation of labour, 6.97–6.98
  decision to allow VBAC,
    6.91–6.96
  generally, 6.85–6.89
  incidence of rupture, 6.90
  induction of labour, 6.97–6.98

Self-determination
  consent, and, 4.04

Shoulder dystocia
  see also **Obstetric brachial plexus
    injury**
  clinical risk management, and, 1.13
  generally, 12.01–12.02

Special damages
  future, 15.35–15.38
  past, 15.28–15.34

Standard of care
  civil procedure, and, 2.11–2.15

Statement of truth
  civil procedure, and, 3.07

Sterilisation failure
  causes
    generally, 14.07
    investigation, 14.12–14.14
  conclusion, 14.50
  counselling, 14.15
  filshie clips, 14.06
  introduction, 14.01
  investigation of cause, 14.12–14.14
  laparosopic sterilisation, 14.06
  legal claims
    compensation, 14.16–14.49
    counselling, 14.15
    introduction, 14.10–14.11
    investigation of cause of failure,
      14.12–14.14
  pre-operative counselling, 14.15
  recanalisation
    generally, 14.08–14.09
    introduction, 14.07
    overview, 14.02
    tubal ligation, and, 14.05
  sterilisation methods
    background, 14.02–14.03
    current approaches, 14.04
    filshie clips, 14.06
    introduction, 14.02
    tubal ligation, 14.05
  tubal ligation, 14.05

Stillbirth
  failure of pregnancy, and, 11.03

Striking out
  civil procedure, and, 2.53–2.66

Succession to claims
  civil procedure, and, 2.97–2.98

Surgery
  causes of action, and, 2.06

Swab counts
  pudendal neuropathy, and, 13.34

T

Taxation
damages, and, 15.52

Tetraplegia
cerebral palsy, and, 5.03

Timing of onset of fetal brain damage
acute near total asphyxia
bradycardia, 9.08–9.10
damage occurring after onset of
insult, 9.11–9.16
elements, 9.07
introduction, 9.01–9.07
other evidence, 9.06
review of evidence that damage
ensue well after bradycardia
lasting longer than 10 minutes,
9.69–9.103
review of working backward
method, 9.24–9.49
review of working forward
method, 9.17–9.23
summary, 9.64–9.68
10–25 minute principle,
9.17–9.23
therapeutic cooling, 9.58–9.63
units of time of less than 5
minutes, 9.50–9.57
use of methods, 9.05
working backward method, 9.04
working forward method, 9.03
chronic partial asphyxia

introduction, 10.04–10.15
overview, 10.01–10.03
timing of damage, 10.16–10.29
introduction, 10.01–10.03

Trespass to the person
causes of action, and, 2.06
consent, and, 4.08

Trials
civil procedure, and, 2.99–2.102

Tubal ligation
failed sterilisation, and, 14.05

'Turtle' effect
obstetric brachial plexus injury,
and, 12.07

U

Umbilical cord problems
abnormalities, 6.55–6.56
introduction, 6.48
obstruction, 6.49–6.54
prolapse, 6.57–6.67

Unborn child
causes of action, and, 2.08

V

**Vaginal birth after Caesarean section
(VBAC)**
clinical risk management, and, 1.13
generally, 6.91–6.96